THE CASE FOR THE UFO

Unidentified Flying Objects

The Varo Edition

by

M. K. Jessup

THE BOOK TREE
San Diego, California

Original Edition First Published 1955
The Citadel Press
New York

© 1955
Morris K. Jessup

ISBN 978-1-58509-438-7

cover image
© Ursatii

Cover layout
Paul Tice

Published by
**The Book Tree
San Diego, CA**
www.thebooktree.com

We provide fascinating and educational products to help awaken the public to new ideas
and information that would not be available otherwise.
Call 1 (800) 700-8733 for our FREE BOOK TREE CATALOG.

FOREWORD

The original version of *The Case for the UFO* was first published in 1955. It is known as an excellent overview of UFO encounters throughout human history. This version, known as The Varo Edition, appeared later that year when just one copy, containing additional material not penned by the author, was anonymously sent to Admiral N. Furth, Chief of the Office of Naval Research. The notes and additional material reflected so much inside knowledge on the subject, that various military people took a special interest in the book. They had it privately published in very limited form, meant only for those with special access. It seems that three different individuals made color-coded notations that are preserved in this edition, now made available to the general public. Over the years this book has been one of the most rare and sought after manuscripts to be found within the UFO field.

In order to distinguish between the three commentators in the book, a woman named Michael Ann Dunn retyped the entire manuscript to include the color coding while working with or for The Varo Corporation, an electronics firm that was engaged in classified military operations for the Navy. Twelve copies were originally produced, and later another 127 or so copies were generated.

Later, in 1973, Gray Barker published a limited number of facsimile copies, which explains the opening Preface found here, which had accompanied his edition. Today, it seems that this particular edition had to have the color coding again restored, which has been attributed to The Quantum Future Group in France, done in 2003. We are grateful to them—and for all those who put work into this book, and for continuing to make it accessible to the public.

Paul Tice

PREFACE

On the evening of April 20, 1959, an astronomer committed suicide in Dade County Park, Florida. Inhaling automobile exhaust fumes, which he had introduced from the tail pipe through a hose into his station wagon, he died in the same academic obscurity in which he had lived, unheralded and almost unrecognized in his discipline.

Ironically, the scientist's only public recognition had come from lay people, who had read his series of four books about unidentified flying objects.

Morris K. Jessup's first book, *The Case For the UFO*, had tended to alienate him from his colleagues, though it came and went with relatively few sales. Its publisher sold it off to second-hand bookstores at $1.00 each. Today it brings $25.00 or better per copy, if you can find one.

It was a paperback edition of the same book, published in 1955 by Bantam Books that enmeshed Jessup in one of the most bizarre mysteries in UFO history. An annotated reprint of the paperback was laboriously typed out on offset stencils and printed in a very small run by a Garland, Texas manufacturing company which produced equipment for the military.

Each page was run through the small office duplicator twice, once with black ink for the regular text of the book, then once again with red ink, the latter reproducing the mysterious annotations by three men, who may have been gypsies, hoaxters, or space people living among men. The spiral bound 8 ½" X 11" volume, containing more that 200 pages, became known as *The Annotated Edition*. The reprint quickly became legend. A few civilian UFO enthusiasts claimed to have seen copies, and it was rumored that a few close associates of the late Mr. Jessup possessed copies. Many people claimed it simply had never existed.

Because you are now holding a virtually exact facsimile of *The Annotated Edition* in your hands, it is most obvious that the book existed. But the big mystery still remains: why did a Government contractor go to so much trouble to reprint a book that had been rejected by the scientific community, and further to include mysterious letters to the author and even more bizarre annotations? And with this mystery goes the suspicion that the book may have been printed by the manufacturer at the request of the military, which implies Government interest in some of the weirdest aspects of "Flying Saucer" study.

Jessup's Background

Not much detail is known of Jessup's life before he emerged as one of the early writers on UFOs, mainly because nobody has taken the trouble to do the needed research. Probably the most that Ufology knows about him prior to his involvement with flying saucers is contained on the jacket flap of his first book.

He is described as having been an instructor in astronomy and mathematics at the University of Michigan and Drake University. The Jacket copy also notes that Jessup completed his thesis for the doctorate degree in astro-physics at the University of Michigan, though it does not state whether on not he was awarded the actual degree. In the academic business, usually the thesis is the thing that comes last, and is the final step in the awarding of the doctorate degree. Sometimes these doctoral candidates are deferentially called "Doctor" by their associates, though it cannot be used officially by them. This would seem to be the case of Jessup, who was often addressed as "Dr. Jessup", but who never used the title in correspondence, nor on the covers or title pages of his four books. Very likely Jessup was never actually awarded the degree.

Apparently, his thesis consisted of a report on his research program which (again according to the book jacket) resulted in several thousand discoveries of physical double-stars "which are now catalogued in the *Memoirs of the Royal Astronomical Society* of London".

The short biography also lists other important research activities by Jessup. It indicates that he was assigned by the United State Department of Agriculture to study the sources of crude rubber in the headwaters of the Amazon, though no date is given. He made archeological studies of the Maya in the jungles of Central America for the Carnegie Institute of Washington.

Without identifying the source of sponsorship or financing, the jacket states that he explored Inca ruins in Peru, and concluded that the stonework he found there had been "erected by the levitating power of space ships in antediluvian times". Also:

"Mr. Jessup's latest explorations have taken him to the high plateau of Mexico where he has discovered an extensive group of craters. They are as large as, and similar to, the mysterious lunar craters Linne and Hyginus N, and he believes them to have been made by objects from space. They are presently under study by means of aerial photography and the study will be ready for publication in approximately eighteen months".

Apparently the further exploration of the craters was never carried out. According to James W. Moseley, former publisher of Saucer News, Jessup sought university, foundation and private sponsorship of the project, but was unsuccessful in gaining sufficient interest and funds.

The Allende Letters

The mystery of the annotated paperback edition of *The Case for the UFO* was preceded by a series of strange letters from Carlos Miguel Allende addressed to Jessup. Two of these, reproduced as part of the *Annotated Edition*, appear in the following pages. The letters claimed that as a result of a strange experiment at sea utilizing principles of Einstein's Unified Field Theory, a destroyer and all its crew became invisible during October, 1943.

"The Field was effective in an oblate spheroidal shape," Allende wrote. He added that "any person within that sphere became vague in form, and that as a result of the experiment some of the crew went insane. Further horrifying aspects of the alleged experiment are detailed in the two letters (See Appendix).

The Allende letters became connected with *The Annotated Edition* when the Varo Manufacturing Company evidently got in touch with Jessup in regard to the latter.

Varo's unusual involvement in the mystery began a few months after February 1956, In April of that year Admiral N. Furth, Chief of the Office of Naval Research, Washington D.C., received a manila envelope postmarked Seminole, a small town in Texas. Written across its face was the notation "Happy Easter". When Furth opened the envelope he found a copy of the Jessup paperback. We are not certain of Furth's reactions, but we can assume that he thumbed through the book and that his interest was piqued by a series of notes, interjections, underscorings, etc., in three colors of ink, apparently written by three different people. Only the name of one of the authors of the annotations appeared in the notes, that of "Jemi".

The paperback had apparently been passed through the hands of the strange annotators several times. This conclusion could be drawn from the fact that the notes indicated discussions between two or all three of the men, with questions answered, and places where parts of a note had been marked through, underlined, or added to by one or both of the other men. Some had been deleted by marking through.

The notes had a tone of absolute weirdness. Sometimes they agreed with Jessup's original text; sometimes they contradicted it, as they referred to two types of people living in space. They specified two habitats for the space people: underseas, and what they termed the "stasis neutral", the latter term apparently in agreement with Jessup's exposition on points of neutral gravity in space.

They mentioned the building of undersea cities and identified two groups of spacemen, "L-M's" and "S-M's". The "L-M's" were designated as peaceful, the "S-M's" as sinister.

Some of the terms used would have been familiar to any ufologist of the 1950's, yet others expressed an alien-like vocabulary which had never been previously used in "saucer" literature.

Some of the terms were: Mothership, home-ship, dead-ship, great ark, great bombardment, great return, great war, little-men, force-fields, deep freezes, measure markers, scout ships, magnetic and gravity fields, sheet of diamond, cosmic rays, force cutters, inlay work, clear-talk, telepathing, burning "coat", nodes, vortice, magnetic "net".

They explained what happened to people and to ships and planes which had disappeared, as discussed in Jessup's original text – and elaborated upon the origin of odd storms and clouds, objects falling from the sky, strange marks and footprints, and other matters Jessup wrote about.

Two Theories

We do not know Admiral Furth's personal reaction to the strangely marked paperback. The history of this matter, again from a confidential source, next surfaces several months later, in July or August of the same year, when the paperback was passed on to Major Darrel L. Ritter, U.S.M.C., Aeronautical Project Officer of ONR. Soon afterward, and no date is available, Captain Sidney Sherby joined ONR, and, along with Commander George W. Hoover, Special Projects Officer, ONR, indicated interest in the book.

Sherby and Hoover were deeply involved in satellite development, and supervising the systems which would later place the first U.S. satellite into orbit. Some UFO buffs have expressed the belief that they were also coordinating gravity research, and that this was the reason for their interest.

The book was evidently taken to the Varo firm by Sherby, possibly in conjunction with Hoover. At that time, Varo was deeply involved in aero-space design and manufacturing for the military. One division was called "Military Assistance", which may have coordinated the firm's activities with the government, and occasionally performed personal services for military personnel (as any commercial organization might do).

At any rate, the Military Assistance Division agreed to run off a limited number of copies of the annotated book, and it was laboriously typed out my Miss Michael Ann Dunn, personal secretary to the president of the company, a Mr. Stanton. (Incidentally, Miss Dunn no longer is employed by Varo. Varo says that personnel records fails to find a record of her employment!)

Two theories evolve as to Varo's role in publishing the Annotated Edition:

(1) Top military brass passed this down through the lower echelon, thus avoiding the responsibility should there be any publicity, and it was published surreptitiously by Varo, the personnel of which may have had top military security clearance – avoiding sending it to a government printing source, where word might leak out. The Military was interested in applications of the notes to secret research being carried out by the U.S. After printing, the limited edition could be passed around to interested persons, and distributed to other contractors engaged in secret military development.

(2) Lower echelon officers, such as Sherby, had deep personal interests in the UFO mystery, and wanted copies to give to other Naval personnel who held similar interests. As a matter of personal interest, they asked the Varo company to make the reprint, knowing that the contractor would comply, as one of the many personal favors they may have extended to military personnel.

The latter of these alternatives is the writer's best guess. No great degree of secrecy seemed to have been employed. Jessup was called in by Varo and shown the book, and nothing in his subsequent writings or reported conversations indicates he was requested to maintain secrecy. Permission was obtained both from the author and the publisher, Citadel Press, to reproduce the text of the original book. Jessup was given several copies, probably the source of the copies a few UFO researchers reportedly possess.

One such copy, according to Riley H. Crabb, Director of Borderland Sciences Research, has been given to the late Bryant H. Reeves, author of two books published by Ray Palmer.

Crabb told me recently that he saw the *Varo Edition* while visiting Reeves at his home in Virginia Beach. Reeves agreed to lend the volume for a brief period, and Crabb, who told me he felt that both he and Reeves were "under surveillance", hesitated to carry it with him back to his home in California. He posted it to himself, but it was lost in the mails.

A tradition of bad luck or strange circumstances is connected with possession of the *Varo Edition*. One person's home, along with the book, was destroyed by fire shortly after he acquired a copy. Capt.

Edward J. Ruppelt, former head of Project Bluebook, suffered a fatal heart attack, allegedly shortly after he read a borrowed copy. Robert Loftin, UFO author, who also died prematurely, was another rumored owner of the book. Of course, except for the deaths, thus is purely hearsay, and, if true, could have been the result of coincidence.

Regardless of the motivation behind printing the *Annotated Edition*, neither Varo nor the military could foresee the zeal of civilian UFO research in its probing of the matter. Intrigued by the mystery, and questioning the untimely death of Jessup, Ufologists began delving. At least two national magazine articles explored Jessup's death and his connection with the book.

Our Personal Involvement

Our personal involvement with the mystery surrounding Jessup began after we heard of his suicide and began looking into rumors involving the above matters. Our findings became the basis for a book, *The Strange Case of Dr. M.K. Jessup*, published in 1963 by Saucerian Books, and reprinted in 1965 and 1967.

The book contained a chapter about *The Annotated Edition* and reproduced the Preface with annotations, though not in facsimile. The Preface was provided by Riley Crabb of the Borderland Sciences Research Associates Foundation, Inc. Our interest continued, though we had never seen an actual copy of *The Annotated Edition*, and often doubted that it really existed.

One of our correspondents claimed to possess the complete volume in photocopy form and sent us second generation copies of a few pages to prove his point. Brad Steiger provided miniature reproductions of three actual pages to illustrate an article, "Fantastic Key to the Flying Saucer Mystery," in *Saga* magazine, November, 1967. He noted that the reproductions were from a microfilm copy owned by Stephen Yankee.

We finally acquired one of the rare original copies in 1971 from a friend of the late Mr. Jessup, to whom he had given one of the few copies supplied him by its publisher. Observing the clarity of the printing and the good physical condition of our copy we began exploring the idea of a facsimile reprint.

I am president of a small publishing company, Saucerian Press, Inc., which specializes in limited editions of works pertaining to unidentified flying objects. Sales of these books rarely exceed 2,000 copies, and the main purpose of the publisher is to provide distribution for works, sales of which do not warrant general trade publication.

Publishing a facsimile of *The Annotated Edition* would present problems. It contained about twice the number of pages of our usual publications; it demanded expensive separation negatives and printing, and its appeal would be much more limited than our usual books. It would demand a run of no more than 500 copies and would have to sell at a relatively high price. While prudence urged that the idea be dropped, two overwhelming considerations urged us on. The original edition of *The Case For the UFO* had long been out of print, was becoming very rare among antiquarian dealers. *The Annotated Edition* was almost legendary, surrounded by excessive mystery and controversy, and unavailable to serious students of the UFO mystery, either in libraries or by their own personal acquisition.

In July 1972, Saucerian Press made the positive decision to publish this edition.

The Facsimile Edition

We have reproduced the original as faithfully as possible, within the photo-mechanical means available to us.

The body of the facsimile edition begins with the Introduction on the following page. No information as to the authorship of this Introduction is given in the original. It is, however, competently done, helps to explain what is to follow and comments further upon the arrangement of the volume.

In our original copy the Appendix is bound between the original Introduction to Jessup's text and Part One of the body of the book. While this could be a mistake in binding, the Appendix, consisting of the two Allende letters, does help set the tone and scene for *The Annotated Edition* and most likely was bound there on purpose. Not having a second coy for comparison, we have included the Appendix at the same place, even though this represents a radical placement.

The writer is happy that this work is going to be printed. He believes it will represent a contribution to the literature of Ufology, some minor monument to those strange and wonderful times that began with Kenneth Arnold in 1947.

                                                                         Gray Barker
                                                                         July, 1973

INTRODUCTION

Notations that imply intimate knowledge of UFO's their means of motion, their origin, background, history, and habits of beings occupying UFO's provide an interesting subject for investigation. Such notations were found in a copy of the paperback edition of M.K. Jessup's "Case for the UFO's". Because of the importance which we attach to the possibility of discovering clues to the nature of gravity, no possible item, however disreputable from the point of view of classical science, should be overlooked.

The annotated copy, addressed to Admiral N. Furth, Chief, Office of Naval Research, Washington 25, D.C., came in a manila envelope postmarked Seminole, Texas, 1955. Written across the face of the envelope in ink was "Happy Easter." In July or August of that year the book appeared in the incoming correspondence of Major Darrell L. Ritter, U.S.M.C. Aeronautical Project Office in ONR. When Captain Sidney Sherby reported aboard at ONR he obtained the book from Major Ritter. Captain Sherby and Commander George W. Hoover, Special Projects Officer, ONR indicated direct interest in some of the material therein.

Varo Mfg. Co., Garland, Texas, offered to re-publish the book together with all notations in a very limited edition as a prelude to consideration of further pursuit of this unconventional material.

Miss Michael Ann Dunn has undertaken the task of rewriting this book including all notes, interjections, underscoring, and etc. By form, position, color, and footnotes as much of the meaning and relationships of the original annotated copy is retained as possible. No attempt has been made, with ultra violet light or other methods, to read material which has been crossed out by one of the correspondents.

It appears that these notes were written by three persons. The use of three distinct colors of ink– blue, blue-violet, and blue-green– and the difference in handwriting lead to this conclusion. Hereafter they will be referred to as Mr. A, Mr. B, and Jemi.

It is assumed that the third person was Jemi because of the direct use of "Jemi" in salutations and references to that name by Mr. A (Green) and Mr. B (Blue) throughout the book. There are many, some of which appear on pages 2, 81, 122, 126, and 162 in the original book. It is possible of course that it is merely a salutation.

It is possible that two of these men are twins. There are two references to this word. They appear on page 6 and page 81 of the original book. The assumption that Mr. A is one of the twins may be correct. On page 81, Mr. A has written and marked through "...and I Do Not know How this came to Pass, Jemi." Then he has written, "I remember, My twin...". On page 6 he writes in an apparent answer to Mr. B, "No, My twin..." We cannot be sure of the other twin.

It is probable that these men are Gypsies. In the closing pages of the book Mr. B says, "...only a Gypsy will tell another of that catastrophe. And we are a discredited people, ages ago. Hah! Yet, man wonders where "we" come from..." On page 130 Mr. A. says, "...ours is a way of life, time proven & happy. We have nothing, own nothing except our music & philosophy & are happy." On page 76 Mr. says "Show this to a Brother Gypsy..." On Page 158 the reference to the word "we" by Mr. A could refer to the "discredited people". Charles G. Leland in his book "English Gipsies and Their Language" states that the Gypsies call each other brother and sister, and are not in the habit of admitting to their fellowship people of a different blood and with whom they have no sympathy. This could explain the usage of the term in the closing notes "My Dear Bothers" and perhaps the repeated reference to "vain humankind."

This book was apparently passed through the hands of these men several or many times. This conclusion is drawn from the fact that there are discussions between two or all three of the men, questions answered, and places where parts of a note have been marked through, underlined, or added to by one or both of the other men. Some have been deleted by marking through.

Shortly after the publication of his book, Mr. Jessup received a letter from a Carlos Miguel Allende. (A copy of this letter and the one that followed appear in the appendix.) Mr. Jessup said that he "had felt from the first that this man was the one who mailed the book to the Navy.." Consideration of the handwriting, style, content, and phraseology of both the notes and letter show a distinct possibility that the letter was written by Mr. A. This conclusion comes from the notes by Mr. A on page 130, 117, and 150. These references to Farraday, Hob-mail or cleated shoes, and catching fire are nearly the same as the ones in the letter.

The letter was received by Mr. Jessup in Miami, on Friday January 13, 1956. It was postmarked Gainesville, Texas, and mailed in an envelope of the Turner Hotel, Gainesville. It is copied as nearly verbatim as possible.

Mr. Jessup received a second letter from Mr. Allende postmarked Du Bois, Pennsylvania, May 25, 1956. Due to peculiar spelling and other idiosyncrasies there can be little doubt that Mr. A. and Carlos Allende are the same person.

These men have been careless in their spelling, capitalization, punctuation and sentence structure; though consistency indicates adherence to custom, perhaps dictated by their original language. The notes are arranged as close to the original as possible. In cases where a word or group of words could not be deciphered footnotes were used.

It might seem that the underscore in the book was in the form of a code or that if read separately that it would have a meaning of its own. Superficial examination has failed to disclose such a code. The underscored text usually refer to the notes by the same man.

The distinction between the original book and the handwritten additions to it is made by the use of red and black type. Black type indicates the type of the original book. Red type indicates any addition made in handwriting by Mr. A, Mr. B. or Jemi to the original.

The placement of the notes indicates the paragraph to which they refer, or to their precise position in the book.

The page numbers of the original book are denoted in parenthesis. The matter on the page numbered follows the number. The page numbers of this edition appear at the bottom of each page.

It had been necessary to disregard the italics of the original.

It might be helpful for you to know a little about the nature of the notes before you begin reading this book. The notes refer to two types of people living in space. Specifically the "stasis neutral" and the undersea are mentioned as habitats. They seem to live in both interchangeably. The building of undersea cities is mentioned. Many different kinds of ships are used as transportation. These two peoples, races or whatever they may be called, are referred to over and over again. They are called L-M's and S-Ms. The L-M's seem to be peaceful; the S-M's are not. It seems that the annotations are inclined toward the L-M's as they speak more kindly of them that the S-M's.

Terms such as: mothership, home-ship, dead-ship, Great ark, great bombardment, great return, great war, little-men, force-fields, deep freezes, undersea building, measure markers, scout ships, magnetic and gravity fields, sheets of diamond, cosmic rays, force cutters, undersea explorers, inlay work, clear-talk, telepathing, burning "coat", nodes, vortice, magnetic "net", and many others are used quite naturally by these men. They explain how, why, and what happens to people, ships, and planes that have disappeared. They explain the origin of odd storms and clouds, objects falling from the sky, strange marks and footprints, and other things which we have not solved.

These men seem to feel that it is too late for man to obtain space flight. They feel that mankind could not cope with "those mind wrecking conditions that space and sea contain" for mankind is to egotistical, values too much the material, wars over mer parcels of the planet, is too filled with jealously, and lacks true brotherhood.

How much truth is there in this? That cannot be answered. It is evident that these men provide some very intriguing explanations; explanations that may be worth consideration.

PREFACE

The subject of UFO's in its present stage is like astronomy in that it is a purely observational "science," not an experimental one; necessarily, therefore, it must be based on observation and not on experiment. Observation, in this case, consists of everything which can be found to have bearing on the subject. *There are thousands of references to it in ancient literature,* but the authors did not know that their references had any bearing, for the subject did not then exist. The writers were recording such things as met their senses solely through an honest effort to report inexplicable observational data.

> *Hoping, in those days, that something would "come of it" Nowadays, Science is afraid that "Something Will Come of it." It will, too. In 1956 or 57 the Air force Will have Ships LIKE these in appearance & Will "feel" safe to announce that Human eyes Have seen Saucers from outer Space BUT to Not be Worried because "we too have these Ships" Oh! Brother What a farce! Ours will be JET propelled not M ◯ propelled.*

Some of my contemporaries have attempted to prove that all of these phenomena are, in some way or other, illusory, and that in any case they do not involve flight, wingless or otherwise, mechanical propulsion or intelligent direction.

I consider their negative case unproven because *there is an overwhelming mass of authentic evidence (B)* which can be cited as: (1) direct observation, (2) indirect observation, and (3) supporting evidence or indication.

There is one sphere of indirect evidence in the form of events of mysterious nature which have never been explained. These things would be easy to explain were we to admit the limitations of our own knowledge, and the possibility of "intelligence" elsewhere in the universe operating space ships — quite possibly more than one kind of "intelligence" and more than one kind of space ship.

This world is full of unexplained oddities. The legends of Atlantis and Mu have been favorite targets of the scoffers. "They" say there are no ghosts, no spirits, nothing falls from the sky but iron and stone meteorites. But for centuries the earth was believed to be flat, there was no America, no heliocentric system of earth and planets, no fossil dinosaurs; *yet we know these beliefs to have been wrong.*

Reliable people have been *seeing* the phenomena known as flying saucers *for a thousand years and more. There are good reports as far back as 1500 BC and before. Thousands of people have seen some kind of navigable contraptions in the sky,* and *some have sworn it under oath.*

> *In a day When oaths were just as good as Money -in- Hand for if incorrect your Neck suffered "The Miracle"[1] from the Church as a knife from the out- raged who took your oath.*

---

[1] Undecipherable: could be Nracle or Nrack.

I cannot agree with any astronomer who insists that all of these things are mirages, planets, clouds or illusions. The majority of the people are articulate enough to tell their stories, and sincere enough to make depositions before notaries public. Even scientists concede that these folk saw something.

I see nothing particularly odd in strange descriptions of phenomena the like of which has no earthly counterpart or for which we have no frame of reference.

If he does not, then he KNOWS the L-M's.

This work is a serious attempt to bring order out of chaos, an attempt to pull all of the facets of this controversy into a basic stratum upon which to make an intelligent evaluation of the subject.

M.K. Jessup

Washington, D.C.
January 13, 1955

If he does succeed in such evaluation Nobody cares enough to bother believing him for that would require the effort of Courage & the Gaiyar are such cowards & conformists. Even if believed, Nobody would dare say so for that would require action & They dare not act in BEHALF OF A BELIEF THAT INTERFERES WITH USUAL LIVING

TABLE OF CONTENTS

Introduction

PART I
The Case for the UFO's

"If It Waddles..."?	1
UFO's Are Real	3
There Is Intelligence in Space	9
Short-Cut to Space Travel	15
The Home of the UFO's	20
Are UFO's Russian?	22
Space Flights: Common Denominator	24

PART II
Meteorology Speaks

Falling Ice	28
Falling Stones	32
Falling Live Things	37
Falling Animal and Organic Matter	40
Falling Shaped Things	45
Falls of Water	52
Clouds and Storms	56
Rubbish in Space	60

PART III
History Speaks

Disappearing Ships and Crews	65
Teleportation or Kidnapping?	75
Levitation	84
Marks and "Footprints"	91
Disappearing Planes	97
Fireballs and Lights	101
Legends	106

PART IV
Astronomy Speaks

The Incredible Decade	115
UFO's Against the Sun	119
Location of UFO's	125
UFO Patrol	128
The Height of the Puzzle	133
The Case is Proved!	137
A NOTE ON SOURCES	144

List of Illustrations

A Flying Saucer photographed over Brasil	2
Passage of Auroral beam, November 17, 1882	13
Cross found in an ancient grave in Georgia.	50
Meteor from an organic cloud, Salford, England, 1877	59
The "Devil's Hoofmarks."	92
Six UFO's seen and drawn by Astronomer Barnard in 1882	136
Comet "B" of 1881	141

NOTE:
Anyone reading this book would have to KNOW that Electron *quatums* (sic), Within Molecular structures, are similar in scope of "field" as Planets *orbits*.
They Would Have to know that, Electrons in Metal go across, What in Planetary Systems, would be BILLIONS OF MILES, Leaving three a Graviational field, Dead-spot *or* Node, or Vortice or Neutral as *this one thing* is variously called. Realizing this as Dr. Albert Einstien did, it shows clearly how solids may become Energy or Dissolute AND How then they May Pass easily out of Visual scope *instantly*. This is Merely one Clue gleamed from *Einstiens Theory of a Unified Magnetic* Field through *all substances* AND throughout Whole inter-Galactic-Universe.U.S. EXPIERMENTS, 1943 ON ONE PART OF IT *PROVED* PLENTY!

Ed: The page numbers in this Table of Contents are the numbers in the original book.

INTRODUCTION

The Case for the UFO is perhaps the **most unusual** and comprehensive volume yet produced on the fascinating subject of the "flying saucers." To bring the rare combination of a scientifically trained mind, plus imaginative, fetter-free thinking to the mysterious subject of possible intelligence from outer space, is something which has been much needed. This is precisely what Jr. Jessup has done.

This book is a sound step forward in the great need to approach, dispassionately, material pertaining to the flying saucers; it goes far toward putting the topic on a down-to-earth basis. I have never before seen such apparently unrelated subject matter brought into focus so skillfully and analyzed so successfully.

> He says "apparently" means "seemingly"

It is the men of insight and the men of unobstructed vision of every generation who are able to lead us through the *quagmire of a in-a-rut thinking. It is the men of imagination who are able to see relationships which escape the casual observer.* It remains for the men of intuition to seek answers while others avoid even the question.

Mr. Jessup's analyses are based on phenomena which were of scientific record many years before the present controversial era, and are therefore objective; thus, the overall picture which we have here will, and should, become the bible for the UFO.

Whereas, I may not necessarily agree with Mr. Jessup *in each* of his startling deductions, certainly there is every reason to believe that his is the correct approach: indeed, many of his conclusions will be difficult, if not altogether impossible to refute!

Having brought to The Case for the UFO his ability to reason clearly, to research assiduously and to write lucidly and effectively, Mr. Jessup has performed a valuable service to all of us who know and believe "There are more things in heaven and earth... than are dreamt of in (our) Philosophy."

FRANK EDWARDS

> Jemi:
> He may reason clearly *but only to the point* where
> Logical deduction stops & Emotionalism takes over,
> as do all Humans. Mortification *or* pride or Lack
> of enough evidence May put him on a Soap-box Level.
> Yet, He *is* a Scientist and as such May show No such
> traits, as are ;usually found in Gaiyari. I see your
> point, Jemi. He could convince the whole thing but
> then have you ever tried to tell the Honest truth
> about Something of which *only* you have observed?
> True enough, It cannot be done. So Let us see What
> *this* man has in ways of Doing So, Eh?

APPENDIX

The first letter received by Mr. Jessup from Carols Allende:

>Carlos Miguel Allende
>R. D. #1 Box 223
>New Kensington, Penn.

My Dear Dr. Jessup,

   Your invocation to the Public that they move en Masse upon their Representatives and have thusly enough Pressure placed at the right & sufficient Number of Places where from a Law demanding Research into Dr. Albert Einstiens (sic) Unified Field Theory May be enacted (1925-27) is Not at all Necessary. It May Intrest (sic) you to know that The Good Doctor Was Not so Much influenced in his retracton (sic) of that Work, by Mathematics, as he most assuredly was by Humantics. (sic)

   His Later computations, done strictly for his own edification & amusement, upon cycles of Human Civilization & Progress compared to the Growth of Mans General over-all Character Was enough to Horrify Him. Thus, We are "told" today that that Theory was "Incomplete".

   Dr. B. Russell asserts privately that It is complete. He also says that Man is Not Ready for it & Shan't be until after W. W. III. Nevertheless, "Results" of My friend Dr. Franklin Reno, Were used. These Were a complete Recheck of That Theory, With a View to any & Every Possible quick use of it, if feasable (sic) in a Very short time. There Were good Results, as far as a Group Math Re-Cheek AND as far as a good Physical "Result," to Boot. YET THE NAVT FEARS TO USE THIS RESULT. The Result was & stands today as Proof that The Unified Field Theory to a certain extent is correct. Beyond that certain extent No Person in his right senses, or having any senses at all, Will evermore dare to go. I am sorry that I Mislead You in My Previous Missive. True, enough, such a form of Levitation has been accomplished as described. It is also a Very commonly observed reaction of certain Metals to Certain Fields surrounding a current, This field being used for that purpose. Had Farraday concerned himself about the Mag. Field surrounding an Electric Current, We today Would NOT Exist or if We did exist, our present Geo-political situation would have the very time-bomish, ticking off towards Destruction, atmosphere that Now exists. Alright, Alright! The "result" was complete invisibility of a ship, Destroyer type, and all of its crew While at Sea. (Oct. 1943) The Field Was effective in an oblate spheroidal shape, extending one Hundred yards (More or Less, due to Lunar position & Latitude) out from each beam of the ship. Any Person Within that sphere became vague in form BUT He too observed those Persons aboard that ship as though they too were of the same state, yet were walking upon nothing. Any person without that sphere could see Nothing save the clearly Defined shape of the Ships Hull in the Water, PROVIDING of course, that that person was just close enough to see yet, just barely outside of the field. Why tell you Now? Very Simple; If You choose to go Mad, then you would reveal this information. Half of the officers & the crew of that Ship are at Present, Mad as Hatters. A few, are even Yet, confined to certain areas where they May receive trained Scientific aid when they, either, "Go Blank" or Go Blank" & "Get Stuck". Going-Bland IE an after effect of the Man having been within the field too Much, IS Not at all an unplesant experience too Healthily Curious Sailors. However it is when also, they "Get Stuck" that they call it "HELL" INCORPORATED" The Man thusly stricken can Not Move of his won volition unless tow or More of those who are within the field go & touch him, quickly, else he "Freezes".

   If a Man Freezes, His position Must be Marked out carefully and then the Field in cut-off. Everyone but that "Frozen" Man is able to Move; to appreciate apparent Solidity again. Then, the Newest Member of the crew Must approach the Spot, where he will find the "Frozen" Mans face or Bare skin, that is Not covered by usual uniform Clothing. Sometimes, it takes only an hour or so Sometimes all Night & all Day Long & Worse It once took 6 months, to get The Man "Unfrozen". This "Deep Freeze" was not psychological. It is the Result of a Hyper-Field that is set up, within the field of the Body, While the "Scorch" Field is turned on & this at Length or upon a Old Hand.

A Highly complicated Place of Equipment Had to be constructed in order to Unfreeze those who became "True Froze", of "Deep Freeze" subjects. Usually a "Deep Freeze" Man goes Mad, Stark Raving., Gibbering, Running MAD, if his 'freeze' is far More than a Day in our time.

I speak of TIME for DEEP "Frozen Men" are Not aware of Time as We know it. They are Like Semi-comatoese (sic) person, who Live, breathe, Look & feel but still are unaware of So Utterly Many things as to constitute a "Nether World" to them. A Man in an ordinary common Freeze is aware of Time, Sometimes acutely so. Yet They are Never aware of Time precisely as you or I are aware of it. The First "Deep Freeze" As I said took 6 months to Rectify. It also took over 5 Million Dollars worth of Electronic equipment & a Special Ship Berth. If around or Near the Philadelphia Navy[2] and you see a group of Sailors in the act of Putting their Hands Upon a fellow or upon "thin air," observe the Digits & appendages of the Stricken Man. If they seem to Waver, as tho within a Heat-Mirage, go quickly & Put YOUR Hands upon Him, For that Man is the Very Most Desparate of Men in The World. Not one of those Men ever want at all to become again invisible. I do Not think that Much More Need be said as to Why Man is Not Ready for Force-Field Work. Eh?

You will Hear phrases from these Men such as "Caught in the Flow (or the Push) or "Stuck in the Green" or Stuck in Molasses" or "I was "going" FAST", These refer to Some of the Decade-Later after effects of Force-Field "ork. "Caught in the Flow" describes exactly the "Stuck in Molasses" sensation of a Man going into a Deep Freeze" or Plain Freeze" either of the two. "Caught in the Push" can either refer to That Which a Man feels Briefly WHEN he is either about to inadvertently "Go-Blank" IE Become Invisible" or about to "Get Stuck" in a "Deep Freeze" or "Plain Freeze."

There are only a very few of the original Experimental D-E's Crew Left by Now, Sir, Most went insane, one just walked "throo" His quarters Wall in sight of His Wife & Child & 2 other crew Members (WAS NEVER SEEN AGAIN), two "Went into "The Flame, "I.E. They "Froze" & caught fire, while carrying common Small-Boat Compasses, one Man carried the Compass & Caught fre, the other came for the "Laying on of Hands" as he was nearest but he too, took fire. THEY BURNED FOR 18 DAYS. The faith in "Hand Laying" Died When this Happened & Mens Minds Went by the scores. The expierement (sic) Was a Complete Success. The Men Were Complete Failures.

Check Philadelphia Papers for a tine one Paragraph (upper Half of sheet, inside the paper Near the rear 3rd of Paper, 1944-46 in Spring or Fall or Winter, NOT Summer.) of an Item describing the Sailors Actions after their initial Voyage. They Raided a Local to the Navy Yard "Gin Mill" or "Beer Joint" & caused such Shock & Paralysis of the Waitresses that Little comprehensible could be gotten from them, save that Paragraph & the Writer of it, Does Not Believe it, & Says "I only wote what I heard & them Dames is Daffy. So, all I get is a "Hide-it" Bedtime Story."

Check observer ships crew, Matson Lines Liberty ship out of Norfolk, (Company MAY Have Ships Log for that Voyage or Coast Guard have it) The S.S. Andrew Furnseth, Chief Mate Mowsely, (Will secure Captains Name Later) (Ships Log Has Crew List on it.) one crew Member Richard Price or "Splicey" Price May Remember other Names of Dec Crew Men, (Coast Guard has record of Sailors issued "Papers") Mr. Price Was 18 or 19 then, Oct. 1943, and Lives or Lived at that time in His old Family Home in Roanoke, VA a small town with a Small Phone book. These Men Were Witnesses, The Men of this crew, "Connelly of New England, (Boston?), May have witnessed but I doubt it. (Spelling May be incorrect) DID Witness this. I ask you to Do this bit of Research simply that you May Choke on you own Tongue when you Remember what you have "appealed be Made Law"

Very Disrespectfully Yours,
Carl M. Allen

P.S. Will Help More if you see Where I can. (Z416175)

---

[2] Could be "Free Freeze"

Days Later

Notes in addition to and pertaining to Missive.
(Contact Rear Admiral Ransom Bennett for verification of info Herein. Navy Chief of research. He may offer you a job, ultimately)

Coldly & analytically speaking, without the Howling that is in the Letter to you accompanying this, I will say the following in all Fairness to you & to Science. (1) The Navy did Not know that the men could become invisible WHILE NOT UPON THE SHIP & UNDER THE FIELDS INFLUENCE. (2) The Navy Did Not know that <u>there would be</u> Men Die from odd effects of HYPER "Field" within <u>or</u> upon "Field." (3) Further, They even yet do Not know Why this happened & are not even sure that the "F" within "F" is the reason, for sure at all. <u>In Short</u> the Atomic bomb didn't kill the expierimentors (sic) thus the expieriments (sic) went on-but eventually one or two were accidentally killed BUT <u>the cause</u> was known as to Why they died. Myself, I "feel" that something pertaining to that Small-boat compass "triggered" off The Flames." I have no proof, but Neither Does the Navy. (4) WORSE & Not Mentioned When one or two of their Men, Visible-within-the-field-to-all-the-others, Just <u>Walked into Nothingness</u>, AND Nothing Could be felt, of them, either when the "field Was turned on OR off, THEY WERE JUST GONE! <u>Then</u>, More Fears Were Amassed. (5) Worse, Yet, When an apparently Visible & New-Man Just walks seemingly "throo" the Wall of his House, the surrounding area Searched by all Men & thoroughly scrutinized by & with & Under an Installed Portable Field developer AND NOTHING EVER found of him. <u>So Many Many Fears were by then in effect that the Sum total of them all could Not ever again be faced by ANY of those Men or by the Men Working at & Upon The Experiments.</u>

I wish to Mention that Somehow, also, the Experimental Ship Disappeared from its Philadelphia Dock and only a Very few Minutes Later appeared at its other Dock in the Norfolk, Newport New Portsmouth area. This was distinctly AND clearly identified as being that place BUT the ship them, <u>again</u>, disappeared And Went <u>Back</u> to its Philadelphia Dock in only a Very few Minutes or Less. This was also Noted in the Newspapers But I Forget what paper I read it in or When It happened. Probably Late in the experiments, May have been in 1956 <u>after</u> Experiments were discontinued, I can Not Say for Sure.

To the Navy this Whole thing was So Impractical due to its Morale Blasting effects Which were so much so that efficient operation of the Ship was Drastically Hindered and then after this occurrence It was shown that even the Mere operation of a ship could Not be counted upon at all. In short, Ignorance of this thing bred Such Terrors of it that, on the Level of attempted operations, with what knowledge was then available It was deemed as impossible, Impracticable and Too Horrible.

<u>I believe</u> that Had YOU <u>then</u> been Working upon & With the team that was Working upon this project With yourself knowing what You <u>NOW</u> know, <u>that</u> "The Flames" Would Not have been <u>so unexpected</u>, or Such a Terrifying Mystery. Also, More than Likely, I must say in All fairness, None of these other occurrences could have happened without some knowledge of their possibility of occurring. In fact, They May have been prevented by a far more Cautious Program AND by a Much More Cautiously careful Selection of Personnel for Ships officers & Crew. Such Was Not the case. The Navy used Whatever Human <u>Material</u> was at hand, Without Much, <u>if any</u>, thought as to character & Personality of that Material. If care, Great Care is taken in selection of Ship, and officers and crew AND If Careful Indoctrination is taken <u>along</u> with Careful watch over articles of apparel Such as rings & Watches & Identification bracelets & Belt buckles, <u>Plus</u> AND ESPECIALLY the effect of Hob-Nailed shoes or Cleated-shoes U.S. Navy issue shoes, I feel that some progress towards dissipating the fearfilled ignorance surrounding this project Will be Most surely and certainly accomplished. The Records of the U.S. Maritime <u>Service</u> HOUSE Norfolk Va., (for Graduated Seamen of their Schools) Will reveal Who was assigned to S S. Andrew Furuseth for Month of either Late Sept. or October of 1943. I remember positively of one other observer who stood beside Me When tests were going on. He was from New England, Brown-Blond Curly Hair, blue eyes, Don't remember Name. I Leave it up <u>to you</u> to Decide if further Work shall be put into this or Not, and Write this in Hopes there Will be.

Very Sincerely,
Carl M. Allen

The second letter received by Mr. Jessup from Carlos Allende:

                                                             Carl M. Allen
                                                             RFD #1 Box 223
                                                             New Kensington, Pa

Dear Mr. Jessup:

    Having just recently gotten home from my long travels around the country I find that you had dropped me a card. You ask that I write you "at once" and So after taking everything into consideration, I have decided to do so. You ask me for what is tantamount to positive proof of something that only the duplication of those devices that produce "this phenomenon" could ever give you. At least, were I of scientific bent, I presume that, were I of Such a Curiosity about something, the which has been produced from a theory that was discarded (1927) as incomplete, I am sure that I would be of such a dubiousness towards that I would Have to be shown these devices that Produced such a curious interaction of Forces & Fields, in operation & their product Mr. Jessup, I could NEVER possibly satisfy such an attitude. The reason being that I could not, Nor ever would the Navy Research Dept. (Then under the present oss of the Navy, Burke) ever let it be known that any such thing was ever allowed to be done. For you see, It was because of Burkes Curiosity & willingness & prompting that this experiment was enabled to be carried out. It proved a White-elephant but His attitude towards advance & ultra-advanced types of research is just "THE" THING that put him where he is today. (Or at least, to be sure, It carries a great weight). Were the stench of such an Experiments results EVER to come out, He would be crucified.

    However, I have noticed, that throo the ages, those who have had this happen to them, once the vulgar passions that caused the reaction have cooled-off AND further research OPENLY carried on, that these crucified ones achieve something akin to Saint hood. You say that this, "is of the greatest importance". I disagree with you Mr. Jessup, not just whole Heartedly, but vehemently. However at the same time, your ideas & your own sort of curiosity is that of mine own sort and besides my disagreement is based upon philosophical Morality and not upon that curiosity which Drives Science so rapidly. I can be of some positive help to you in myself but to do so would require a Hypnotist, Sodium Pentathol, a tape recorder & an excellent typist-secretary in order to produce material of Real value to you.

    As you know one who is hypnotized cannot Lie and one who is both hypnotized AND given "Truth serum" as it is colloqually (sic) known, COULD NOT POSSIBLY LIE, AT ALL. To boot, My Memory would be THUS enabled to remember things in such great detail, things that my present consciousness cannot recall at all, or only barely and uncertainly that it would be of far greater benefit to use hypnosis. I could thus be enabled to not only Recall COMPLETE names, but also addresses & telephone numbers AND perhaps the very important Z Numbers of those sailors whom I sailed with then or even came into contact with. I could too, being something of a Dialectician, be able to thusly talk exactly as these witnesses talked and imitate or illustrate their mannerisms & Habits of thought, thus your psychologists can figure IN ADVANCE the Surefire method of dealing Most Successfully with these. I could NOT do this with someone with whom I had not observed at length & these men, I lived with for about 6 months, so you are bound to get good to excellent results. The mind does NOT ever forget, Not really, As you know. Upon this I suggest this way of doing this with Myself but further, the Latter usage of Myself in Mannerism & Thought pattern illustration is suggested in order that the Goal of inducing these Men to place themselves at & under you disposal (HYPNOTICALLY OR UNDER TRUTH-SERUM), is a Goal, the Which could Have FAR greater impact, due to co-relation of Experiences remembered Hypnotically by Men who have NOT seen or even written to each other, at all, for Nearly or over TEN years. In this, With such Men as Witnesses, giving irrefutable testimony It is my belief that were, Not the Navy, but the Airforce, confronted with such evidence, (IE Chief of Research) there would be either an uproar or a quiet and determined effort to achieve SAFELY "that which" the Navy failed at. They did NOT fail to, I hope you realize, achieve Metallic & organic invisibility nor did they fail to, unbesoughtedly, (sic) achieve transportation of thousands of tons of Metal & Humans at an eyes blink speed. Even though this latter effect of prolonged experimentation was (to them) THE thing that caused them to consider the experiment as a failure, I

BELIEVE THAT FURTHER EXPERIMENTS WOULD NATURALLY HAVE PRODUCED CONTROLLED TRANSPORT OF GREAT TONNAGES AT ULTRA-FAST SPEEDS TO A DESIRED POINT THE INSTANT IT IS DESIRED throo usage of an area covered by: (I) those cargoes and (2) that " Field" that could cause those goods, Ships or Ship parts (MEN WERE TRANSPORTED AS WELL) to go to another Point. Accidentally & to the embarrassed perplexity of the Navy THIS HAS ALREADY HAPPENED TO A WHOLE SHIP, CREW & ALL. I read of this AND of THE OFF-BASE AWOL ACTIVITIES OF the crew-Men who were at the time invisible in a Philadelphia NEWSPAPER. UNDER HARCOHYPNOSIS I CAN BE ENABLED TO DIVULGE THE NAME, DATE & SECTION & PAGE NUMBER of that Paper & the other one. Thus this papers "Morgue" Will Divulge EVEN MORE POSITIVE PROOF ALREADY PUBLISHED of this experiment. The Name of the REPORTER who skeptically covered & Wrote of these incidents (OF THE RESTAURANT-BARROOM RAID WHILE INVISIBLE & OF THE SHIPS SUDDEN AWOL) AND WHO INTERVIEWED the Waitresses CAN THUS BE FOUND, thus HIS and the Waitresses testimony can be added to the Records. Once on this track, I believe That you can uncover CONSIDERABLY MORE evidence to sustain this, —— (what Would you call it —SCANDAL or DISCOVERY?) You would Need a Dale Carneigie to Maneuver these folks into doing just as you wish. It would be cheaper than paying everyone of all these witnesses & Much more Ethical. The Idea Is, to the Layman type of person, utterly ridiculous. However, can you remember, all by yourself, the Date of a Newspaper in which you saw an interesting item more than 5 years ago? Or recall names of Men, their phone #'s that you saw in 1943-44.

  I do hope you will consider this plan. You will Progress as Not possible in any other way. Of course, I ealize that you would need a Man Who can cause people to want to have fun, to play with Hypnotism, one that can thusly dupe those he-you need to: #1 come to His Demonstrations & thus call on them to be either or both "Honored" as Helping with the show" & for doing Him a Great favor, &/or being part of the act for the mite of a small fee He would HAVE to be a Man of such an adroit ingenuity at Manufacturing a plausible story on the-instant-he-sizes-up-his-"personality-to be dealt-with THAT had cost PLENTY. The ability to convince people of an outright Lie as being the absolute truth would be one of his prime prerequisites. (Ahem.) Yes, some such skulduggery (sic) would have to be thought well out & done. THE ULTIMATE END WILL BE A TRUTH TOO HUGE, AND TOO FANTASTIC, TO NOT BE TOLD. A WELL-FOUNDED TRUTH BACKED UP BY UNOBFUSCATIVE PROOF POSITIVE. I would like to find where it is that these Sailors live NOW. It is known that some few people can somehow tell you a mans name & his Home address UNDER HYPNOSIS EVEN THOUGH NEVER HAVING EVER MENT OR SEEN THE PERSON. These folks have a very high or Just a High PSI factor in their make-up that can be intensified under stress or strain OR that usually is intensified under extreme fright. It also can be RE-intensified by Hypnosis, thus is like reading from the Encyclopedia Britannica. Even though that Barroom-Restaurant Raid was staged by invisible or partly invisible men, those men CAN SEE EACH OTHER THUS NAMES, In the excitement, were sure to have been Mentioned, whether last or first Names or Nicknames. A check of the Naval Yards Dispensaries or Hospital or aid stations or prison RECORDS of that particular day that the Barroom-Restaurant occurred May revela (sic) the EXACT NAMES OF PRECISELY WHO WERE THE MEN, THEIR SERVICE SERIAL NUMBERS & THUS THE INFORMATION ON WHERE THEY ARE FROM BE SECURED & by adroit "Maneuvuerings" (sic) of those still at Home, THE NAME OF THE PLACE where they are at present can be secured.

  HOW WOULD YOU LIKE TO ACTUALLY SPEAK TO (or some of THE MEN) A MAN WHO WAS ONCE AN INVISIBLE HAMAN BEING? (MAY BECOME SO IN FRONT OF YOUR VERY EYES IF HE TURNS-OFF HIS HIP-SET). Well, all this fantastically preposterous sort of rubbish will be necessary, Just to do that, the Hypnotist-psychologist & all that. Maybe I suggest something too thorught (sic) & too Methodical for your taste but then I, as first subject, Don't care to be Hypnotized at all, But too, feel that certain pull of curiosity about this thing that, to me, is irresistible. I want to crack this thing wide open. My reasons are simply to enable more work to be done upon this "Field Theory".

  I am a star-gazer Mr. Jessup. I make no bones about this and the fact that I feel that IF HANDLED PROPERLY, I.E. PRESENTED TO PEOPLE & SCIENCE IN THE PROPER PSYCOLOGICALLY EFFECTIVE MANNER. I FEEL sure THAT Man will go where He now dreams of being—to the stars via the form of transport that the Navy accidentally stumbled upon (to their embarrassment) when their EXP. SHIP took off & popped-up a minute or so later on several Hundred sea travel–trip miles away at another of its Berths in the Chesapeake Bay area. I read of this in another newspaper & only by Hypnosis could any Man remember all the details of which paper, date of occurrence & etc., you see? Eh. Perhaps already, the Navy has used this accident of transport to build your UFO's. It is a logical advance from any standpoint. What do you think???

              VERY RESPECTFULLY
              Carl Allen

PART ONE

The Case for the UFO's

"If it waddles..."?

If it looks like a duck, waddles like a duck and quacks like a duck, swims and has webbed feet—then perhaps it is a duck!

But a child, seeing his first platypus, will say, "It looks like a duck with four feet and fur! But what is it?

But what happens when a man sees something for the first time and asks, "What is it?"...and there is no one who can supply the answer?

Fortunately, our experience and knowledge enable us to explain the seeming inconsistencies of this freak of nature.

The controversy about the s0-called Flying Saucers began in just such a fashion with Kenneth Arnold-s startling announcement in 1947.

A businessman of Boise, Idaho, Mr. Arnold was on his way from Chehalis to Yakima, Washington. Flying in his private plane, he was startled to see a bright flash on his wing.

Looking in the direction of Mount Rainier, he was astonished to see nine gleaming disks, each approximately the size of a C-54. They were clearly outlined against the snow.

As he later told the story, "it was as if they were linked together. They flew close to the top of mountain in a diagonal, chainlike line."

Mr. Arnold estimated their speed to be around twelve hundred miles per hour, and he thought they must have been about twenty to twenty-five miles from his plane.

"I watched them about three minutes," he said. "The were swerving in and out around the high mountain peaks. They were flat, like a pie pan, and so shiny they reflected the sun like a mirror. I never saw anything so fast!

Thus, as of June 24, 1947, Flaying Saucers were born.

"I saw them—but what are they?" Mr. Arnold undoubtedly asked. And no one had the answer.

Since that memorable day, thousands of other sightings have been reported and verified, and still the question must be asked, "What are they?" But more importantly, where do they come from, what is their purpose here, and if they can do it, why can't we? Are they Russian secret weapons?

Not Worry, Jemi, those were L-M Ships, Not "S" Men.
They are an improved type & were only on a training
Flight. That is why their leader inter-connected
their force-fields-to teach them Ion Level Tele-

<u>Control without inducing a fear-block[1] which they,
too, get When "Mowing the Lawn."</u>

Several well-documented volumes have been devoted to listings of sightings, to reports by everyone from boy scouts and families on picnics to astronomers and a man who claims to have had a conversation with a Saucer passenger from Venus.

But our answers to the questions, our evaluation of the potential answers to the fascinating and sometimes frightening questions, end where others begin. In other words, we shall not devote ourselves to the recent sightings and reports which have flooded newspaper offices, official bureaus of the government and, for some strange reason, airports. (Presumably, the public feels that anything which takes place in the air is the business of the airport!)

I have long been interested in the study of the unexplained areas of human existence, and <u>as an astronomer</u> with special interest in the moon, the early reports of flying saucers caught my attention. References in dusty volumes in the Library of Congress flashed through my mind, references I <u>had noted years ago</u> and which <u>now, in the light of these developments, seemed to offer a new field</u> of research, <u>of analysis and co-relation</u> which might throw light upon the matter.

<u>I began to ask myself questions</u> ... <u>and</u> I began to see a shape, a form, take place in the entire field of observable phenomena <u>which had remained obscure and previously unrelated.</u>

This flying saucer was <u>photographed</u> over the Brazilian Jungle

Desmond Leslie, in the book, "Flying Saucers Have Landed," reviewed some of the interesting material gleaned from old manuscripts, many of which referred to sightings of unidentified objects flying through the air. The most cursory examinations of such material, when collected and organized into a readable whole, made it <u>quite evident</u> that conclusions could be drawn.

<u>Does it follow</u>, I wondered, that <u>still further conclusions</u> could be drawn if one were to collect and sift and evaluate data from many different fields? Would there be any indication that life does, in fact, exist in space? If so, would that life have direction, control, intelligence? Or would it be amoebic in nature, lacking intelligence, be a form of vegetable or animal-mineral life? Would a thorough study of material in many fields <u>reveal a pattern</u>, a consistency of any sort which would provide clues to the future activities of these Unidentified Flying Objects?

I wanted to know the answers. I wanted to know if the somethings existed, and if they did, what they were. <u>I wanted to know where they lived and how they lived</u>. I wanted to know what they were doing when we didn't see them. I wanted to know why some people saw them and some people didn't see them. I wanted to know why they appeared in one place and not another. <u>I wanted to know whether they were friendly or hostile.</u>

<u>L-M? PALS: S-M?[1]</u>

<u>Even if he knew he nor any number of men could ever do anything, Jemi</u>.

---

[1] Clearest Translation

[1] This note is quite ambiguous. It may be interpreted as the above or as: L---M: PALS S-M? or since L-M closely follows the word hostile it might be: Hostile L-M? PALS: S-M? From the similarity of the marks following L-M and S-M the first interpretation is most likely the correct one.

> For first they would refuse to even believe.
> Requires true Humility or active[2] fascination.

I wanted to know, further, if they might be a Mark Twain-like hoax which a gullible public was swallowing, having tired of ordinary pursuits of happiness and excitement.

I wanted to know, too, whether we would have to wait until the things decided to visit us, or if we could possibly expect to pay them a surprise visit in their own territory in the near future.

Like a child seeing his first platypus, I asked myself questions. But unlike the child, I searched for my own answers.

UFO's Are Real

A serious approach to the question of Unidentified Flying Objects demands, first of all, that we face a fundamental change in concept as regards the world of our environment. We must loosen out thinking, let our imaginations fly with the winds, and, above all, we must want to think!

No human being with a closed mind need read further, for he will be asked to think as he has never thought before, to admit to possibilities which will shake the very foundations of his being.

For countless generations mankind has been confronted with an endless series of events, the causes of which have been obscure, if not altogether outside any casual sequence which his mind was able to imagine. In varying degrees, these happenings have generally been called supernatural: in more modern terminology, paranormal. This convenient phraseology may name them and, to a lesser extent, classify them; however, it does not explain the events, nor does it transmit and real knowledge to a groping mankind.

To gain understanding, therefore, we must do more than classify; we must analyze and theorize.

To do these things we must courageously invade a field which has so frightened formal science that it has been omitted from man's professed and organized cognizance. Only a few have dared to admit these phenomena and to investigate them Of the few, a large proportion have become outcasts from their chosen field of study. They have become nonconformists, and few sins are considered more basic. Yet the mass of our qualitative knowledge has come through nonconformity.

> Don't Worry those few DO NOT COUNT. He again
> asks too much of Proud, Vain Humankind

In this volume, we are going to confront, for the first time, a number of hitherto incorrigible facts. We shall relate, for the first time, previously unrelated data and draw startling conclusions therefrom.

To begin such a leap into the maelstrom of the "supernatural," we must first clarify our use of the word "world." We must no limit it to a state or a continent. And, despite the fact that it may disturb our complacency and arouse vague fears, we can no longer limit it to a single planet. The earth is not alone, nor has it been for some time.

---

[2] Clearest translation. Could be actual.

Next, we segregate paranormal experiences into groupings having some family likenesses. Only by so doing can we give them the merciless scrutiny necessary to determine their significance. If there is enlightenment to be had from the, we shall have it. (If this be nonconformity, let us make the most of it; our orthodox opponents may try to make the worst.)

This segregation of "erratics" or "oddities" into groups having some similarity serves a two fold utility. First, it simplifies our problem of analysis, because it helps t bring order out of chaos-chaos which is the product of centuries of accumulated data with no co-relation, with no purpose other than that of cataloguing facts for posterity. We may now assume, and with great assurance, that we are the posterity for whom these data were recorded. The time has come when these isolated ? and lone facts, so long orphaned, must be brought into the light, marshaled, and made to serve our purpose. This heterogeneous mass of data has doubtless been preserved for some purpose, if life has any meaning at all, and the solution of the mystery of the UFO's may well be that purpose.

The second utility of grouping is to establish emphasis and striking power, for any one of these innumerable events is too weak to stand alone in the face of scientific scoffing. It does not matter, evidently, that a thousand, or even ten thousand, people observe and report paranormal events. One self-confident, assertive and arrogant scientist, backed by the tacit support of his esoteric profession, can deny the occurrence, obfuscate its record, *nullify* its import, and come close to convincing the ten thousand people that they did not see what they *plainly* saw. This, of course, is not really science. It comes close to a kind of intellectual dictatorship, and imperialism of the intellect. Thus, by relating the previously unrelated, we can build a wall unscalable by such conformists.

> Such contempt for those badly frightened or
> Strictly Orthodox Namby-Pamby Scientists,
> The Shade of Galileo Walks again in the Name
> of Better Science.Will he arouse & Enlighten
> as before?

> No, my twin, He Walks throo clouds!

But let us not be over ambitious. We can as easily overstep the bounds of our capabilities as we can shirk our responsibilities. Some of the unexplained phenomena do seem to lie in what, for lack of a better terminology, we must still call the paranormal or psychic fields. One must be on guard not to commit the prime fallacy of all analysis, that of evolving a theory and then proceeding to find facts by which to substantiate it. Therefore, we must sort our observations into two groups. One group will contain everything which can be attributed to physical action by intelligent beings or an undeified and nonspiritual status. The second group is the residue which, as far as one can judge after careful consideration, must remain associated with the psychic or spiritual realm.

Even a cursory survey of the vast and scrambled field of strange events--oddities, we can call them--shows us at least three major areas. One of these relates to things which fall from the sky, some of which come from space and which may be roughly classified as organic and inorganic. We use "organic" in the sense of something which is part of, or associated with, a living, thinking entity, and "inorganic" as being merely the debris of space. An ordinary iron-nickel meteorite from space is inorganic within the sphere of our present definition; but if this meteorite arrives on earth shaped like a seven-headed Malayan goddess, or a compound microscope, it's organic.

A second major category stands out in the bibliography of oddities. It is the great area of events which encompasses disappearing people, and ships; airplanes and airships crashing and disappearing without trace and without warning; instantaneous and mysterious transportations of people and things; inexplicable tracks and marks, such as the Devil's Footprints of Devonshire, and the "cup-marks" found in stone over much of the world; the organically shaped meteorites found in Tertiary rock and coal formations; evidences of levitation and flight from prehistoric antiquity; and many other phenomena which appear to us to be, or resemble, acts rather than things.

All of these are terrestrial events—manifestations more or less on the terrestrial surface.

But there is a third great area of observational data. It is that vast conglomerate of purely astronomical observations which relates to things and phenomena in space or on planets and satellites other than earth. These are the unpopular, poor relatives of orthodox astronomy, the untouchable erratics. These have come to be regarded with such disfavor that there are few published records of them within the past fifty to seventy-five years.

We may consider that the sciences of meteorology and mereoritics, whose nature we will discuss later, speak almost eloquently in behalf of the case for space life and UFO's. It is within these fields that we have found the greatest volume of detailed observation and data. And it is just here that we have found the most difficulty in grouping and organizing. Even here, however, we can not a primitive pattern and by simple use of it as a guide, we begin to separate acts of intelligence from "natural" acts of statistical nature.

Whereas the actual groupings are given in Parts Two, Three, and Four, the problems involved in the initial research are of interest. The resolution of those problems is still another key to the fact that we are on the right track, that by relating the previously unrelated we have discovered pattern and form.

ED: The following has no obvious reference or necessary position.
> All men of renown had two things, Courage & Conviction, often so Much that they were ridiculed. This Man opens & invites same merely by Saying what his observations, Records & Data *have shown* him, WhatCannot be escaped. There are, of course, such Men who like the one that Would not permit himself to View the Planets Circling the sun Lest it interfere with his religious "Dogmas of the day."

An example of the way such things develop is our experience in classifying falling objects. Our first thought was that this was a minor field which could be disposed of with a casual perusal. Not so. It soon developed, as the pattern began to evolve, that we could not coordinate these onslaughts from the sky, nor interpret them, unless we gave consideration to their effect, their origins, and to concomitant phenomena. Not only that, but very shortly we were forced to acknowledge that falling objects and other phenomena in the sky must be considered in three categories if order was to ensue from chaos. In short, there seemed to be a class of objects which were merely physical debris cluttering up space and moving in orbits of varying shapes and which had little, if any, relationship to or association with intelligent being. A second group was obviously the product of thinking, if not, indeed, of higher mental characteristics such as purposefulness, determination, morality, and perhaps even humor. Then, especially in those instances where space phenomena appear to intermingle with our native meteorological condition, it became necessary to consider, as a third group, the less spectacular terrestrial events and to clarify our thinking by segregating these and getting them out of our way.

The upshot of this coercion was that we found more than half a dozen subcategories wherein we were allied with the sciences of meteorology which is the terrestrial science of the air, and meteoritics which is a branch of astronomy.

Let us, then, consider briefly these segments of our problem. To most of you who read this book, falling ice has been limited to hailstones, mostly small, perhaps the size of marbles. But in trying to organize data on ice which falls from the sky, we ran head-on into cases where chunks of ice weighing from a few pounds to some tons were known to fall, and without final proof we were forced to give thought to "spacebergs" which might weigh thousands of tons each, maybe hundreds of thousands, and which arrived from space in swarms of hundreds or even thousands, and left vast scars on the surface of the earth. We were compelled to consider some of these falling blocks of ice as having been produced by, or at least associated with intelligent entities. It was even necessary to consider various sources for the orbital ice, depending on whether it came from the exploded fifth planet, whether it was blasted off the earth by prehistoric atom scientists, whether it was detached from the earth by tidal action when the earth and moon were united, whether it fell off the moon, or just where did it come from? In sifting out these cases where intelligence seemed to be involved, we found the process to have certain resemblances to panning gold nuggets from alluvial gravel. At least if the nuggets were there, we had to do our own sifting.

ED: The following has no obvious reference or necessary position.

I am Not adverse to saying that a Force-Field Can Make a Man to fly FOR I HAVE SEEN IT DONE & I know the cause of this flight & Am Not disturbed Paris Exhibition, 1951, Scientiest from Paris Universigy Demonstrated this. An AP PHOT WAS SENT TO U.S. SHOWING THIS ACTION.

U.S. NAVYS FORCE-FIELD EXPEIRIMENTS 1943 OCT. PRODUCED INVISIBILITY OF CREW & SHIP. FEARSOM RESULTS. SO TERRIFYING AS TO, FORTUNATELY, HALT FURTHER RESEARCH.

We went through similar compelling experiences with regard to falling stones, falling live animals, and falling animal or organic matter. We found that life arriving from the sky was almost universally of a low order, such as reptilian or aquatic, and we found that some of it involved such intellectual elements as functionality, localization of target and repetition in fixed areas. The only common denominator for all the observed conditions turned out to be -- of all things --hydroponic tanks in space craft!

ON *THE* HEAD!

And if we are confronted with a falling object of crystalline rock obviously shaped as an optical aid, are we to cravenly call it an erratic, and discard or ignore it? And are we to cringe before the deposition of a few hundreds of dead birds from the heavens, all on one city, but of species completely scrambled and mostly unknown within hundreds of miles of that city?

What would you do with a piece of meteoric iron, unmistakably shaped by intelligent hands, but which was equally unmistakably removed from solid formations of geological Tertiary Age of 300,000 years ago? Wouldn't you perhaps reshuffle your conception of the antiquity of intelligence and wonder whether it was, for a fact, indigenous to this planet?

If you found raw meat, with hair attached, falling over a two-acre space, from a clear and undisturbed sky, wouldn't you struggle even harder to find some kind of category for it, and a common denominator of explanation relating it with other phenomena?

SPOILED FOOD, DROPPED.

If you found that water sometimes arrives from the sky in solid masses, flooding little brooks until they washed away villages, but neglecting the brooks a half mile away, wouldn't you look for a category outside routine meteorological storms?

These problems all had to be faced. Something had to be done about them -- and they all arose from objects falling from the sky. Also, they had to be distinguished from meteorological storms -- for some of the clouds which we studied just appeared, spat a stone or two and passed on. They were not thunderstorms, What were the?

Those were the problems which we faced in a welter of data on things coming from the sky, but they were, on the whole, less puzzling than events which directly involve people, or which were clearly current actions and not merely things which may have been operated in distant times and places. Among those phenomena involving people, the sudden disappearances are probably the most amazing. Some have disappeared instantly, while being watched by friends and close relatives. Crews have mysteriously disappeared from ships— sometimes within sight of their home port--without warning and without trace.

HEH! IF HE ONLY KNEW WHY, HE'D DY OF SHOCK.

There are too many instances of planes and ships disappearing for us to ignore them. One plane is reported to have flown into a cloud from which it never emerged, while the crew of a blimp disappeared before the eyes of dozens of watchers. We are still wondering what happened to about fifty passengers from a plane whose wreckage was found recently on a mountainside in the Pacific Northwest.

These are several of the instances which have prompted some writers to postulate that UFO's were on the attack. My contention is that, at the very worst, such an attack is no more organized or malicious than that of a redcapped hunter stalking deer in the Pennsylvania mountains is an attack by the human race against the deer; and there may be elements of similarity.

It is almost an inseparable corollary to our thesis that we admit to an unfathomable antiquity for mankind, or at least intelligence, upon the earth, and its vicinity. This conclusion is made unavoidable by the antiquity of records of UFO's and wingless flight. It is apparent in the innumerable megalithic works of stone which involve masses too huge to be moved by means other than levitation and which have been standing for ages before any written record now available.

THE MAN IS CLOSE, TOO CLOSE.

As these pieces of the jigsaw puzzle make themselves known, and as we realize fully that this is an old, old problem, we can begin to take comfort. If UFO's have been here for 300,000 years and have not yet chosen to launch a mass attack on humanity, it is scarcely likely that they will do it now – unless they are forced to do something to prevent the world's experimenting militarists and scientists from destroying the earth through ignition of its hydrogen, thus crating another nova or new star in the galaxy, a may well have been done when the fifth planet disintegrated at an incalculable time in the past.

So there are two elements of importance in our study of the antiquity of intelligence: the proof that superior beings have been here longer than mankind has been civilized, and the demonstration that forces were at work in those millennia, the magnitude and nature of which are only suspected today.

Is this, then, a hint that we are at this moment awakening and, like a chrysalis, emerging into a new and much more powerful state of existence and cognizance? Are, therefore, our current troubles, domestically and internationally, but the excruciating birth pains of such a renaissance, as we could not have imagined one short generation ago? Will we, then perhaps be welcomed rather than repelled by the intelligences which inhabit the UFO's or which may even be the UFO's?

> Man's Emotional structure is such that he *cannot*
> awaken to Powers of 'True-'Thinking.'

> Alright so it was not thougth that man would
> *ever* mature. Don't worry, Jemi.

Probably the oldest, and almost surely the most prolific of sources bearing on wingless flight, are the records of the Indian and Tibetan monasteries. These in themselves are almost conclusive. Records of 15,000 years ago imply wingless flight at least 70,000 years prior to that. Add this to the recorded visit of a space fleet to the court of Thutmose III, approximately 1500 B.C., and we are close to paralleling the sightings of today. Evidence of continued interest by the space dwellers comes from medieval France where Adamski was completely scooped by elements of the French populace who were given rides in the UFO's.

ED: The following has no obvious reference or necessary position.
> No Not pals but the French are such of an general Pholosophic attitude Even in that Day that they were chosen to be contacted. Now, some L-M's live in france out of preference *in* field of Philosophical Study. *They* like it.

If early visits to Asia, subsequent contacts with the Egyptians at the peak of their culture, rumored associations of flight with the disappearance of Atlantis, and tours of France some centuries ago, indicate a pattern, then it may be of little wonder that the civilizations of today, perhaps the most spectacular of all, are receiving attention.

In many ways, the most intriguing data of all comes from the skeptical astronomers. Their observations do tend to be quantitative, timed, and documented. The astronomical data is more than merely qualitative. In other words, the astronomers themselves, being conscientious data hounds, were not content with merely seeing things move in space. Although unaware of the true nature of what they saw, they recorded as much as time and equipment would permit, and, as a result, they have enabled us to locate the habitat of the UFO's.

As with out own observations today, any single sighting by an astronomer could be a mistake or an illusion. But hundreds of sightings are involved, and dozens of serious, reliable astronomers.

BOY! IF ONLY HE KNEW THE THOUSANDS.

Many round things have been seen crossing the discs of the sun and moon, and some in space with no background. Roundness implies spherical or discoid shapes. Lights have been seen in space, some of them near Mercury, Venus, Mars, and the moon, and some between us and those orbs, so that they might be on their surfaces. In the case of the moon, lights have been seen on the surface. There have been shadows on the moon and on the earth which could have been cast only by manipulated space contrivances. The advent of the great comets and the red spot on Jupiter in the late 1870's was coincident with the mysterious appearance of a new crater on the moon precisely the size of the UFO's seen by astronomers between the earth and the moon.

The astronomers have seen two distinct classes of objects: the spherical, definitely outlined ones, and the hazy, nebulous ones. Both have appeared to undergo intelligent manipulation and exhibit erratic motions. In all of these are features that have counterparts among the sightings listed by lay observers since 1947. Simultaneous observations by tow or more observers have at times established the approximate distances of the UFO's through study of parallax. ("Parallax" is the displacement, often measurable, caused by looking at an object from too different points; e.g. hold up a finger and view it with first one eye and then the other. The displacement against a distinct background is parallax.) All-l-all, the astronomical evidence for UFO's while less voluminous than other types, is better grounded in factual and quantitative data. It must be given great weight.

If, in reality, the astronomical profession is to be forced into the position of being the principal witness for the defense, in the case of the UFO's its members will suffer a most peculiar type of embarrassment, for theirs is the unenviable position of having been most dogmatic and derogatory.

It seems unfortunate that astronomy, once the leader in the search for qualitative knowledge, is apparently degenerating into opposition to pioneering. Yet, astronomy, while strictly an observational and not an experimental science, takes front rank in denying authentic observational data which threatens in the slightest to upset its own scientific applecart.

IT SEEMS QUIOTICALLY RELIABLE OF HUMANS TO WAIT

> **TILL THEY THEMSELVES HAVE KNOWN FLIGHT & THINK NOW OF SPACE-FLIGHT BEFORE ADMITTING THAT OTHERS TOO HAVE FLIGHT. NOT, OF COURSE, (HE!-HEH) THAT *THEY* ARE SURPASSED,NO NOT WHEN THEY NOW ARE CLUED TO AN EQUALING IDEA IN FORCE FIELDS. THEY NOW HOPE TO BECOME EQUALS. *ALAS!*

In an observational science such as astronomy, laws have to be built from innumerably repeated observations and not, as is partially true in physics and chemistry, on the basis of duplicative laboratory experiment. In such cases, as the astronomer knows only too well, repeated observations must be accepted as tantamount to proof.

> H-K HAS Enough observations, as he says. They ignore them

Many of astronomy's tenets are in such a category. To take only one example, the hypothetical life history of stars is based entirely on the so-called spectral sequence built solely upon spectroscopic observations of thousands of stars and the subsequent grouping and arranging of these into some logical structure. Even in this ponderous sequence there are erratics, or stars with peculiar spectra, whose real nature is a matter of speculation even after a hundred years of spectroscopy. Yet, the astronomer can hardly deny the existence of the obviously shinning star, no matter how recalcitrant may be its light waves.

There Is Intelligence in Space

The vast amount of material from the past, in all categories, shows clearly that intelligence exists in space! "Intelligence" is the sine qua non of our analysis. Without it our thoughts may be meaningless. Wit it, our corollary postulates are automatic.

> Is Nothing, Harvard expiereiments show that only a few Humans Have Pie factors of any depth. They cannot tele-talk to any Clarity. Nor thusly are they able to "see" beauty of Each others Souls. Thus they are forced into Matierialistic Values & concepts & and Lack any SORT OF REASONABLE PHILSOSPHY TO LEAD THEM UPWARDS. SAVE THE GREAT BOOK.

Throughout this book, we make some rather fine distinctions. The difference between rain and "falling water" is one. For our concepts of **our** spatial environment we have to make a similar division between "mind" and "intelligence." "Mind," for our purposes, is the thinking function of the brain of mankind, or perhaps of lower animals. By "intelligence," we must conceive more broadly of an ability to think, construct, direct, analyze, plan,, navigate, laugh, etc., which is not necessarily a part of, or associated with, a carnate brain. In short, we must adjust our ego to the possibility that intelligence exists in space, that it may be and probably is superiour to our own, and that it may inhabit physical entities of a discarnate nature such as the nebulous or cloudlike bodies observed by Barnard (described later.)

Throughout, we are searching for objects, bodies, events which have been made, shaped or guided by forces obviously controlled by an "intelligence" which has the power of decision as opposed to those which have merely been acted upon by "physical" forces and "physical" laws, such as gravitation, and the Keplerian or Newtonian laws. Only thus can we establish "intelligence" as a universal component of neighboring space.

ED: The following has no obvious reference or necessary position.
Einstiens Theory of Unified Field throughout all Space & atmosphere WAS SO WELL PROVEN that upon realizing Mans Misanthropic emotionality He Withdrew it. 1927

Nobody know the precise nature of this spatial intelligence, much less the nature of the physical body within which its resides. This intelligence seems to manifest itself in many ways. In our study of storms we have been driven inexorably to admit that some storms have an artificial aspect, as sort of organic appearance, an air of being manufactured for a purpose and to be carrying out that purpose. We therefore postulate some percentage of artificiality, or intelligence, among that small percentage of storms which suddenly appear in otherwise undisturbed skies, proceed with a purposeful manner, as though concealing something, and discharge peculiar materials. They seem to concentrated, perhaps too directive, to be entirely meteorological in their orgins (sic).

DEAD GIVE-AWAY! *HE KNOWS*, SAYS AS MUCH, TOO.?

As a means, then, of assuring that we do not knowingly overlook any possible contributory evidence in the case for the UFO's, I ask you to keep these storms and cloud formations in mind, and, if possible, to fit them in to the basis of any comprehensive conclusions which you may eventually draw.

I believe that space structures of five to twenty miles in diameter are sufficiently large to produce such storms, and there may be elements of purposefulness in so doing, if only for camouflage or concealment.

THE L-M GREAT ARK=*BIGGER*!

It may be difficult to see the significance of antiquity in the consideration of space flight or space inhabitance. But failure to consider the sprawling background of the UFO problem is the greatest single factor in the appalling chaos which engulfs this enigma. Take but one small item: the little piece of meteoric iron which was found deep within a tertiary coal bed. The locale and the finding are authentic. The shape is purely artificial. It is but an inch or so square, practically a cube. Four sides are squarely faced, and the other two are convexly shaped, with complete symmetry. Around the four surfaced sides runs a groove, geometrically contrived. Here are three established facts:

1. Placement in an incipient coal bed some 300,000 years ago.
2. Made of meteoric iron, identifiable by structure and chemical content.
3. Clearly shaped by artificial means.

The number of explanations as to how it got into that coal bed may be few or several, but there is one underlying fact which cannot be scoffed into oblivion: This piece of natural steel was shaped by an intelligent instrumentation at least 300,000 years ago!

BEFORE STEEL WAS KNOWN TO H.S.

We can go on, but somebody has to make a choice, or deny and ignore the entire factual substratum. Science has ignored it. The choice is most galling to face: Was this gadget, created as it was by intelligence, placed there by man indigenous to earth, or was it dropped from space by a space traveler?

You choose to say: placed by Man? Then there was a race of men here 300,000 years ago who knew enough to shape steel, and, by inference, make machinery. If they could do that, they most likely had locomotion of some sort, and there is no good reason to deny that they could have found space flight either by research or accident. At worst there was time to develop a civilization of any preassigned refinement. Science doesn't like that. Alternative to that horn of the dilemma, we must contemplate space flight of 300,000 years ago,

> TO WIT: THEY HAD THE WHEEL IN MANY FORMS.
> SUCH AS MACHINE TOOLS OR FORCE FIELD (sic) "SHAPERS"
> & CUTTER-BURNERS WHICH?
>
> —BROTHER! THEY SURE DON'T!

capable of bringing this little machine part to the earth, or of bringing civilization itself and planting it here within that type of animal life judged most likely and suitable to perpetuate and develop mental capacity. **It is indeed a nasty choice for inhibited minds.**

> EINSTIEN WASN'T ALIVE THEN, BUT THE NATURAL
> FUNCTIONS OF OUR UNIVERSE & this planet Worked
> Well without him.

We can conclude that space habitation has existed for many a millennia. We do not care whether earthmen took to space as a matter of convenience, comfort, and safety after blowing off a portion of the planet; or whether space inhabitants created terrestrial intelligence "in their own image." Bluntly: "What's the difference?" The basic thought is that **man is living in a world in which he is neither the completely dominant nor the supremely intellectual being.**

> HUH, HE'LL *NEVER ADMIT IT*, THOUGH: PRIDE.

There has been a raging controversy for generations between pro-Atlantians and anti-Atlantians as regards the antiquity of civilized mankind upon this planet. **The archaeological remains of those nuclei civilizations,** which have, for 7,000 years or more been recovering from the celestial impact which caused the traditional flood, redistributed the surface soil of the earth, destroyed continents and made new ones, sunk Atlantis and Mu and raised hob in general, **are readily available in quantity**. They offer **easy materials for study**. Archaeology and ethnology, sharing with astronomy the feature of being observational and not experimental, have built their entire framework upon the study of those remains. Yet, underlying and intermingled with this vast array of material, there **are remnants of cultures of almost unspeakable age**. Their artifacts have been subjected to geological and cosmic cataclysms of almost incomprehensible violence and few major relics remain for perusal. Those few, however, are cast aside as the erratics of archaeology and ethnology, and their very existence is buried or denied in efforts to avoid toppling the house of cards so laboriously established by those branches of learning.

> THAT'S JUST IT, NO ONE HAS DARED SPEAK, EXCEPT
> IN COMMENTS TO ONE ANOTHER. *TILL NOW*.

INSTANCE:

> (DARWIN WAS CASTIGATED, OSTRACIZED)

These studies break down almost completely at an antiquity of approximately 7,000 years, at which point they meet with what the mathematician calls discontinuity. Many of the oases of culture thus studied appear, suddenly, in final analysis, as going concerns, with little indication of forward development and **considerable to show** that **they were degenerate remnants of something already lost behind the misty curtain of antiquity**. It is my belief that we must admit to the "doings" of man in the eons prior to the collision of the earth with a vast aggregate of meteoric material which struck the Western Hemisphere some 10,000 to 15,000 years ago.

Books have been written, **libraries of them**, to **show this antiquity**, but it has not yet been accepted, even in principle, by any branch of science. Geology opposes any type of cataclysmic change in the structure of the earth and **will go to any extremes to avoid coming to grips with its erratics.**

Yet every science breaks down when it is forced to contemplate the origin of man's intellectual development. (Printing in Red is A & J)

IE. WHAT INSPIRATION CAUSED MAN TO BECOME MAN BY STARTING TO USE TOOLS. WHENCE CAME THE IDEA. SCIENCE SAYS "OF NECESSITY" BUT THE SAME NECESSITY EXISTS FOR APES.... *EVEN NOW*.

The few erratics in the following pages show that there have been very ancient cultures, or civilizations, which may have and could have developed methods of flight much simpler and more effective than ours, and more directly associated with forces which we do not yet comprehend. Again we are dealing with indirect evidence, not always of the greatest clarity. Yet in support of an antiquity of such an order I have seen and touched stonework carved out of the solid mountains of rock in South America, which certainly antedate the Andean glaciers, and almost as certainly predate the formation of the mountains themselves. This work is superior in technique to that accomplished by our currently machanized civilization. Much of that construction, sculpture and tunneling could only have been accomplished by "forces" different from those in use by us today. The quandary is largely resolvable by admitting to a levitating force developed and used by the same common denominator--space flight--which simplifies so many other puzzles for us.

ED: The following has no obvious reference or necessary position.

SUCH PRE-GLACIAL AGE WORKS OF CIVILIZATION ARE GENERALLY KNOWN BUT MUST BE DENIED A PLACE IN HISTORY FOR THEY ALL ARE--MYSTERIES.

PRIDE IGNORANCE

On the basis of the evidence of an antiquity involving epochs of 50,000 to 200,000 or 300,000 years or more, we postulate the ancient development of some kind of science which either produced space flight or was brought to this third planet via space flight. I do not believe it is of great significance to our thesis at the moment whether one, or the other, of these assumptions is most likely to be true. Either is abhorrent to science and to some religions, yet either presents a background of conditionality favorable to an extremely ancient development of wingless flight. Nothing else answers all of the conundrums presented by observed and recorded facts.

As you will see, history is replete with stories of another great category of phenomena: the mysterious and ghostly disappearances of people, singly and in groups, publicly or in unobserved obscurity. These skin-ting-ling episodes seemed at first to have little in common with the falls of objects and the antics of storms. Many are incidents which, if their reality has been admitted at all, are in the view of scientists, spiritualists, and students of the occult, considered to belong to or border on the so-called supernatural. Within these segregations we must place the disappearance of the crews of ships, such as the Sea Bird and the Marie Celeste; the disappearance of individuals while in the company of their peers. There is not much hypothecating to be done with these. The stories can be told, and the cases lumped together as one big unexplained group of events. No explanation other than that of abduction by intelligently navigated aerial or celestial craft can be advanced: It is almost a case of proof by default.

With planes, there is perhaps some added element other than metal fatigue which involves striking some apparently solid object while in the air, or being rent by unimaginable forces just before falling. (Because of this additional evidence I have put the accidents to planes into a separate section of Part Three, below.)

Planes seem to hit something which crushes them or tears them apart, which is nevertheless invisible, and which strikes with such suddenness that the pilots do not have time to make an outcry via

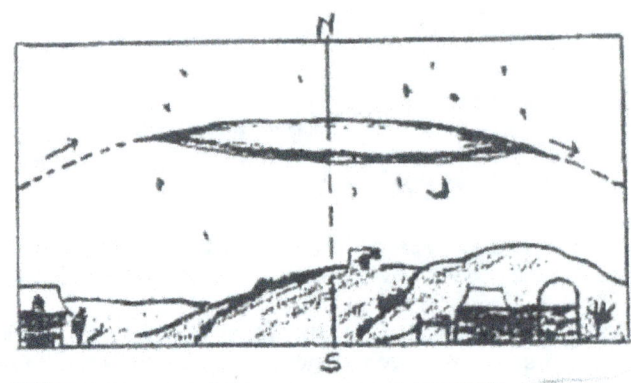

Passage of Auroral beam, November 17, 1882, as seen from
Guildown Observatory, Lat. 51 31' 39" N., Long. 0 28' 47" W.

their ever-live radios.

Then, too, there are cases of dead or frightened birds, and the cases of people being struck by unseen forces, as with seventeen marching soldiers in eighteenth-century France who were simultaneously struck down by an invisible agency.

One had a compass on him, fouled a "SWEEP"
made L-Ms ANGRY

After analyzing these things, one speculates as to new types of obstacles as well as new forces. Take the mysterious Maunder object, which moved deliberately across the sky above southern England in November 1882. Rand Capron, an authority on auras, said it was auroral, while other equally competent scientists said it was a physical or material object. Then there are the many modern sightings of things which seem to manifest intelligent action, and to possess all normal physical characteristics except mass or weight. We recollect that radar sees things which are not visible to the eye.

ARK IN STASIS, THEN CAME OUT OF STASIS.

From such analysis we come by easy stages to conceive of a force, ray, or focal point, in some force-field either; unknown to us, or at least not understood, which produces rigidity in a localized or sharply delimited volume of air, or possibly in space itself. We are thinking of something like crystals of ice freezing within a body of water. The element remains the same but its physical attributes change suddenly and drastically.

DEH O'. They Can't Prove it yet!

Another example might be the passage of a limited but powerful magnetic field through a scattering of iron filings or iron powder. Before the approach of the magnetic flux, the powder lies loose, flexible, and penetrable. Yet, when the flux enters it, invisibly and imperceptibly to the senses of man, this docile powder become rigid, tenacious, coherent, and at least semisolid. Do the space dwellers have a force which produces this temporary rigidity in the air, or even possibly in the gravitation field itself? Or do they create "local" concentrations of the gravitational field as we are able to do with the magnetic field?

REVERSE MAG. FORCE?

Suppose that some intelligent entity was directing a concentration of potential which could make small volumes of rarefied air rigid, could set up a sort of island in the gravitational or magnetic field, moving the island about as the spot of a searchlight is moved on thin clouds. Such a thing would be invisible, would have many of the physical attributes of a solid body, but very small mass. For example, its movement through the air would be wavelike, and would not envolve translation of the medium any more than the spot of the searchlight would require movement of the cloud which enabled the beam to attain visibility. In moving, this island would simply "freeze" on the advancing edge and "thaw" on the trailing edge. In this way it could have almost infinite velocity, and also acceleration, just as the spot of the searchlight. In this manner it would appear to be free of mass, and actually it would be free of mass, because only the force beam would move, not the air. Yet in resisting the impingement of a bird, a plane, or perhaps a meteor, it would have mass, and a very destructive mass at that. A pilot flying a plane into such a body would have no warning. Yet if such a thing were a few hundred yards in diameter, its mass in resisting the plane would be thousands of pounds, perhaps tons. The analogy to a ship hitting an iceberg would be very close.

If such a force island were formed in the upper atmosphere, it might be very possible for it to have many of the physical characteristics of a solid body, and yet in matters of illumination it could behave exactly as any other auroral phenomena. In this connection we must remember that auroral phenomena are magnetic and may be caused by streams of electrons from the sun which are, in effect, precisely the type of force beam upon which we are speculating.

> Yes, He is Close, but doesn't think of Mag. Inductors
> or of Gravity as "air" Or thought of in Jet propulsion.
> He doesn't know gravity & Magnetizm (sic) can be drawn into
> a ship, built up to High Power, While being converted
> & used as a Force-Propulsive HE MAY KNOW OF FORCE-
> SHIELDS of Primitive Ancient type.

It seems obvious that a single beam could not have the effect which we have suggested, else the freeze would take effect along the entire length of the beam. However, it is possible that the three-dimensional volume enclosed within the intersection of two beams might create such a congealed island.

Speculating further on this weird possibility, remember that oxygen is a magnetic substance. It is not, perhaps, paramagnetic like iron, manganese and nickel, but nevertheless sufficiently magnetic that it can be separated from the other constituents of air by means of a magnetic field.

ED: The following has no obvious reference or necessary position.
> 2000 Watt Cyclotron, built 1948, N.Y. STATE
> GIVES PROOF OF THE *ACTUALITY OF "SOLIDITY"* IN
> FORCE-FIELDS (sic) HOWEVER, IS NOT RECOGNIZED YET,
> OR THOUGHT OF YET AS TOOL.

If such a congealment were possible, consider the result of crossing the two beams at the exact aerial position of a flying plane and congealing the air around and in the plane. Could you, in this way, hold a plane in suspension, or even carry it away? Could you, by a similar concentration of beams, freeze two aviators on the sands of the Arabian Desert, and carry them away? Could you freeze a man and instantly lift him out of sight, or cause him to be invisible within the block or frozen air or oxygen? Could you freeze the crew of a ship, and remove them from the vessel? Could you catch or kill birds, quickly and over a vast area, with such a thing, and dump them on a city in Louisiana? All these peculiar things happened, but we don't know how, or why.

> Heh! If he only knew by experience he'd keep
> Silent & Not write or speak of it *ever* again in
> his Lifetime. He COULDN'T SPEAK OF IT, for you
> see, Jemi, It paralyzes ones Sense of time &
> Nulifys Mental Cognition, functions & Memory, SO HE
> HAS NO KNOWLEDGE, HE COULD NOT HAVE. *ONLY* GUESSING.

Before we leave this tantalizing topic, give thought to the nature of an aurora borealis. As early as the time of Maunder's object, it was recognized that auroras are magnetic phenomena, or at least associated with the earth's magnetic field. It has been further ascertained that they are related to sunspots, and that they are probably due to the interaction of electronic streams from the sun or from sunspots. Is not an aurora, then, something very much akin to the congealed islands which we have just postulated? Is it not a delimited volume of rarefied air caught within the tripping reaction of an electron stream passing through a magnetic field? Was Maunder's object, then, in a sense both material and nonmaterial; both massive and nonmassive? Is it the incounter with the "pockets" which makes meteors explode? Do they make blips on a radar screen?

S-F REGARDED AS FANTASTIC DREAMERS. D-W

Have we a clue here, or are we dangerously close to science fiction?

Short-Cut to Space Travel (He has "hit the nail")

It is but a step from such contemplations to a similar analysis of the "Foo" fighters, fireballs, the comet-like objects usually seen in groups of six or eight, and the darting evanescent things seen now and then over Washington D.C. Such phenomena must be considered as most likely due to intelligent manipulation, or remote control, from distant structures, and technically trained observers have often said as much. We do not entirely rule out a self-contained intelligence, but many of these manifestations have more the quality of something which, for want of an established terminology, we might call the searchlight type of UFO. Many reports have described objects or UFO's as appearing to have been operated by remote control. I believe that they are exactly that.

It is by no means clearly established that all apparently self-luminous phenomena are of this nature. There are still a number of luminous spheres and discs which seem to have a more material nature and to contain the intelligences which operate them. The widgets seen by astronomers in space are examples, and I think, too, of such things as the ruddy disc which buzzed Captain Manning's DC-3 near south Bend, Indiana.

The "Devil's Hoofprints" and related phenomena, discussed below in Part Three, offer another key or clue, and in segregating them from the mass of unclassified data we can, again, remove a considerable segment of the load which burdens the psychic and paranormal field. The misinterpretation adherent to the Hoof marks are more fantastic than the phenomenon itself. It is unbelievable, to me at least, that people intelligent enough to make a living among their fellows would try to interpret a linear sequence of exactly duplicated marks, crossing roof tops, walls and haystack unfalteringly and indiscriminately as animal tracks. These marks were equally spaced, occurring singly, not in twos or fours. Even in the old mythology there is no tale of a one-legged animal.

The Measure-Marker was accidently Left Idling, that time. Nowadays, Measure-Markeres are Not used, except by Undersea-Explorers. *(Italics by A)*

Here is something clearly mechanical. With equal clarity it is something maneuvering in the sky. Since the mysterious phenomenon occurred half a century before our race developed mechanical flight, this, to me, is an isolated and clear-cut indication of space flight.

Throughout the series of modern (after Arnold) sightings of UFO's there is a thread of frequent references to "Mother Ships" and huge superconstructions. The vast thing chased by Mantell and the ten-mile-long thing/over Kansas are examples. There can no longer be serious doubts of their existence. It seems probable that these constructions are the domiciles of the small-fry discs, spheres, balls of light, etc., which are so frequently seen in proximity to the earth's surface and to our planes, rockets, air fields and cities.

It is my belief that these constructions are few in number, not many (there is some possibility, in fact, that there may be only two of them) and that they do not come from distant planets such as Venus, Mars, Jupiter or the vastly more distant stars. It is my belief that they are usually globular, sometime spindlelike, and that they are an indigenous part of earth-moon binary-planet system. I make this statement on the basis of hundreds of astronomical observations in which the rough determinations of parallax can be made. Parallax shows these objects to be somewhere between a few hundred miles away and a maximum of something less than the distance of the moon. While I believe that these space islands probably use both earth and moon for their own convenience, I suggest that their most natural and permanent habitat is at the gravitational neutral of the earth-sun-moon, three-body system which is well within the orbit of the moon.

> Why Not, The Neutral has Less wearing effects on
> Tissue, Nerves & Lets one Live Much, Much Longer.
> Humans Die Due to Gravitational Wear & tear,
> too.

Dean Swift was prescient in regard to his astronomy, predicting that Mars had two small satellites, one of which was close to Mars' surface and made two revolutions daily. It has been pointed out that this inner body is too close to Mars to be in adjustment with any known postulate of the natural distribution of satellites relative to their parent body. This may be an indication that Mars' inner satellite is artificial.

> Also an old "Dead-Ark" S-M MAKE

It has been postulated that gravitation need not be considered as acting with uniform continuity, from the center of the attracting body outward, even if subject to the inverse square law. Such a concept, today, would be especially horrendous to physics and astronomy. Yet, there is a suspicious rhythm to the distribution

> TODAY IS When it could be if the Most Technical
> use Tomorrow is too-Late for these War-Lovers.

of planets, outward from the sun. This has been somewhat crudely expressed in Bode's "law," and in spite of scientific protestations there is a similarity between atomic structure as we comprehend it and the obvious structure of the solar system.

> & HOW ABOUT MOLECULAR STRUCTURES & ITS "FIELDS"???

Refinements of Bode's law indicate nodes in the gravitational field, at which planets, asteroids, and possibly comets and meteors tend to locate themselves. An extension of the theory to the satellite systems of the major planets indicates a similar system of nodes on smaller scales, where planets, rather than the sun, are gravitational centres. This indicates a sort of generality, and since these smaller planets, such as Venus, Earth, Mars, do not have satellite systems (the moon is more of a companion than satellite and may have joined the earth through acquisition rather than formation), it might well be that these gravitational nodes are occupied to some degree by navigable construction.

> "Nodes," are the old Traps & burial "Grounds"
> Here Lay quite a few Dead-Ships they cannot
> get away. The old types couldn't but these
> new types can. It was nodes in great number
> on Surface of this Earth that gave the clue to
> L.-M's of How to Neatralize forces but a floor
> pattern in METAL ACTUALLY SHOWED THE MEANS.

Over a period of almost two hundred years there have been many modifications of Bode's law, in an effort to completely generalize it, and to make it theoretical as well as empirical. Many researchers have extended the law so as to establish nodes right down to the surface of the central bodies, and in so doing the nodes become closer and closer together so that there may be many of them at short distances from the parent body. Thus, if the law or its derivatives have significance, there could be a number of these orbital nodes between the moon and the surface of the earth.

We can therefore, take it as highly probable that there are many zones of convenience around the planets, as well as around the sun, which are presently unoccupied by planets or satellites of any considerable size and which may well be used by enlightened space dwellers. Such zones, if they exist, are in addition to the demonstrable earth-sun-moon neutral. Since this system of nodes appears to be some function of the radius of the attracting body, it may be that there is a complete series of them in concentric circles starting at the surface of a parent body such as the earth, but their existence or true nature can hardly be known to us until we can in some way determine the nature of gravity itself.

> No, they are Part of Same Physics Principal.
> They DO Extend outward concentrically, Usually
> stay in position, Not, always.

There may even be hints available to us regarding gravity. For instance, no final settlement has ever been made of the argument over the opposed wave and corpuscular theories of the propagation of light. An assumption that the ether, a necessary adjunct to the wave theory, is identical with the gravitational field, whatever that may be, would reconcile the opposing theories and a quantum of light would then be merely a pulsation or fluctuation in the gravitational field. Intense studies of the movements of space-navigable UFO's might furnish vital clues to such problems.

> It would only tell all, What this one has guessed.

Let us go back for a moment to the matter of masslessness of some of the UFO's. Their ability to achieve enormous acceleration has been one of the greatest puzzles to scientists. Time after time we are told that the UFO's could not possibly contain living bodies of flesh and bone — that such bodies could not withstand the stresses imposed by the observed accelerations. Yet such argument can well be based on entirely erroneous ideas as to the nature of the propulsive forces used by the UFO's. Acceleration is damaging only because the forces necessary to produce it are applied externally to the living body, or to the structural members of any flying machine. Any force which would simultaneously accelerate every molecule of either the living body or the mechanical structure would avoid all such stresses, and both the living and the mechanical could undergo any amount of acceleration without the slightest damage or discomfort!

> Ei! Yeih:
>
> *UNLESS* THOSE BODIES WERE *TINY, MATURE*, &
> ENCASED *IN LIQUID*. LIQUID USED AS A SHOCK
> ABSORBER. *(Italics by A)*
>
> GOTTEN FROM "TANKS" & in the tiny "Life-boat-
> ships. Was seen.
>
> IT WORKS FINE.

Since the UFO's, even the material, structure like ones, are observed to sustain acceleration without mishap, we cannot but conclude that whatever the force used for such violent propulsion may be, it must be of such a nature that all fractions of the accelerated bodies are acted upon individually. This could only come about through reactance with the gravitational field, because nonmagnetic materials do not react to a magnetic field. Therefore, since such movements are observed, we have to stop thinking in terms of jet or rocket propulsion, or reactance with a magnetic field, any of which subject both flesh and metal to outside pressures, and instead, ascertain how space craft obtain reactance with gravity. (red is A&B)

DO MOST CERTAINLY REACT.

ED: The following has no obvious reference or necessary position.

Proof of Reactance of Non-Magentic Materials is in Mag. Chamber, Cyclotron, 2000 WATTS, NEW YORK STATE.

A Man *cannot* Move in a *concentrated Mag.* Field & too, Mag can be connected to Grav. & VICE-VERSA Concentrated Magnet causes "Freezing of Man

The Man is on the right track but thinks of Mag. as a Minor force.

Either this guy KNOWS OF MAG. ATTRACTORS & GRAV. CONVERTERS & Force Field Functions

or

& He wants to Mislead or He knows Very Little & shows it —Which?   ?

It should be obvious to all engineers and scientists that rocket propulsion will never solve the problems of space travel, not only because of the unavoidable problems of acceleration, but because of the impossibility of transporting the necessary fuel and carrying the heavy reactance motors. Few laymen realize that, for rocket flight, the fuel is of dual purpose. Its ability to produce energy is no whit more valuable than its ability to produce inertial reactance when expelled through a jet, and therefore, any rocket propulsion craft must carry mass in some form for the purpose of being expelled so as to create reactance. Using fuel for both energy and reactance is only a partial solution of the problem, and obviously limits both the range and speed of a space craft. (Red is A & B).

QUITE TRUE, ROCKET *CARGO (word illegible)* DO.

Atomic power is certainly not the answer, at least not as regards jet or reactance propulsion, for all of the atomic power in the world will not move a space craft, by reactance propulsion, unless there is an enormous mass to be ejected and lost. The amount of such expendable mass is proportional to the weight of the craft and the square of the speed obtained. It is exactly here that the great cost and impracticality of current attempts at rocket flight occur.

True, in the way he thinks of applying. Can XXXXXX Worked in Combination.

A cheap power must, therefore, be found. By cheap power we have in mind something like the effect of the winds on sailing craft, [1] or the reactance of revolving cylinders with the winds, as was tried on a Scandinavian vessel twenty to thirty years ago. Such a force or power will have to originate in reactance directly with the gravitational field, since magnetic fields will not account for the observed accelerations nor are they, so far as we know, extensive enough in space.

---

[1] This probably refers to the series of notes on the preceding page.

39

ED: The following has no obvious reference or necessary position.
> GRAV. CONVERTER, TURNING GRAV. SUCKED IN ON
> THE GRAV. FIELD ATTRACTORS, HAVE BEEN IMPROVED
> & PUSH BETTER.

If the money, thought, time, and energy now being poured uselessly into the development of rocket propulsion were invested in a basic study of gravity, it is altogether likely that we could have effective and economical space travel, at a small fraction of the ultimate cost which we are now incurring, within one decade.

Our present path of development will not give it to us.

Science has consistently scoffed at any thought of gravity control or levitation, and such scoffing has had to be accepted as authoritative in the absence of proof to the contrary. Such proof now seems to be within sight, or at least there is increasingly strong evidence that gravity is neither so continuos so immaterial nor so obscure as to be completely unamenable to use, manipulation and control. Witness not only the documented movements of UFO's in the form of lights, discs, nebulosities, etc., but the many instances of stones, paper, clothes baskets and many other things which have been seen to leave the ground without apparent cause. The lifting of the ancient megalithic structures, too, must surely have come through levitation.

ED: the following has no obvious reference or necessary position.
> I should have enjoyed seeing Lemis Chieftran
> trying to Maneuver The first Craft before
> directional field induction was discovered.
> That, to Me, is a Classic tale of Howlingly
> Good Humor.

The same inhibited thinking which has consistently aroused our protests is responsible for the maladjusted direction of our attack on the problems of space flight through rocket power. There must be, and almost certainly is, a better, shorter way of accomplishing it. The difference between the pre-Incan methods of handling huge stone masses and those of our present-day engineers offers a kind of parallel. We should be looking for the simpler, more direct course-- not wasting our resources on unworkable methods.

In the magazine, Look, August 24, 1954, there was an article entitled "How Close Are We To Space Flight?" by J.Gordon Vaeth. He thinks we are not very close. If we accept his reasons we have to agree with him. He says the problem is too massive, too expensive, too intricate. We might add, ponderous. And--he is quite correct if we continue along present channels of research and development. Our procedure is expensive, cumbersome, tedious, and extremely wasteful of money, time, manpower, and intellect.

If, on the contrary, we shift our concentration to the intensive study of gravity, and put on that problem brains and education comparable to those which have solved the problems of fission and atomic structure, it is my honest belief that we can whip the problem of space travel inexpensively within a decade. It is my belief that something of the sort was done in the antediluvian past, through either research or through some fortuitous discovery of physical forces and laws which have not as yet been revealed to scientists of this second wave of civilization.

It is always easier to uncover a principle, or a fact, if it is known in advance to exist. This is certainly a fact that helped the Russians in their development of the atomic bomb and the H-bomb. It probably helped Columbus in his quest for the "Indies," even though he found something slightly different. It is my belief that the possibility of gravity control, or at least gravity reactance, has been strongly indicated by the phenomena listed in this book.

He May know of this principle but he needs to

> Have a permanent or Very Close "Node" to fathom
> the thing. Or one that *frequently* touches Earth
> in the same spot or even General Area. Nowadays
> Such "Dead-spots" don't revisit the Planetary sur-
> face as described & so Now this Principle cannot
> be discovered, eve*n if known*.

The Home of the UFO's

There seems to be something of periodicity in events of celestial and spatial origin. This has been called to our attention by John Philip Bessor in the *Saturday Evening Post* as early as May, 1949; but no one has thus far been able to catalogue and classify enough of this data to determine for certain whether such cycles exist, much less their time period or cause. It is not particularly astonishing that these phenomena should be cyclic, for practically everything astronomical is periodic. If periodicity could be firmly established for these phenomena, that fact alone would be proof of their reality and integration with the organic world about us.

The rush of oddities and unusual events in the decade 1877 to 1887 is very much in evidence. Perhaps it does seem to be drawing the long bow a bit if one tries to make out that the presence of the great comets, or the activity of the Red Spot on Jupiter, were influential in causing such events, but that all of these were concomitant is undeniable. If space life is limited to the earth-moon system, there is probably no common cause, but it must, however, be borne in mind.

Of greater pertinence is the observed and authenticated activity on the lunar surface during those and the immediately preceding years. Not only were there appearances and disappearance of lunar craters abaout the size of some of the larger space craft which have been seen but there is some evidence that nebulous entities hover over these evanescent craters and contribute to their obscuration.

Observations of UFO phenomena and related events on or near the earth's surface may be distorted by excitement, emotionalism and prejudice. But the direct observations of space life and its contingent activity, as seen by astronomers are more objective and more coolly recorded. We can feel more relaxed in dealing with them, on more solid ground.

Astronomical observations break naturally into three categories: lights, shadows, and bodies. Lights and shadows, perhaps, in reality comprise one group since one is the counterpart of the other, while bodies, on the other hand, tend to divide into two groups, one made up of solid contrivances and the other of nebulous or cloudlike units.

Lights seem to be especially representative of intelligence, particularly when they appear to have independent movement, or to shine in places where there seems to be no natural organic activity, for lights have to be created as well as manipulated. The hundreds of observations of lights on or near the moon and in other parts of nearby space —lights which seem to exhibit volition, purposefulness and direction — are extremely difficult to explain on any other basis than intelligent activity in space. On the other hand, they become a natural corollary to such activity. Again, since science has failed utterly to offer any other acceptable explanation, we ask that these lights be taken as one more phenomenon which can be simply adapted to our organic environment by the one common denominator of space flight and space life.

ED: The following has no obvious reference or necessary position.
> They have built there, now that peace has come
> these past 70 years. I would Like to see their
> Great Port City but I am too old to travel &
> even if so could not return. As always, Its
> underground

Shadows are almost as easily identified with intelligence as are lights, and one is pretty well the counterpart of the other. Their validity cannot be denied. Russell's shadow on the moon, 1,500 miles in diameter, holding a steady position for hours, cannot be lightly dismissed. The shadows on our own clouds, as seen in Texas and England, are irrefutable proof that some kind of dirigible bodies are moving in our upper atmosphere or in nearby space.

Bodies seen in space may be considered to have more direct and obvious connection with intelligence than do lights and shadow. There was a time when astronomers, seeing these by the dozens, thought them to be intra-Mercurial planets, or asteroids. Keen analysts have long since dispelled that misapprehension, but they have not discouraged nor discredited the sightings. These have remained without explanation for many decades, and some for hundreds of years. All of these observations gradually came to be regarded as erratics, to be ignored if possible. Astronomers who did not make any such observations liked to call them hallucinations, especially the spindleshaped ones whose configuration did not resemble that of more commonly known celestial objects. Mass passages, such as those seen be Herschel and Bonilla, were laughed off as being bugs, birds or seeds; or at worst, meteor swarms.

Ship frames, unfinished & being pushed or turned to new bases, during the Last War.

Little effort was made to determine the parallax of such objects, so their distance was never fairly established. We cannot blame the individual astronomer too much for this, particularly since many of those observations were made by amateurs. In those days it had not entered our comprehension that any of these spatial wanderers could be so close to the earth that parallax would be noticeable between observers only a few score miles apart. It has remained for us, awakening to the importance of those old observations, to make what we can of parallax studies for determining the distance of the objects sighted. It is not astonishing that our findings substantiate earlier analyses, but there may be an element of amazement in finding that these bodies are being navigated within the earth-moon system.

There is something more of astonishment, however, in finding that the astronomical observations include two distinct and divergent types of bodies: the solid, geometrically shaped structures, and the ill-defined nebulous clouds. Both have been recorded by impeccable witnesses. Both have been shown to exhibit evidences of intelligent direction or control. Both have their parallel instances among the current observations of UFO's seen by the man in the street, since 1947, and by our forebears as shown in historical records.

Strangely enough, however, the cloudy types have been seen really far out in space, and rather probably associated with such large comets as that of 1882. But whether seen two-thirds of an astronomical unit away or hovering over New York Harbor, they have had peculiar characteristics. Some of those seen by Schmidt in the neighborhood of the great comet in 1882 were moving both with the comet and at right angles to it, and there were undoubtedly objects moving about within the head of the comet.

The astronomical observations are so definite that we must leave them largely to speak for themselves, other than to point out again their concentration in certain years. It may be that further investigation will disclose other years of concentration, but the task is an enormous one. It is possible to say, however, that the search has been fairly exhaustive for the years 1877-86. There is reason to think that the next intensive investigation might bear fruit if concentrated around the prior years 1845-1860.

It is my contention that these observations of space movements are well explained by the existence of controlled space clouds and space structures, and that nothing else known to man does explain them. That the structures are the habitat of some kind of intelligence seems reasonable enough, but we also begin to wonder if intelligence is also inherent in the big clouds. If it is, then we are almost certainly going to have to adjust ourselves to a new type of intelligence and "life."

> Have refused acceptance for 200 ages, *How could* they ever adjust to What they refuse to accept?

Observations by Harrison, Gould, Perrine, Swift, Brooks and others demonstrate incontrovertibly that some of the objects seen by astronomers are subject to volitional and purposeful controls, whether they are cometary (nebulous) (sic) type (as per Harrison, Perrine, Gould, Bone), or of the planetary (structural) sorts (as per Watson, Swift, Lescarbault, Gruitheinsen, et al.).

The astronomical literature from 1885 to the present has been but sketchily included and researched. If it is but a fraction as prolific as that of the "comet years," there is, indeed, a wealth of UFO lore awaiting some research. It is to be doubted if there is as much in later years, because it became increasingly unfashionable to publish such information. It is barely possible that the editorial offices of some scientific publications may retain some of their old correspondence, and, if so, readers who have enough interest and access to those files might reap a rich reward from a bit of browsing. Search of observers' notebooks and observatory files might also bear fruit, and the old files of daily and weekly papers, especially where there are professional observatories or active amateur clubs, might disgorge some valuable information. I welcome reports of such items.

I suggest an alliance between amateur astronomers with telescopes and UFO enthusiasts, for the purpose of keeping eyes on the gravitational neutral of the earth-sun-moon systems. At times of new moon and of solar eclipse, this neutral point will be directly in line with the sun and moon, which will either be superimposed in the sky or be very close to each other. As the moon approached first quarter the neutral will swing to the east (left) of the sun and will move back into line between first quarter and full moon. After full moon and until third quarter the neutral will move to the west (right) of the sun, and will again swing toward the sun between third quarter and new moon. The neutral will reach its maximum distance to left of right at first and third quarters, but will not follow the moon around the earth. At new moon the neutral will be very close to the moon and that will be the time to watch for objects landing or taking off from the moon, although it is the worst time of all to see anything in that region because of the glare of sunlight. On the other hand, at the time of full moon the neutral will be closest to the earth, and directly in line with the sun, and that will be the time to watch for objects crossing the disc of the sun, probably from left to right. All of this on the assumption that space structures do make use of the neutral on account of the lessened navigational problems. Look for formations and groups which are especially indicative of intelligent action.

Cometary masses, on the other hand, will be more easily seen in other parts of the sky and are less likely to be using the neutral. Look for them in the northern sky on dark nights and expect them to look exactly like small comets without tails, or like a small nebula. Their rapid motions will give away their nature. Watch the regions of terminator on the moon for lunar surface activity. You might get a surprise.

> "What are we (humans) that Thou hast *placed* us only a Little *"Lower than the Angels"*

Are UFO's Russian

The October 1946, issue of the *Intelligence Digest* said:

The Soviets have ordered the building of a special centre of Astronomical research—in which will be a number of institutes, observatories and special airdromes where flying observatories, special balloons and airships are to be based for carrying out protracted studies at high altitudes.

Special machinery was acquired and there were further reports of work with monster mirrors. *Intelligence Digest* reported that the Russians were known to be working on a highly secret project involving cosmic rays, which (without much proof) was surmised to be related to atomic development. They were reported to have made some discoveries far in advance of the atomic research. One of their reported accomplishments was said to be a method of freezing large areas of ground to subzero temperatures, killing everything therein.

> If that is so then they also have a Heat
> Generator all in one IF this is Like to
> what I'm thinking about, in Principle.

The reporting agency, *Intelligence Digest*, of London, has proved remarkably accurate in many instances, as for example their prediction in November, 1948 of the explosion of a Russian atom bomb which did actually occur during the following August, within two months of the time predicted.

This is not to say that the UFO's are definitely Russian. But it does appear that Russia has had something during the postwar years, which was worth some very extreme efforts to conceal. Since we were presumably ahead of them in atomic research and development in the late forties, it does seem unlikely that concealment of their own atomic work would have justified such tremendous effort.

One wonders if their vast military deployment has been of that nature—for if they intended to use it against us, their ideal time was in 1950-52 when the United States was weak and spread most thinly over the world. There was just enough ostentatious secrecy about their military operations to make them appear to be the major interest.

UFO's, as we have seen, and as has been pointed out by Palmer and Arnold, Leslie, Wilkins, Fate, and others, have been around for thousands of years. It has been no secret that some principle of space flight or levitation was in existence; the problem was to rediscover it for contemporary civilization. As we have said before, it is easier to discover a scientific principle if it is *known* to exist. The Russians have known this as well as we have known it.

We are contemplating space travel via cumbersome methods within a few years— at most a few decades. If earthlings can be that close to it now, other races, either nonterrestrial or of great terrestrial antiquity, can already have it. If the U.S.A. can foresee space navigation in such a short time, there is no reason why Russia's mathematicians and physicists cannot have stumbled onto the principles which makes it possible.

But there is another, and much more plausible, possibility. Have the Russians captured a space ship? Or have space people taken over the Red Empire?

> NUTS.

The secrets of ancient flight and levitation, according to researchers into very ancient oriental records and reported by Churchward, Leslie, and others, have been preserved in the monasteries of the Himalayas: in Tibet, Nepal, India and China. Can there be a direct relationship between this fact and Russian anxiety to capture and control those mountain fastnesses?

> Could easily be so.

ED: The following has no obvious reference or necessary position.
> Russia FINALLY admits atomic Warfare would
> obliterate Civilization from the Earth, No Winner
> & etc. Would they admitt such if they knew of
> Nothing better?

Russia may have discovered such a new force or principle, either through accidental scientific discoveries or through capture of a space ship or association with "Space People."

If the UFO's are, indeed, interested in preventing disintegration of the earth through atomic warfare, it is but natural that they would act through control of one or both of the nations now throwing around their atomic weight. Do they, then, control the United States, secretly? Or do they control the Soviets? Or have the Soviets captured a space ship? Whether we like it or not, and whether or not our governments admit the true state of affairs, these are *some* of the possibilities which we must consider.

If such a condition exists, then even the development of atomic and hydrogen bombs could be diversionary.

Space Flight: Common Denominator

If I should be asked to state my thesis in one word, I believe that this word would be isolationism, or if I could squeeze in a hyphen, anti-isolationism.

Whatever else we may do or think, we have to extend our ideas of one world to include at least one solar system, and maybe more. But, whether or not, it is beyond the comprehension of our weary minds to go further at the moment, and we will just have to be content to consider our solar system as one living entity. This war-weary, heartsick and bedraggled planet is not alone—it is just one cell in a multicellular unit.

GALACTICLY SPEAKING

Let us revive from the sedative idea fostered by both science and religion that man, homo sapiens, of here and now, of the United States and today, is the final, glorious, end-point in the work of an omnipotent and benevolent creator, all alone in an infinite universe. It cannot be true and in our honest hearts all of us know that it is not so.

IT IS NICE TO HAVE COMPANY, EH? DRAGA?

Were I to be granted one more word, that word would be Truth. I am interested in true knowledge, for its own sake. It is my philosophy that science and religion should have at least one thing in common: the untiring, unceasing, unwavering quest of unbiased, undistorted true knowledge of the world around us... and, again, I use the word world in its old, original and all-comprehensive sense.

To cry out that we have discovered the truth about UFO's would be to invite ridicule, even for our effort. Therefore, let us summarize our conclusions and preface them with the same statement of open-mindedness which we demand of others whom we invite to immerse themselves in our studies of historical, meteorological, and astronomical erratics. We believe that our analyses have taken every possibility into account and have provided us with the most logical answers. (Red is A and B)

> What this guy Believes he has knowledge to Prove his beliefs in the Main.
>
> Psychological appeal to be Man enough to keep an open Mind, Lively with wanting to know, and to try Not to form any opinion until book is concluded.

Our general conclusions then, are:

1. A vast number of hitherto unexplained phenomena are readily accounted for by admitting that they result from intelligent action on the part of being living in space in navigable contrivances.

2. Abundant observations by accredited astronomers, despite the general attitude of the profession, indicate both the existence and location of the parent structures from which UFO's come.

3. UFO's inhabit the space between the earth and the moon, probably at the approximate region of the earth-sun-moon gravitational neutral, about 165,000 to 170,000 miles from the earth.

4. While some of the larger widgets (like the one chased by Mantell and the ten-miler seen over Kansas) may occasionally come close to our terrain, we see, mostly, the small, agile observers of both solid and nebulous types **which they send** on exploratory **missions**.

5. They have developed a source of power much superior to anything of which we aware.

6. UFO's have pointed the way too a shortened research program which might give us space travel in a decade, at a small fraction of the cost of trying to develop rocket flight, if we will only concentrate our research into the proper channels.

7. Russia may well have captured a UFO and be developing the resources gained therefrom, employing atomic experimentation as a diversionary measure.

> NOT SO or else she'd have cornered the Worlds
> Diamond Market by Now as a dead-Give-away that
> she'd Caught one. (Takes a Powerful Magnetic
> "Net" to do so)
>
> one with a reverse "snap Neutralizer" in it.

8. The very number and variety of the UFO's which are constantly seen is almost a priori proof of an origin close to the earth. Even the distance to nearby planets such as Venus and Mars seems too great to permit of such promiscuity.

We can conclude that the UFO's are permanent because they have been here for many centuries. That we have so suddenly become aware to them may be due in part to an increased activity, but it is more likely the result of our own slow awakening from intellectual immaturity. Exhaustive research has disclosed records of sightings covering thousands of years, and occasionally actual visits and contacts with our race. More of these incidents are coming to light constantly as research is pursued with UFO's in mind. Now that we are aware of UFO's and know what to look for the uncorrelated data of our predecessors takes on a meaning hitherto lacking and becomes significant. It is now up to us to discover and analyze all the data, and to correlate it with current observations.

We can allay our fears of present-day "Flying Saucers." They have been here since before the dawn of our civilization, so what is there to get excited about? If we haven't been molested seriously in two thousand centuries, why get excited now? If anything is at stake, it is our ego, not our physical welfare. (Red is A&B)

Yet, it is hard to discourage the innate feeling that there has recently been a great surge of activity on the part of UFO's as if in preparation for something big. One does not have to look far for a motive. These entities have probably been living in the solar system long enough to have seen the fifth planet explode, destroying itself and perhaps jeopardizing life throughout the system. They may have originated on that planet. Should one be astonished if these space dwellers are preparing to prevent a few fearstricken human beings from blowing up another planet, perhaps the only remaining one which offers supplies and a haven to space navigators? If we are incapable of the self-control necessary for our preservation, are we to assume that superior neighbors will permit their safety to be imperiled by our immature behavior?

Matches our own thoughts.

It is no longer necessary to explain them as visitors from Mars, Venus, or Alpha Centauri. They are a part of our own immediate family— a part of the earth-moon, binary-planet system. They didn't have to come all of those millions of miles from anywhere. They have been here for thousands of years. Whether we belong to them by possession, like cattle, or whether we belong to each other by common origin and association is an interesting problem, and one which may soon be settled if we keep our heads.

He *Knows* Something but *How* Does He know.

In final summary, the UFO's have been around us for a long time and probably are a connecting link with the first wave of terrestrial civilization. They have been used against us in some very minor and insignificant cases, but, on the whole, have either been friendly or indifferent. They are operated by forces currently unknown to us, but of vastly greater efficiency than anything we now contemplate. Space contains enough miscellaneous debris to supply many of the requirements of space life, and the remainder are obtained from the surfaces of the earth and moon, while the UFO's spend most of their time at the neutral points in space. The Russians have something which they have determined to conceal at all costs. The Russians have been doing very advanced experimental research with cosmic forces; UFO activity was stepped up greatly just a year or so after intelligence reports noted the unusual Russian scientific activity. It is not necessary to assume that the Russian basic science is far ahead of our own if we can believe that a space ship has landed in inner Asia and that they have captured it and are studying its principles and experimenting with models — or that the space people have taken over the Russian high officialdom and are directing their efforts and supplying know-how.

We do have the UFO's. They are of several kinds, always have been, so they may come from various sources. They are either terrestrial, extraterrestrial, or both. We think they are extraterrestrial, but remotely of terrestrial origin.

We believe they are both, and that the Russians may have captured one or more. We think that some new scientific principles are with us, perhaps even now operating within our military laboratories, and may burst forth at any moment — and that as a race we may be on the verge of something akin to what the modern atomic scientist calls a "quantum expansion"!

No other set of conclusions will serve as a common denominator for all observable facts.

The possibility of the Ruskies have FOUND an *old* "Dead-Ship" is Not without the realm of probability. His admittance to other forms of Humanoid Life is near-revealatory to what I surmise: *He* is *being Lead* by his short-Wave Telepathic nose, so to speak; too "SEE" these things. He says, "WE" and that could imply anything from one friendly L-M to a fellow scientist or his Wife or Some Member of U.S. Government.

If What I, now, surmise, is true, then the L-Ms are in trouble *or* the S-Ms Wish to War upon the L-Ms & are USING this Man, telepathically, to "get help." Whether this consideration is of import to him only remains to be seen. If is isn't , then, He will be Left out on a Emotional Limb, trying to say "See, I am right, "They" are Wrong" & will forget what IS important here.

PART TWO

Meteorology Speaks

Falling Ice

It has been postulated that there are "lands in the sky" from which ice falls to earth periodically. But there has never been a positioning of these lands. No one tells us what kind of lands, where they are, why ice falls from them or why ice exists on them. The lands in the sky theory is based solely on the locale of the falls and the kind of ice noted.

Read the following citations, bearing in mind our thesis that intelligence or intelligent direction does explain the selectivity of materiel and locale.

Selectivity can be intelligent or nonintelligent. The affinity of hydrogen and oxygen, which produces water, is what we consider nonintelligent selection. The direction which makes rifle bullets strike on or near a target is what we believe to be intelligent direction or selectivity.

Repetition of falls on the same pinpointed area from fixed regions above a spinning and revolving earth is incredible. But repeated showers, selectively directed by intelligence, is a probability within the grasp of the uninhibited thinker.

We list these occurrences with two thoughts: first, to show that there is a great amount of activity in space which has origins difficult to explain on the bases of Newtonian or Keplerian laws, second, they indicate that the simplest explanations common to all of these puzzles is that they originate from the actions of space contrivances or the intelligence directing such mechanisms.

The following reports are from The Books of Charles Fort:

1802: During a storm in Hungary on May 8, a mass of ice fell which was three feet long, three feet wide, and more than two feet thick.

1808: The sun suddenly turned a dull brick red on May 16. At the same time there appeared, on the Western horizon, a great number of round bodies, dark brown, and seemingly the size of a hat crown. They passed overhead and disappeared on the Eastern horizon. It was a tremendous procession lasting two hours. Occasionally one fell to the ground. When the place was examined, there was found a film which soon dried and vanished. Sometimes, on approaching the sun, the bodies seemed to link together in groups not exceeding eight. Under the sun they were seen to have tails, Away from he sun, the tails were invisible. Whatever their substance may have been, it is described as gelatinous "sopy (sic) and jellied."

1811: Lumps of ice, a foot in circumference, fell in Derbyshire, England, on May 11.

1828: A mass of ice about a cubic yard in size fell in Candeish, India.

1829: A block of ice weighing four and one-half pounds fell at Cazorta, Spain, on June 15.

1830: A profound darkness came over the city of Brussels, on June 18, and flat pieces of ice, an inch long, fell to the ground.

1844: A block of ice weighting eleven pounds fell at Cette, France, in October.

1849: An irregular-shaped mass of ice fell at Ord, Scotland, in August, "after an extraordinary peal of thunder." It was said that this was homogenous ice, except in a small part, which looked like congealed hailstones. The mass was about twenty feet in circumference. The story, as told in the *London Times*, August 14, 1849, is that, upon the evening of August 13, 1849, after a loud peal of thunder, a mass of ice, said to have a circumference of twenty feet, has fallen upon the estate of Mr. Moffat, of Balvullich, Rosshire. It was said that this object fell alone, without hailstone.

1851: Ice the size of pumpkins fell in Gunfalore, India, on May 22.

1851: Masses of ice, each piece about a pound and one-half in weight, fell in New Hampshire, August 13.

1853: Masses or irregularly shaped piece of ice fell at Pouen, France, on July 5. They were about the size of a hand and described as looking as if all had been broken from one enormous block of ice.

1854: At Pourhundur, India, December 11, flat pieces of ice, many of them weighing several pounds each, fell from the sky. They are described as large "Ice-Flakes."

1857: The *London Times* of August 4 reported that a block of ice, described as "pure" ice, weighing twenty-five pounds, had been found in the meadow of Mr. Warner, of Cricklewood. There had been a storm the day before. As in some of our other instances, no one saw this object fall from the sky.

1860: January 14, in a thunderstorm pieces of ice fell on Captain Blackiston's vessel. "It was not hail, but irregular-shaped pieces of solid ice of different dimensions, up to the size of half a brick."

1860: In a snowstorm in Upper Wasdale, England, on March 16, blocks of ice fell which were so large that at a distance they looked like a flock of sheep.

1864: During a storm at Pontiac, Canada, July 11, pieces of ice fell which were one-half inch to two inches in diameter. What is most extraordinary is that a respectable farmer, of undoubted veracity, says he picked up a piece of ice, in the center of which was a small, green frog.

1869: Near Tiflis, large hailstones fell which had long protuberances. The most remarkable point is that a very long time must have been occupied in their formation.

1877: Ice as large as men's hands killed thousands of sheep in Texas on May 3.

1880: In Russia, June 14, red hailstones, blue hailstones and gray hailstones fell in profusion.

1882: A mass of ice weighing about eighty pounds fell from the sky near Salina, Kansas, in August. Mr. W.J. Hagler, a North Santa Fe merchant, collected it and packed it in sawdust in his store.

1882: Pieces of ice eight inches long and an inch and one-half thick fell at Davenport, Iowa, on August 30.

1883: A lump of ice the size of a brick, weighing two pounds, fell in Chicago, on July 12.

1883: There was a storm at Dubuque, Iowa, on June 16. Great hailstones and pieces of ice fell. The foreman of the Novelty Iron Works stated that in two large hailstones, melted by him, were found small living frogs.

The pieces of ice which fell at that time had a peculiarity as bizarre as anything in this book. They seemed, evidently, to have been motionless for a long time floating somewhere.

There could be no more perfect description of ice suspended in meteoric orbits.

1886: In a small town in Venezuela, April 17, hailstones fell, some red, some blue, and some gray.

1887: In Montana, in the winter, snowflakes fell which were fifteen inches across and eight inches thick. (Snowflakes?)

1889: Intense darkness at Aitkin, Minnesota, April 2; sand and "solid chunks of ice" fell.

1889: At East Wickenham, England, on August 5, an object fell, slowly, which was about fifteen inches long and five inches wide. It exploded, but no substance was found from it.

1891: Snowflakes the "size of saucers" fell near Nashville, Tennessee, on January 24.

1893: A lump of ice weighing four pounds fell in Texas, on December 6.

1894: From the Weather Bureau of Portland, Oregon, a tornado was reported on June 3. Fragments of ice fell from the sky. They averaged three to four inches square and about an inch thick. In length and breadth they had smooth surfaces and "gave the impression of a vast field of ice suspended in the atmosphere, and suddenly broke into fragments about the size of the palm of the hand."

ED: The following has no obvious reference or necessary position.
Crystal, Ice in Great Curved sheets is used at odd times as a Gigantic Lens for close observation of Humankind or Merely for amusement.

1897: Rough-edged, but smooth surfaced pieces of ice fell at Manassas, Virginia, August 10. They looked much like the roughly broken fragments of a smooth sheet of ice. They were two inches across, and one inch thick.

1901: On November 14, lumps of ice fell during a tornado in Victoria, New South Wales, which weighed a minimum of one pound each.

1908: A correspondent wrote that, at Braemar, Switzerland, July 2, when the sky was clear overhead and the sun was shining, flat pieces of ice fell. Thunder was heard.

1911: Large hailstones were noted at the University of Missouri. They exploded like pistol shots. The reporter had seen a similar phenomenon at Lexington, Kentucky, eighteen years before.

The entire report below, from the *Science Record* of 1876, is worthy of note.

At Potter Station, on the Union Pacific Railroad, recently, a train was just pulling out from the station when a storm commenced and in ten seconds there was such a fury of hail and wind that the engineer deemed it best to stop the locomotive. The "hailstones" were simply great chunks of ice, many of them three or four inches in diameter and of all shapes: squares, cones, cubes, etc., and the first "stone" that struck the train broke a window and the flying glass severely injured a lady on the face, making a deep cut. Five minutes later there was not a whole pane of glass on the south side of the train, the whole length of it. The windows of the Pullman cars were of French plate three-eighths of an inch thick, and double. The hail broke both thicknesses and tore the curtains to shreds. The wooden shutters were smashed and many of the mirrors were broken. The deck lights on top of the cars were also demolished. The dome of the engine was dented as if pounded with a heavy weight, and the woodwork of the south side of the cars was ploughed as if someone had struck it all over with sliding blows of a hammer. During the continence of this fusillade, which lasted fully twenty minutes, the damage amounted to several thousand dollars and several persons were injured.

Note, particularly, the size and shapes of the "hailstones." This was obviously not a hailstorm. Winds strong enough to have torn mountain icesheets to bits and carried them across the country, would have lifted the train from its tracks. Note, too, the suddenness of the attack.

A more definite case of meteoric ice could scarcely be imagined.

Lest we fall into the trap of suspecting these reports merely because of their age, I shall depart from my desire to draw upon material reported before the present flying saucer phenomenon, and reproduce this letter in *Fate Magazine*, August, 1950.

The Great Hail

On Sunday, September 11, 1949, three acquaintances, Dr. Robert Botts, Dr. John Tipton, and Dr. T.J. Treadwell, went dove hunting on the Eugene Tipton Ranch in northwest Stephens County, Texas.

Dr. Botts told me about it, and said that it was a fairly clear, hot afternoon on the ranch when the skies let loose with about forty pounds of ice, all in one chunk. Dr. Tipton and Dr. Treadwell substantiate what Dr. Botts says that he saw.

Dr. Botts was sitting by an earthen tank, waiting for birds. He said that he "heard a whistling sound, and when I looked up, I saw a glistening, whirling object falling. It landed fifteen feet from me and shattered into hundreds of pieces." He added that the ice knocked a hole several inches deep in the ground. He immediately called his companions, and, when they arrived, all three saw that the ice was milky white, and when they tasted it they found that it had a soapy flavor.

Botts said there were a few thunderheads in the sky, but none overhead. He declared that no airplanes had passed overhead.

The ice fell about 4:30 P.M., and had not completely melted when Dr. Botts and his friends left, about two hours later.

Treadwell, said that he did not hear the sound of the ice falling, but he arrived on the scene immediately after and saw the chunk where he was sure there had been no ice when he walked by the tank earlier.

Tipton, whose uncle owns the ranch, said that the ice did not look like the truck-delivered variety, but did have something of the appearance of hail, except for the dimensions. All three declared that the pieces were not dry ice, and both Drs. Tipton and Treadwell agreed that there had been no airplanes heard overhead, before or after the ice fell.

After hearing this story, I turned to *my* Bible, Revelations 16:21 — "And there fell upon men a great hail out of Heaven, every stone about the weight of a talent." According to a dictionary definition, a talent is fifty-eight pounds.

Can you explain this mystery?

Lewis W. Mathews,
Fort Worth, Texas

Now... how do we interpret these strange falls of ice? What, after careful consideration, do they mean to us?

We have already enough data to indicate three classes of falling ice:
(1) real hailstones, from thunderstorms, or normal meteorological phenomena,
(2) large and small blocks of meteoric ice, which may have been blasted from the polar regions, or oceans, when scientists of Mu invented the first series of atom and hydrogen bombs, and removed Mu, plus a few million square miles of surrounding land and seascapes from the southwest corner of our harassed planet, and (3) ice from some superstructures which make repeated visits to the atmosphere of the earth.

Since some of the pieces of ice, which show evidence of some contact with a smooth surface, fell long before the days of modern mechanical flight, we are forced to assign their origin to some other, older type of space inhabiting, moving mechanism.

It seems most natural that a space contrivance, if made of metal, and coming in from cold space, would soon become coated with ice. That ice should fall, or be pushed off by de-icing mechanisms, or even melt off when the space ships are heated by friction with the air, or become stationary in the sunshine, seems equally natural. If these contrivances are drawing power from surrounding media via an endothermic process, the space structure will become colder and colder to more power it draws, and, in the atmosphere, ice would tend to form on it, just like the frosting of the coils in a refrigerator.

I am fully convinced that huge ice swarms are moving around in space, in orbits like those of meteors. Somewhere in space there is a borderline—beyond it the sun's rays will not melt ice: on the sunward side of the line, melting takes place slowly.

I cannot accept the idea of a floating ice field permanently near the earth. In contrast, I postulate vast masses in orbital motion, so that when they approach the earth they are held against its attraction by the dynamic force of their velocity. Meteoric and cometic orbits are of what we call very high eccentricity, which is to say that the material following such paths varies extremely in it distance from the sun, as compared to the movement of the earth and other planets, which have orbits almost circular. Then, as the ice swarm approach the sun, in its periodic orbital circuit, tiny amounts of ice are melted and, being fluid, the film of melted ice is pulled toward the side of greatest gravitational attraction, probably earthward or sunward. This melted ice flows toward the direction of greatest gravity, on the surface of the spatial iceberg exactly as, and for the same reasons that, the sun and moon pull water toward the proximate side of the earth in their production of ocean tides.

We come to the inevitable conclusion, therefore, that this series of falling ice cannot be explained other than as vast masses of ice in orbital motion, in which case they are an intrinsic element of the space life or space craft, and that their very inconsistency indicates intelligence in space. Since they are not consistent with natural laws, there must be direction behind them.

Falling Stones

What, indeed, do "falling stones" have to do with UFO's?

We shall list, herein, but a few of the more interesting and entertaining examples of stones having fallen from space, and we can note that quartz and other materials not of usual meteoric types indicate something other than meteors. Where else, then, but from UFO's?

> Yes, quartz, it has its uses Electro-Magnetically
> and otherwise on the Home-ships.

It is essential, too, to keep reminding ourselves that because we attribute intelligence too these otherwise inexplicable phenomena, it does not necessarily mean human Intelligence. It is a blow to our ego to accept the fact that our racial intelligence is anything but the supreme summation of creation; however, the quicker we adjust to the notion that the human body and the human mind are but incidental in a limitless welter of space life and activity, the quicker we shall approach a true grasp of the nature of the Universe and our own true purpose in it.

> "WHAT IS MAN THAT THOU HAST PLACED (planted)
> HIM A LITTLE LOWER THAN ANGELS." "angelic"
> is a good discription of the Little-Men *when*
> they aren't *on* business.

On June 20, 1887, during a violent storm, a small stone fell from the sky at Tarbes, France. It was thirteen millimeters in diameter, five millimeters thick, and weighed two grams. It was reported to the French Academy by M. Sudre, Professor of the Normal School, Tarbes.

It is difficult for the conventionalists to press the old, convenient expostulation that the stone was there in the first place. Such a dodge must be resisted, for...the stone was covered with ice.

The object had been cut and shaped by means" similar to human hands and human mentality." That expression, "similar to," begins to tell a story. It was a disc of worked stone, "tres regulier." "Il a ete assurement travaille." There is no word of any known whirlwind or tornado, or notes of any other objects or debris which fell at, or near, this date, in France. It was a single entity. It had fallen alone!

Can part of our trouble with the acceptance of miscellaneous falls lie in our definition of "sky" and our use of the word sky instead of space? When we get far enough out into space, Only a few hundred miles, the word sky becomes meaningless.

To the surface dwellers, sky is essentially something opposed to earth, or the solid understratum of dirt and pavement on which we live. It is usually thought of as the immediate layer of air above us. But out in space, the earth, with its air and sky is but a minute detail. If you were in a space ship remote from planets, completely surrounded by the blackness of infinity, but nevertheless bathed by the sea of sunlight, what would be your concept of sky?

Monthly Review, 1796: "The phenomenon which is the subject of the remarks before us will seem, to most persons, as little worthy of credit as any that could be offered. The falling of large stones from the sky, without any assignable cause of the previous ascent, seems to partake so much of the marvelous as almost entirely to exclude the operation of known and natural agents. Yet a body of evidence is here brought to prove that such events have actually taken place, and we ought not to withhold from it a proper degree of attention."

That was one hundred and fifty-nine years ago! It is a part of a paper read to a very learned society. These were intelligent and erudite men. They had to overcome their own prejudices, and those of even more bigoted people. They had to undergo a change of concept and to accept a less egocentric or geocentric, viewpoint. They had to attain an increased degree of objectivity. And they had to do it innately, spontaneously, on the basis of accumulating evidence which ran contrary to their every belief and tenet.

1846: Something described as "slag" fell at Darmstadt, Germany, on June 6.

1875: Ashes fell on the Azores.

1879: A quantity of "slag" fell from the sky near Chicago, on April 9. A professor who did not see the fall and who was not there, said that the slag was there all the time. But the *New York Times* of April 14, 1879 said that about two bushels had fallen.

1881: Two silver crosses were found by Charles C. Jones in Georgia. An unintelligible inscription was upon them and they were definitely not Christian since both arms of the cross were of equal length.

1884: *Nature*, of January 10, quotes a Kimberley newspaper: "Toward the end of November, 1883, a thick shower of ashy matter fell at Queenstown, South Africa. It was in marble-sized balls, soft and pulpy, and crumbled when dry. The shower was confined to one narrow strip of land, and thus hardly attributable too Krakatao almost halfway around the world. With the fall, loud noises here(sic) heard."

It is most significant that this shower was confined to a narrow strip of land.

1908: A white substance, like ashes, fell at Annoy, France, on March 27.

1910: Charles F. Holder wrote that on September 10: "Many years ago a strange stone, resembling a meteorite, fell into the valley of the Yaqui, Mexico, and the sensational story went from one end of the country to the other, that a stone bearing human inscriptions had descended to the earth... The stone was brown igneous rock, about eight feet long, and on the 'eastern' face was the deep-cut inscription... I submitted the photographs to the Field Museum and the Smithsonian, and others, and, to my surprise, the reply was that they could make nothing of it."

A lot of coke, cinders, ashes and slag fell in, the proximate to, the decade of the 1880's. There are too many cases of stones, fire balls, and other things falling in storms. It is useless to argue that storms pick these things up. The list is too selective. So we have to think of some reasons why these things fall during storms; and one wonders if the storms were created by something outside of what we are commonly calling meteorological conditions?

1885: It was reported that a good-sized stone, of clearly artificial form, had fallen at Naples, in November.

La Science Pour Tous, 5-264: At Wolverhampton, England, June, 1860 a violent storm, there fell so many little pebbles that they were cleared away with shovels... Rept. Brit. Assoc., 1864. Great numbers of small black stones which fell at Birmingham, England, in August, 1858 – in a storm... Mon. Weath. Rev., July, 1888: Pebbles of the water-worn variety, not common to the locality, fell at Palestine, Texas, July 6,1888...Am. Jour. Sci., 1-26-161: Many round smooth pebbles fell at Kandahar in 1834...Mon. Weath. Rev., May, 1883: "a number of stones of peculiar formation and shapes, unknown in this neighborhood, fell at Hillsboro, Illinois, May 18, 1883."

Concentrate on the selectivity—a function of intelligence—and possibly shape. Possibly, we should consider the coincidence of storms, to which we can hardly attribute this selectivity nor the dexterity with which to implement it.

1815: Hailstones the size of baseballs, which were said to contain small pebbles, fell near Annapolis, Maryland.

1824: Small symmetrical objects of metal fell at Orenburg, Russia, in September. A second fall of these objects at Orenburg, January 25, 1825.

Selectivity, repetition, symmetry, timing: attributes of intelligent action!

1884: A report from the *Signal Service* observer at Bismark, North Dakota, states that at 9:00 P.M., May 22, sharp sounds were heard throughout the city, caused by the fall of flinty stones at Bismarck. Fifteen hours later there was another fall of flinty stones at Bismarck. None reported falling anywhere else.

1860: Professor Sayed Abdulla, Professor of Hindustani, wrote an account of the fall of stones at Dhurmsalla, India, which were of "divers forms and sizes, many of which bore great resemblance to ordinary cannonballs, just discharged from engines of war."

Note that some of these Dhurmsalla stones were spherical. Spherical stones are most likely shaped by intelligence. It is further noted that, within a few months of the fall of the Dhurmsalla "meteorite," there had been a fall of live fish at Berares, a shower of red substance at Furrackabad, a dark spot observed on the disc of the sun, an earthquake, "an unnatural darkness of some duration," and a luminous appearance in the sky that looked like an aurora borealis.

1855: A series of explosions in the sky, fall of debris, slag, cinders, powder, discolored rain, reported at and near Crieff, England.

Recurrence, in a localized area, of unusual events, mostly of celestial, or mysterious origin.

1858-1868: Dr. C.M. Inglsby, a meteorologist, wrote: "During the storm on Saturday (12) morning, (May), Birmingham was visited by a shower of aerolites. Many hundreds of thousands must have fallen, some streets being strewn with them." Many pounds of stones gathered from awnings. Greenhouses damaged. The same type of stones fell again at Wolverhampton, thirteen miles from Birmingham, June 9, 1860, two years later. Eight years later they fell again in Birmingham. Birmingham Daily Post, May 30, 1868: Letter from meteorologist, Thomas Plant, who said: "I think for one hour the morning of May 29, 1868, stones fell from the sky at Birmingham. From nine to ten o'clock, meteoric stones fell in immense quantities in various parts of town. They resembled, in shape, broken pieces of Rowley ragstone...in every respect they were like the stones that fell in 1858." In the Post, June 1, Mr. Plant says the stones of 1858 did fall from the sky, and were not washed out of the pavement by rain (although of the same shape) because many pounds of them were gathered from a platform which was twenty feet above the ground.

This phenomenon may have continued in driblets, for in the *Post* of June 2, 1868, a correspondent wrote that on the first of June, his niece, walking in a field, was struck by a stone that injured her hand severely. In the *Post*, June 4, someone else wrote that his wife had been cut on her head by a stone while walking down a lane.

Some of these big falls occurred in storms, and all of the falls are identified as being of the same appearance as the Rowley ragstone with which Birmingham was paved, and the old explanation of whirlwinds is invoked. But regardless of the origin, there is again repetition and a selectivity of material which is inexplicable except through intelligent manipulation. Why anyone or anything would pick up Rowley ragstone and dump in on Birmingham and Wolverhampton, repeatedly, is more than we can say! There must be a reason.

1896: On February 10, a tremendous explosion occurred in the sky over Madrid, and throughout the city windows were smashed. A wall in the building occupied by the American Embassy was thrown down. The people of Madrid rushed to the streets and there was a panic in which many were injured. For five and a half hours a luminous cloud of debris hung over Madrid, and stones fell from the sky.

Here we have stone falling from the sky, a hint of a localized cloud, luminosity, and definitely the suggestion that some violent activity had come from space. There is also a haunting resemblance to the circumstances of the Great Heresford Quake, in England, of December 17, 1896.

A disc of quartz fell on the plantation, Bleijendal, Dutch Gueana,(sic) and was sent to the Layden Musuem (sic) of Antiquities. It measures six centimeters by five millimeters by about five centimeters. I am puzzled by these dimensions, unless the disc is slightly oval and is six cm. in its major axis and five cm. in the minor axis. This seems to be a good datum. It has some individuality. Even if we omit space ships from our cognizance, this thing could have been blasted into space by our progenitors in Mu when they lost control of the atom.

> The Muaneans *Never knew What* an atom was &
> Niether did the Atruscan-Lems. They only know
> & knew Force-field work as their top accomplishment
> & found that throo Inlay work in Metal that the
> Design had been Hit by Lightning causing it to
> Have No weight somehow. THEY WENT ON
> FROM THAT FLOOR Design or floor pattern which
> may have been Laid in Lodestone for all I know.

Anything about quartz that appears to come from the sky is interesting because it helps to illustrate the diversity of debris which drifts around in space. Quartz, as celestial debris, is scientifically damned at present, for science has not yet admitted, openly, the existence of meteoric material other than the two conventional types. Certainly, we do not find meteoric quartz to be plentiful. It's so scarce that if you encounter it, you almost feel instinctively that it has some connection with intelligent being. That may seem an arbitrary assumption; however, worked quartz is something else again!

> As I said; it has its uses.

There is the instance of a man, his wife, and his three daughters, of Casterton, Westmoreland, who were looking at their lawn during a thunderstorm when they saw a stone fall from the sky, kill a sheep, and bury itself in the ground. They dug. They found a stone ball. The object was exhibited at a meeting of the Royal Meteorological Society and is described in its Journal as a sandstone ball and it is described as a sandstone by Mr. Symons.

There is a suggestion of symmetry and structure in this object, and it had an external shell separated from a loose nucleus.

Science maintains that it is impossible for quartz to come from any place other than earth. I offer that quartz not only can, but has come from elsewhere. There are two possible sources: (1) that items such as quartz, closely resembling our own geological specimens, may have been blown off this planet by erratic Muvian scientists when they erred in their explosions of hydrogen, and that some of these things are coming home after several eons in orbital isolation, and (2) they may be a part of the space ships or be attracted by them as they pass, drawing them up and then, through some spatial phenomenon, dropping them at a later date.

Bode's law indicated a gap in the planetary sequence between Mars and Jupiter, and near the beginning of the nineteenth century small planetoids began to be discovered at the designated place. They now number much over a thousand, and it is suspected that millions of small pieces of space debris occupy this belt. Astronomical science has never fully accepted the idea that a planet exploded in that location, but a case can be made for such a cataclysm, and it would explain the origin of stones which fell to the earth.

The asteroid zone is the only gap in the Bode systems, but some of the derivatives of that system, which seem to fit observed data a little bit more snugly, have gaps which do not seem to be filled. Furthermore, such systems indicate zones surrounding the larger planets which are not always occupied by satellites, and which may contain interplanetary debris.

The earth-moon system is unique. It is really a binary planet, and while we speak of the moon as being earth's satellite, it may be that this is a misnomer, and the result of a misconception of the formation of the little system. There are a number of traditions, among ancient tribes and races, to the effect that their forefathers were thriving before there was a moon. This would hint that the moon was picked up by acquisition and not formed in the original coagulation of earth-material. At any rate, neither the earth nor its twin Venus formed satellite systems such as accompany the outer major planets. Nevertheless, the laws, such as Bode's <u>imply physical conditions in which either satellites or belts of debris could exist</u>. If this is true, then we see no reason for not suspecting that there may be gravitational nodes around the earth, as around the sun, and major planets; and these nodes may very well be the abode of all manner of particles, either directed or undirected.

<u>Bodes Law to that extent is Proved.</u>

Most of the material in these belts would doubtless be meteoric material, but our experience is that meteoric material includes a much broader category than has heretofore been accepted, and that mixed with it are things associated with intelligence.

<u>MOON NOW *RECOGNIZED* AS RECENT ACQUISITION OF EARTH. NOT KNOWN FROM WHENCE IT CAME. *STRONGLY* SUSPECT QUANTUM "GAP" indicated Bodes Law as original position of *our* Moon.</u>

Falling Live Things

<u>Food expieriments (sic) to compensate for Growing Population of L-M and Mutations.</u>

In the reported falls of live things, we find again selectivity and localization.

There are recorded, by Charles Fort, two hundred and ninety-four distinct reports of showers of living things. The reports are authenticated and are quoted in magazines of learning, substantiated by countless eyewitnesses and newspaper articles, contemporary with the falls. This is excluding, or course, the numerous ancient and biblical references. The latter, for the uninhibited thinker, are not difficult to allow.

Live things falling from the sky have been almost exclusively confined to sea life and lower forms: snails, worms, reptiles, fish, crabs, and a few insects. Most of these have high reproductive rates, simple living habits, and require a minimum of attention to raise.

In case someone is thinking "hoax!" why was it, or would it be, confined to these lower forms? Why not rabbits or groundhogs or cats? Why snails, fish, worms?

Accepting as I do the veracity of the many reports of live things having fallen from the skies, I <u>submit that they are the inhabitants of celestial hydroponic tanks and that their falls come from one of two things:</u> (1) when the tanks are dumped and cleared for refilling, for whatever reason there might be, <u>(2)</u> that the falls may be the residue from the collection from earth while the monitors of the tanks are replenishing their supplies.

<u>Some of Both & of Wrecks & repair-Jobs on Most Ships.</u>

Again we are faced with the admission of intelligence and direction. An intelligence in space controlling either the collection, dissemination, or nurture of sea life, either for study or for food or both, is the only answer which satisfies all the elements of all the reports.

Let us scan but a few of the more dramatic of the falls.

1886: There was a shower of snails, during a heavy thunderstorm, in Cornwall, England, on August 13.

1890: Fish showered over Montgomery County, California, on February 6.

1891: A great shower of fish took place at Seymour, Indiana. They were completely unknown and remain unidentified. This was August 8.

1892: At Coalburg, Alabama, on May 29, a tremendous shower of enormous eels took place. The eels were of a variety unknown in Alabama, though somebody said he knew of such eels in the Pacific Ocean. There were piles of eels in the street, and farmers came with carts and took them away to use for fertilizer.

1892: A yellow cloud appeared over Paderborn, Germany, and a torrential rain fell from the cloud in which there were hundreds of mussels.

1921: Innumerable little frogs appeared in the streets of northern part of London during a thunderstorm on August 17. A thorough search of newspapers of the day indicated no whirlwinds or storms, nothing but frogs!

1922: Toads dropped for two days at Chalon-sur Saone, France.

1924: A shower of red objects fell, with snow, at Halmstead, Sweden, on January 3. They were red worms varying from one to four inches in length.

1925: Mr. C.J. Grewar reported, on March 21, from Uitenhage, Transvaal, that on "The Flats" about fifty miles from Uitenhage he noted some springboks leaping and shaking themselves unaccountably. At a distance he could conceive of no explanation for such eccentricities. He investigated and found that a rain of little frogs and fish had pelted the springboks. Mr. Grewar heard that, sometime before, at the same place, there had been similar shower.

It is interesting to note that this localized repetition; the yellow cloud over Paderborn, Germany, appears to have been an artificially created cloud which might well conceal a navigable structure. It makes us think again of someone opening a vast hydroponic tank in which mussels are grown.

1842: Enormous numbers of fish were reported to have fallen at Derby, England.

1873: A shower of frogs was reported during a rain storm in Kansas City, Missouri. The sky was exceptionally dark.

1877: It was reported that during the winter of 1876-77 at Christiana, Norway, worms were found crawling upon the ground. The worms could not have come up from the ground because the ground was completely frozen at the time and, too, the fall of worms was reported from Sweden.

1877: In Memphis, Tennessee, after a violent storm during which rain fell in torrents, thousands of snakes were found in the space of two blocks! They were crawling on sidewalks, in yards and in streets, masses of them.

Again note the localized area, as if a "dumping" had taken place.

Perhaps the most glamorous of all falls in this category took place in Geneva, Switzerland, on March 21, 1922. The incident, as reported in the *Boston Transcript*, reads as follows:

"Geneva, March 21. During a heavy snowstorm in the Alps, recently, thousands of exotic insects resembling spiders, caterpillars and huge ants fell on the slopes and quickly died. Local naturalists are unable to explain the phenomenon..."

There are several other records of similar falls in the Alps, and usually in late January. It is interesting to note that most falls of worms and insects are recorded in late winter and often in the snow. It may be that this is merely because we are unlikely to see or notice them otherwise.

Again we encounter selection and segregation, despite the fact that we have a mixture of species. These falls, nevertheless, do indicate selection as they are always of relatively the same order and remain unmixed with twigs, grasses, or other debris from space.

The reports are too lengthy and detailed for inclusion in such a volume as this; however, we should at least mention the many unexplained records of eels appearing in inland ponds and mountain tarns; seals and squids in Onondaga Lake; sudden appearances of plants in unexpected areas; a five and one-half foot alligator found frozen on the bank of Rock River, Janesville Wisconsin; parakeets, one after another, appearing in Scotland, These are all verified, substantiated reports.

But, as we have pointed out, most of the falls of animal life have been reptilian, insect, or other low-grade life forms, especially of marine varieties. Fish are among the highest types. There must be significance in this. Are these things indicative of the eating habits of the beings that run space contraptions? Or are they representative of the operators themselves?

We almost drift into fantasy with the "tremendous red rain" in France, October 16-17, 1846. It is said that this rain was so vividly red and so blood-like that many persons in France were terrified. Two analyses were given. One chemist noted a great quantity of corpuscles—whether blood-like or not—in the red rain. The other chemist set down the organic matter at thirty-five percent. Of significance is the fact, that with this substance, larks, quail, ducks, and water hens, some of them alive, fell at Lyons, Grenoble, and other places.

Chico, California, must be a crossroads for celestial phenomena. Not only are there very extensive falls of stone in Chico, but there have been other phenomena there. In the *New York Times*, September 2, 1878, it was said that on August 20, 1878, according to the *Chico Record*, a great number of small fish fell from the sky, covering the roof of a store and falling in the streets and upon an area of several acres. Perhaps the most important part of the observation is that the fell from a cloudless sky.

Hah! Even yet they Honor their Heros of
The Great Battle.

1917: A Baton Rouge correspondent to the *Philadelphia Times* reported that in the summer of 1896, into the streets of Baton Rouge, Louisiana, and from a "clear sky," hundreds of dead birds fell. There were wild ducks, catbirds, woodpeckers, and "many birds of strange plumage," some of them resembling canaries.

Usually one does not have to look very far from such an event to learn of a storm, but the best that can be done in this instance is to point out that there has been a storm on the coast of Florida.

Isn't there more than just a hint of intelligent action in the fall of these birds? Especially such a heterogeneous collection of species from widely separated places of usual habitat which are not usually found flocking together? Doesn't this smack of dumping, as in the many cases of fish, frogs, periwinkles, etc.?

I have seen reference to live birds which flew head-on into a locomotive, as though frightened into complete panic; also a group of starlings flying as though completely terror-stricken into suicidal collision in New York streets. What had they seen, or encountered? Something real, but invisible to, or unnoticed by man? Have we some clues in the apparently unmaterial things which are being reported today under the misnomer "flying saucers"?

1921: A shower of little frogs fell upon Anton Wagner's farm, near Sterling, Connecticut.

By way of coincidence, Professor Campbell of Lick Observatory, Ace Aviator Eddie Rickenbacker, conservative astronomer, Colonel Marwick, and Dr. Emmert, of Detroit, all reported from widely separated points of the earth that an unknown, luminous object had been seen near the sun on August 6 and 7. "Near the sun," means, in astronomical parlance, something more or less in line with the sun as seen from terrestrial observation. It actually means "apparently near the sun," not necessarily physically close to that orb.

In conclusion, let us summarize the vital features of these phenomena as they relate to our thesis.

Most falls involve only low forms of life, most of which require water for their environment, or at least a moist habitat. Many falls are reported in clear weather from a clear sky, but most are associated with torrential downpours of water – not an ordinary rain. In some cases, isolated and strange-looking clouds are responsible, and some of these suddenly appear in otherwise cloudless skies. The descriptions of these storms and clouds have an element of similarity and the haunting suggestion arises that these storms and clouds are the result of artificial conditions as opposed to ordinary meteorological forces.

This does not prove that hydroponic tanks exist for the convenience of our space race; however, whether these tanks are for supplies or experimentation, it substantiates our thesis for either a race originally from earth which drove itself to space, or a race which originated in space and keeps in touch with earth.

> If he has "seen" them, it does not seem
> that he has managed "clear-talk" with them
> & Mistakes their or its actual meaning
> Their spoken tongue is rough from Disuse
> and only a True—"Thinker" could see their
> complete Lingo. Besides, When they are
> Hungry they Don't "speak" well.

Falling Animal and Organic Matter

Perhaps the least substantiated, but most fascinating, of the itemized falls include animal and organic matter for which no real explanation is yet available. This material is usually considered, but without real thought, to be the result of whirlwinds picking up the material in one locale and dropping it elsewhere. It has also been suggested that buzzards have been disgorging the matter, particularly the bits of bone and bloody flesh. That no whirlwinds were reported at the time of the falls, and that no flights of buzzards have been reported seems to have been of little consequence.

It is up to us, therefore, to ask: Is there another explanation?

1887: On December 13, in Cochin, China, a substance like blood, somewhat coagulated, fell from the skies.

1888: There was a repeated "red rain" in the Mediterranean region on March 6, and again on March 18. The substance, when burned, had a strong and persistent odor of animal matter.

It is in the records of the French Academy that, on March 17, 1669, in the town of Chatillon-sur Seine, a reddish substance fell which was "thick, viscous and putrid." Only organic matter can become putrid.

There is also a story of a highly unpleasant substance which fell from the sky in Wilson County, Tennessee. A Dr. Troost visited the place and investigated the reports. He declared that the substance was clear blood and that portions of bloody flesh were scattered upon tobacco fields.

On March 3, 1876, at Olympian Springs, Bath County, Kentucky, flakes of a substance that looked like beef fell from a clear sky. Nothing but this falling substance was visible in the sky. It fell in flakes of various sizes; some two inches square, and some four inches square. It was a thick shower, on the ground, on trees, on fences, but it was narrowly localized on a strip of land about one hundred yards long and about fifty yards wide. For the first account see the *Scientific American*, 34-197, and the *New York Times*, March 10, 1876.

It is very important to consider the familiar landmarks of selectivity and localization. The geometric shape of distribution, fifty yards by one hundred yards. It corresponds to the size of many of the well-defined falls of toads, fish and frogs. Note, too, the thick shower on trees, fences, and the ground.

In the American Journal of Science of 1833-1834, in many observations upon the meteors of November, 1833, are the following reports of falls of gelatinous substance: (1) that according to newspaper reports, "lumps of jelly" were found on the ground at Rahway, New Jersey. The substance was whitish, or resembled the coagulated white of an egg; (2) that Mr. H.H. Garland, of Nelson County, Virginia, had found a jellylike substance of about the circumference of a twenty-five cent piece; (3) that according to a communication from A.C. Twining to Professor Olmstead, a woman at West Point, New York, had seen a mass the size of a teacup, which looked like boiled starch; (4) that according to a newspaper of Newark, New Jersey, a mass of gelatinous substance, like soft soap, had been found. "It possessed little elasticity, and, on the application of heat, it evaporated as readily as water."

A story from California, reported in the San Francisco *Evening Bulletin*, August 9, 1869, tells of flesh and blood which fell from the sky, upon Mr. J. Hudson's farm, in Los Nietos Township—a shower that lasted three minutes and covered an area of two acres. The conventional explanation was that these substances had been disgorged by flying buzzards. "The day was perfectly clear, and the sun was shining, and there was no perceptible breeze"; and if anybody saw buzzards, buzzards were not mentioned.

Has anyone ever seen buzzards in one flock to disgorge over an area of ten square yards – much less two acres?

The flesh was in fine particles, and also in strips from one to six inches long. There were short, fine hairs. One of the witnesses took specimens to Los Angeles, and showed them to the editor of the *Los Angeles News*, as told in the *News*, August 3. The editor wrote that he had seen, but had not kept, the disagreeable objects. "That the meat fell, we cannot doubt. Even persons of the neighborhood are willing to vouch for that. Where it came from, we cannot even conjecture."

> S-M's Work. They eat so revolting amount of Sea Food that Red-Meat is a Madness in Them?

The bulletin also said that about two months before flesh and blood had fallen from the sky in Santa Clara County, California.

These falls of flesh and blood coincide, temporally, with a vast fall of dead birds in Baton Rouge, Louisiana.

Again we have a familiar pattern: segregation, isolation, clear sky, "about two acres of ground."

There is an interesting item from the Journal of the Asiatic Society of Bengal, 1847. On March 16, 1846, at about the time of the fall of edible substance in Asia Minor, an olive-gray powder fell at Shanghai. Under the microscope it was seen to be an aggregation of hairs of two kinds: Black ones, and rather thick white ones. They were supposed to be animal fibers, but, when burned, they gave out "the common ammoniacal smell and smoke of burnt hair or feathers." The writer described the phenomenon as a "cloud of 3,800 square miles of fibres, alkali, and sand."

According to Professor Luigi Palazzo, head of the Italian Meteorological Bureau, on May 15, 1890, at Massagnadi, Calabria, something the color of fresh blood fell from the sky. The substance was examined in the public health laboratories of Rome and found to be blood. Some said that migratory birds were caught and torn in a violent wind, but there was no record of a violent wind at the time, nor any feathers or dead birds. Later, more blood fell from the sky in the same place.

The *Literary Digest* of September 2, 1921 published a letter about a fall of a substance resembling blood in southwest China on November 17. It fell upon three villages, and was said to have fallen forty miles away as well. The quantity was great, and in one village it covered the ground completely. The writer in the Digest accepts that this substance did fall from the sky because it was found on rooftops as well as on the ground. He rejects the conventional explanation of dust because the material did not dissolve in several subsequent rains.

In the *American Journal of Science*, 1-42-196, we are told of a yellow substance that fell in great quantities over a vessel one "windless" night in June, in Pictou Harbor, Nova Scotia. The writer of the article analyzed the substance and it was found to "give off nitrogen and ammonia, and an animal odor."

I don't think there is much intelligence required in the matter of depositing "a yellow substance giving off nitrogen, ammonia, and an animal odor," on a ship. But there could be purposefulness! I feel that there may have been intent or necessity, either of which implies some kind of control or cognizance

Monthly Ship-Cleaning.

In these few examples of flesh and blood having come from the sky, we can readily see that it is not beyond the realm of possibility that our space friends are flesh and blood: however, it is a more likely assumption that these "disgorged" materials have more to do with experiments and "captures" than anything else.

Kuts, Sky burial impossible.

It is possible that there we may have a clue to the whereabouts of the people who have vanished suddenly under mysterious circumstances that have baffled witnesses and those seeking to explain these mysteries.

ED: The following has no obvious reference or necessary position.
>Burial in Space Not possible. So the L-M's *had* to
>grind-up any proof of their existence & drop
>it. THEY Do not Do so now, except in case of attractor
>failure but deposit their dead undersea in the
>"Vaulted City"

Other organic materials have frequently been attributed to meteoric activity, but again we are faced with the simple fact that materials fall which do not exist in meteors.

In 1872, on March 9, 10, and 11, something fell from the sky and was accompanied by dust. It was described as red iron ochre, carbonate of lime, and unidentifiable organic matter.

In the *American Journal of Science*, 1-2-335 (1819), is Professor Graves' account, communicated by Professor Dewey, that on the evening of August 13, 1819, a light was seen in Amherst — a falling object — with accompanying sounds as if from an explosion. In the home of Professor Dewey this light was reflected upon a wall of a room. The next morning in Professor Dewey's front yard, in what is said to have been the only position from which the light could have been reflected, a substance was found "unlike anything before observed by anyone who saw it." It was a bowl-shaped object, about eight inches in diameter, and one-inch thick, bright buff-colored, and having upon it a "fine nap." Upon removing this covering, a buff-colored, pulpy substance of the consistency of soft soap, was found — "of an offensive, suffocating smell," A few minutes of exposure to the air changed the buff color to a "livid color resembling venous blood," It absorbed moisture quickly from the air and liquefied.

Note that the "thing" fell with a burst of light. It is not reported to have come with a storm. It was obviously of either organic or artificial character, and the "sounds as of an explosion" were scarcely normal or commonplace.

But it is interesting to compare that report with another; that in March, 1832, there fell in the fields of Kourianof, Russia, a combustible, yellowish substance, covering an area at least two inches thick, and six hundred or seven hundred square feet. It was resinous and yellowish so one inclines to the conventional explanation that it was pollen from pine trees — but, when torn, it had the tenacity of cotton. When placed in water it had the consistency of resin. "This resin had the color of amber, was elastic, like India rubber, and smelled like prepared oil mixed with wax."

ED: The following has no obvious reference or necessary position.
> Stuff causing "Explosion" was "Force-Impacted"
> Material Expanding back to Natural "size".
> Thus,Explosions where no Sound is heard, only
> seen close by.

In *Philosophical Transaction* of 1695 there is an extract from a letter by Mr. Robert Vans, of Kilkenny, Ireland, dated November 15, 1695, that there had been "of late," in the countries of Limerick and Tipperary, showers of a sort of matter like butter or grease ..."having a very stinking smell." There follows an extract of a letter from the Bishop of Cloyne, Leinster, that for a good part of the spring of 1695 there fell a substance which the country people called "butter" — "soft, clammy, and of a dark yellow" — that cattle fed "indifferently" in fields where this substance lay. "It fell in lumps as big as the end of one's finger." It had a "strong, ill scent." His grace called it a "stinking dew." In Mr. Vans's letter, it is said that the "butter" was supposed to have medicinal properties, "and was gathered in pots and other vessels by some of the inhabitants of the place."

The yellow substance at Kourianof, combustible (organic_ covering six or seven hundred square feet — about the size area we have so often noted — some characteristics of pine pollen... but who ever saw pine pollen of fibrous nature which "when torn had the tenacity of cotton"? Two inches thick means tons!

I am inclined to think that there is something of an indication in these buttery things. There is a haunting quality which says that these substances were formed by some guidance of a higher intellectual grade than the chemical law of averages.

The constant references to substances, rather than naming definite elements, compounds, or natural organic products, is significant. Why, if all this stuff that admittedly falls from the sky is commonplace, natural material or life, is it usually so difficult for experienced and trained scientists and naturalists to give it positive definite identity?

There have been many reports of so-called "spider-webs" and "angel hair" that have fallen from the sky. To give but one example, let us look at the *Montgomery* (Alabama) *Advertiser* of November 21, 1898, which reported numerous batches of a spider-weblike substance which fell in Montgomery. Some of it fell in strands and some in masses several inches long and several inches broad. According to the writer, it was not spiders' web, but something like asbestos. It was reported, too, as phosphorescent.

> Force-extruder expieriment in Plastic cloth fibreswhich, faild, (sic) then, but Later was successful. Boy! My socks wear for 3 years *or* so!

It has been suggested that all of the "falling material" is the result of occasional wrecks of interplanetary, super-space contraptions, or even the dumping from them while in route from planet to planet. If one considers this proposition carefully, the natural question is: why so often?

On the other hand, if adjacent space toward the gravitational neutral at the edge of the earth's sphere of influence, perhaps 180,000 to 200,000 miles away from here, should be the habitat of a vast number and considerable variety of intelligently operated space widgets or urban concentrations of the like, then the whole proposition begins to take on a certain amount of plausibility.

In the past two or three decades, there has been a great discussion about miniature fossils found in meteorites, and something about spores and mono-cellular organisms, maybe alive, or at least viable. Everyone, but those whose weak ego demands that they maintain scientific dignity by making categorical denials with professional aplomb, will concede that this question is debatable, and has been since the findings were first announced. But, debatability is something different from inconceivability, incredibility, negative proof, positive proof, or even smug denial. It is an important point to settle.

If settled positively — that meteorites do contain fossils, viable spores or dormant protozoa — than we have proved that life, or remnants of it, does come from outer space. This is obviously a qualitative decision. It is on the periphery of science, especially astronomy, biology, and geology. It can be an anthropological question if it can be shown that human life has mergers with life in outer space.

If one or more of these fossils or elements of incipient life can be shown to arrive on this planet via meteors, we are confronted with a major problem of deciding whether the meteorites were thrown off this earth in the remote past, whether they originated in the explosion of another planet, whether they arrive from interstellar space, whether they grew spontaneously in the general melee of the origin of the solar system — or where, in fact, did they originate?

A Dr. Hahn has claimed to have found miniature fossils in meteorites, including corals, sponges, shells and crinoids, all microscopic, which he photographed. Some, who didn't see them, taking an attitude of professional scorn, claimed they were not valid. Some trained and intelligent men, like Francis Blingham, who did see them, agree that they are real and were contained in meteorites.

Much miscellaneous junk does seem to come from space, and, with all of this material in space, it is but a step to acceptance of intelligence, or life, some of it in control of vast assemblages of spatial objects or of individual little ones.

One supposes organic material to be a product of life processes, associated with life, or the abode of life. Life implies intelligence, even of an incipient, primitive or rudimentary type. Our contention is that some kind of intelligence has adapted itself to this environment, if it was not actually indigenous thereto.

We shall close this section with a mystery. The following is from *Fate*, of April 1951.

The Mystery of the Falling Grain

One day last summer construction men were working on the top of the Empire State Building tower, 1,467 feet above the street, preparing to put up a new television mast. Suddenly, something stung the check of one of the men. Then another reached into his shirt collar and picked out a grain of something or other. He looked at it in puzzlement, then flung it aside.

Then other men began to notice the kernels falling upon them. While they looked in bewilderment, nearly a peck of grain fell upon the men. It stung their faces and necks and bounced off the steel floor.

Where was it coming from? They heard no airplanes overhead nor did they see any. There was no wind or storm, though the sky was overcast. Meanwhile the grain continued to fall. Tenants along the north side of the building heard it rattling against their windows.

Samples of the grain were taken to Dr. Michael Lauro, official chemist of the Produce Exchange, who identified it as barley. Dr. Lauro suggested that it might have come from one of the great breweries of New York — possibly carried up through cyclone chimneys — but hastened to add that he was just guessing. Ernest J. Christie, of the U.S. Weather Bureau, said that the winds that day were too light to have borne the grain aloft. He did not consider it likely that it had blown in from the Midwest. One scientist suggested, but dropped the idea hastily, that birds had dropped the barley.

Of a reasonable satisfactory explanation, there was none.

> This Man hints much at there being two distinct species or groups of Similar species to be involved in his observation. Why does he presist in Mere Hinting so strongly. I believe that he KNOWS FOR CERTAIN *but* can do Nothing. L-M's ARE in for a surprise *if* he does do *something.*

Falling Shaped Things

I use the word "shaped" here to mean forming by intelligence.

I suggest the following classifications of things that have fallen from the sky:

    A. Object unassociated with intelligent action.
1. Substances of inorganic nature, shaped or moved by random forces: e.g., inorganic dust, "true meteoritic material," etc.
    2. Miscellaneous objects.
      B. Object associated with intelligent action.
1. Symmetrical Objects: wedges, spheres, discs, threads, carvings, works of art, nails; any object not obviously the product of the unguided forces of nature.
    2. Objects and substances of organic or functional nature.
    3. Objects, lights, substances, or groups of these, of any kind, which demonstrated motions, control, accumulation placing, selection, delimitation, direction, defiance of gravity or other natural forces, locomotion, gregariousness, purposefulness, or any dynamic or volitional characteristic not attributable to recognized physical forces alone.

We have to consider some of the utilitarian or functional categories as including items which might be used for food: shrimps, periwinkles, snails, etc., or edible substances.

Two purposes will be served in this chapter. We will consider shapes and functional things as related to intelligence and to falls from space, but will also include gadgets which indicated the extreme antiquity of some type of intelligence or intelligent life on earth; and items found in locations and strata where falls from space, or space ships, might have placed them.

In some of these cases we have to decide between several possible alternatives:

(a) Extreme antiquity, attributable to ancient civilizations without space flight;
(b) The same, but with space flight developed internally;
(c) Space flight independent of man on earth, bringing occasional widgets from extraterrestrial sectors of intellectual development;
(d) Falls of items originally on the earth but previously expelled by explosion or other force;
(e) Falls of items blown off other exploding planets.

We cannot forever ignore the immense antiquity of some archaeological items. It is not fashionable with archaeological circles, which is anything but an exact science, to admit the existence of culture or rather civilization, more remote than that of the historically recorded Egyptians and Orientals: four to seven thousand years at most; and heaven forbid if one suggests advanced races in eras of ten, twenty, forty, or one hundred thousand years ago. Yet no scientist has found a logical common denominator for the various races, cultures, and civilizations of which we have unmistakable records, except that of a common source predating the Egyptians, the Chinese, the Indians (Asiatic), the Incas, and the Mayas, and in fact all branches covered by the study of anthropology and ethnology. Much as we may deride writers such as Churchward (as per De Camp; Lost Continents) in his rather crude presentation of his hypothesis of the Lost Continent of Mu, his is the only general explanation of terrestrial intellectual development and distribution to be advanced which in a broad way explains the observed data. Such explanations, however desirable, are ruled out by the fashion of the day which decries emphasis on qualitative knowledge in favor of quantitatively investigating the fifth place of decimals or other exaggerated refinement of classified knowledge.

Who is Churchward or this DeCamp? Some "Gaiyor"
Baini who guessed or knew right???

Because we feel so strongly on this subject, we list some of the obstreperous items which prove that articles created by intelligence existed tens or scores of thousands of years ago. These things prove either, or both, of two things: there was a vast and advanced civilization on the earth in those distant times; or those articles have come here from space, via ships, or from a scattering of debris in space. Anyway you look at it, the arrogant omnipotence of homo sapiens takes a beating – for our present egotistical state of culture was preceded by another of unfathomable age.

If intellectual development is that old, isn't it logical that it may have created a form of flight not yet known to our engineers? Let's forget the fifth decimal place – go back to unity – to the objective assimilation of qualitative data; back to philosophical generalizations and the divination of natural law; back, in fact, to the mentality of a Humboldt, a Newton, a Copernicus. Science is starved for such ability, more than at any time in the past century.

A Dr. Gurlt, in 1877, reported an object found in a tertiary coal bed. In several magazines of that general period there were questions from speculative scientific men as to why, if meteors have been encountering the earth from remote times, there are no meteorites in tertiary coal deposits. Subsequent finds have answered the questions. Well, anyway, this object, incongruous in its carbonaceous environment, is a fossil meteorite. There has been much debate, some of it venomous, as to whether it can be more than merely that. The find has been placed in the Salzburg Museum, after being taken from a block of coal in Lower Austria.

The specimen was examined by many interested persons and scientists, who did not fully agree on its origins. Some said that it was a meteorite; some said that it was an artificial production; others remarked that is resembled a meteorite modified by the hands of man. (Nobody, so far as I know, ever suggested that modification could have been effected through the agency of intelligence other than human.)

The object is an almost perfect cube, and many examiners consider it too geometric in shape to be entirely natural. Two opposite faces are a little bit rounded, reducing the size of the other four. A deep incision runs around the cube. The material is of a variety conventionally conceded to be meteorite iron and nickel, roughly three by two by two inches. It weights 785 grams, has a specific gravity of 7.75, and it is hard as steel, as are all iron-nickel aerolites.

I can't help thinking of the little stone of Tarbes: are most of the things, which come from space of a little more physical delicacy than most of the indigenous items of the same types?

This cubic meteorite is most disturbing to conservative science. Its tertiary age cannot be denied, nor its authenticity – that much is firm. That is, it was certainly placed in the coal bed in tertiary times, but no one knows how much older it may be. Equally firm is its nature as meteoritic iron, nickel and carbon (it is really a form of steel.)

The greater puzzle is its geometric shape, including the circumscribed groove, so regularly and doubly "artificial" that it seems certainly to have been shaped by hands.

"Hands"? Human hands, in the tertiary era? No! say the anthropologists. Extraterrestrial hands, maybe on an exploded planet, or blasted off this bedeviled old earth when Mu went up in cosmic glory?

Hands with 3 fingers & thumb

To uninhibited thinkers, facts remain facts. This specimen is artificially shaped; it is a fossil of tertiary coal beds; it is of meteoritic structure and material which even conservative science has reluctantly admitted as being from outer space. So this must have been shaped by intelligence either before or after falling, but certainly prior to or surely concomitant with the formation of tertiary coal.

For our purpose, we do not care whether one says it was fashioned by extraterrestrial hands or terrestrial hands, for we are just as much interested in proving the extreme antiquity of civilized man as we are in indicating the existence of extraterrestrial intelligence. This obstreperous whickeroo was dropped into an embryonic coal bed, either from an indigenous civilization or by an off-shore agency of some kind.

If there was civilization in tertiary times – terrestrial or spatial – the sequel of intelligence in space, then or evolving later from the ground variety, is a quantitative development, and the emergence of space travel is inherent in the later case and an almost inevitable emergence in the former.

It is recorded in the *Annals of Scientific Discovery*, 1853-71, that Sir David Brewster had made a startling announcement at a meeting of the British Association for the Advancement of Science in 1853. He had, he said, to call to the attention of the meeting an object of so incredible a nature that nothing short of the strongest evidence was necessary to render the statement at all probable. He claimed that a true crystal lens had been found in the treasure house at Nineveh. It is on record that many of the temples and treasure houses of old civilizations were in the habit of preserving things which fell from the sky and things which, to these ancient peoples, were already antiquities.

This egocentric race has been so imbued with its own importance that it cannot believe that optical equipment could have evolved in times prior to the Renaissance. We will concede that such items were not in use during the Dark Ages, nor, apparently, during the centuries from that period backward to some thousands of years BC. But such a concession is, in fact, a victory, for it then becomes necessary to concede a knowledge of optics some millennia before the incarceration of this lens at Nineveh. And that is a major part of our whole tenet.

In *The Microscope and its Revelations*, Carpenter presents two drawings of the lens, but he argues that it is impossible to accept that optical lenses have ever been made by the ancients. He says the object must have been an ornament. Brewster says it was a true optical lens.

Then we are right back where we started with the little worked meteorite. If either, or both, of these shameless trinkets are indigenous to our planet we must, perforce, accept a civilization with a knowledge of optics, predating all presently recorded history.

Lens was Atruscan.

ED: The following has no obvious reference or necessary position.
Mirror Silvering of Crystal (Rock or Force-Made Crystal) *Unknown to Atruscans*.

It was Crystal & It was a Lens. Atruscans used them to Make fine Gold & Silver earrings & Gold wire inlays. Also were used to Make fire for the 'Smiths.

This lens is just as much, in its small way, a relic of the first wave of civilization (if not from space) as is the Great Pyramid which embodies more astronomy and mathematics than was possessed by those people to whom its construction is attributed.

MAN SPEAKS FROM GENERAL CONCENSUS.

Wilkins, in *Secret Cities of South America*, reports the finding of optical lenses and mirrors in a submerged city on the coast of Equador, and others in archaic ruins of Central America. These appear to be pre-Incan and pre-Andean.

These Were Muanian in Make

The *London Times* of February 1, 1888, has reported the finding of a roundish, or ovate, object of iron which was found in a garden at Brixton, after a violent thunderstorm on August 7, 1887. It is described as an oblate spheroid about two inches across its major axis. An oblate spheroid is the shape generated by an ellipse if rotated about its minor axis, and a prolate spheroid is similarly generated by rotation about its major axis. A football is shaped something like a prolate spheroid, while a flattish pumpkin or tomato is close to being an oblate spheroid.

The paper discussed this object at length, while also describing an "iron cannon ball," found in a manure heap after a thunderstorm. Both items seem to be too shapely, or symmetrical, to have been created without the aid of intelligence. There may be some significance in the fact of their all being small, a couple of inches or so in diameter.

The Scientific American, 1851-52, has the following to say, which is contributory to our theme:

A few days ago, a powerful blast was made in the rock at Meeting House Hill, in Dorchester, a few rods south of Reverend Mr. Hall's meeting house. The blast threw out an immense mass of rock, some of the pieces weighing several tons, and scattered small fragments in all directions. Among them was picked up a metallic vessel in two parts, rent asunder by the explosion. On putting the two parts together, it formed a bell-shaped vessel, four and one-half inches high, six and one-half inches at the base and two and one-half inches at the top, and about an eighth of an inch in thickness. The body of this vessel resembles zinc in color, or a composition material, in which there is a considerable portion of silver. On the sides there are six figures of a flower or bouquet, beautifully inlaid with pure silver, and around the lower part of the vessel a vine or wreath, inlaid also with silver. The chasing, carving, and inlaying are exquisitely done by the art of some cunning workman. This curious and unknown vessel was blown out of the pudding stone fifteen feet below the surface...there is no doubt but that this curiosity was blown out of the rock as above stated...the matter is worthy of investigation, as there is no deception.

Inlay Work the Mark of Atruscan-Lemurians.

The *London Times*, for June 22, 1844, reports that some workmen, quarrying rock close to Tweed, not far from a place called Rutherford Mills, had discovered a gold thread embedded in the stone at a depth of about eight feet. A piece of the gold thread had been forwarded to the office of the *Kelso Chronicle*. That is a very simple item, indeed! Just a wee bit of gold thread in solid rock!

Matching the gold thread in interest is something found inside a lump of coal by a Mrs. Culp, at Morrisonville, Illinois, in 1891. When the lump of coal for her cooking range fell apart she was startled to find embedded in circular fashion, a small gold chain about ten inches long and of quaint workmanship. If the cubical Austrian meteorite is not enough to convince you that things of intelligent manufacture were falling into coal beds in tertiary times, then surely this one will.

Cube shaped by Mag. Force compressor.Caused tremendous Heat, thus the regard of it as being a Meteorite.

It is further reported that James Parsons, and his two sons, exhumed a slate wall in a coal mine at Hammondville, Ohio, in 1868. It was a large, smooth wall, disclosed when a great mass of coal fell away from it, and on its surface, carved in bold relief, were several lines of hieroglyphics. Nothing further seems to have been reported, and if any reader knows more of this incident the author would welcome a report (send care of the publisher) – perhaps from some local newspaper of that date. This item, at least, we will concede was not dropped by space ships. It must represent the work of contemporary, indigenous civilization in tertiary times.

In their hearts, all Miners know this!

Ref. to Ohio incident Miners See these things EACH Year, Many or Most speak Little English & "It ain't coal & ITS IN THE WAY SO GET IT OUT of there.

Some Miners Save parts or all of these above curiositys & they May be found *in their homes*. They are *used* to seeing them.

In the *London Times* of December 24, 1851, it is stated that a citizen of Springfield, Massachusetts, a Mr. Hiram de Witt, had returned from California bringing a chunk of auriferous quartz about as big as a man's fist. It was accidentally dropped and broke upon. It had a nail in it. A cut iron nail, about the size of an ordinary six-penny nail, a bit corroded, "straight and with a perfect head."

DISCARDED FORCE-CRYSTAL

According to the *Reports of the British Association*, 1845-51, Sir David Brewster astounded the assembled brethren with an account of a nail which was found in a block of stone from Kingoodie Quarry, in North Britain. The block of stone was nine inches thick. There was little, if any, evidence as to what part of the quarry it came from, except that it could not have come form the surface. The quarry had been worked for about twenty years, and consisted of alternate layers of hard stone and a substance called "till." The point of the nail extended upward into the till and was badly eaten by rust. Part of the nail lay on the surface of the stone, but about an inch, including the head, was embedded in the stone.

> Head imbedded thus could Not have been pounded
> in Head first, It *Would Not go in.*

This till intrigues me. Once upon a time I read the book, *Raganork*, by Ignatius Donnelly, who was a U.S. Congressman with time on his hands, and who spent that time in the Library of Congress, making himself one of the most literate Congressmen ever to invade Washington. His theme was of Atlantis, and he built up a case for this till having been splattered all over the Atlantic hemisphere of the earth by collision with a comet. In this splash were transported the erratics of the till which are so annoying to geologists. Maybe this nail was one of these erratics.

> The Learned Rep. Was right, save that It was
> done by MANY "Comets" in The Great War.

Under the title "Mysterious Monoliths," *Fate Magazine*, March 1950, shows a photograph of some spherical sandstone balls which were blasted out of solid rock by a highway crew near Hornbrook, California. The balls appear incredibly ancient. Sandstone balls of nearly spherical shape are not especially rare, and they are oblate spheroids which used to be sought after for garden ornaments throughout the Middle West. They were called concretions, and were shaped either by the action of water or by successive deposits of sand which later solidified, according to geologists. We can believe in their natural formation, since the condition in which they were found seem to indicate that this is true. But these balls in California were apparently found in quantity, in solid rock. Their symmetry indicates artificial shaping, they are an indication of antiquity, rather than a proof.

> *Balls* were compressed Earth, Used as Ammo for
> Force-"Guns" During "The Great War" The success
> of *that*, was so fast, that these were never used.

W.S. Forest, in *Historical Sketches of Norfolk, Virginia*, reports the finding of a coin at a depth of thirty feet, by well borers, in September, 1833. It was about the size of a shilling and unlike anything seen before. Although buried for many centuries, the markings were well preserved, represent a warrior or hunter, and had a Roman appearance.

> "ROANOKE" a Whole Colony kidnapped.

There are a number of these coins which have been found in unexplained places, and where

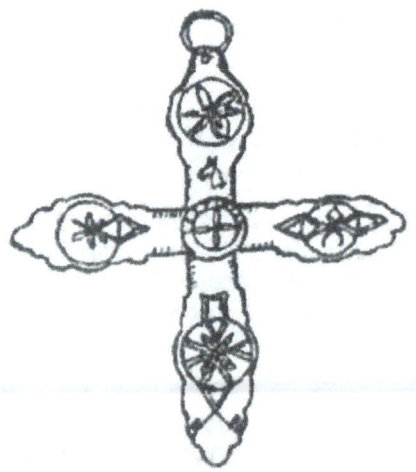

The Cross found in an ancient grave in Georgia. The inscription is undecipherable. The horse's head is crudely scratched by an unskilled hand at a later date than the original. Was it dropped by a UFO?

burial at very early dates is indicated. A coin described by Donelly is fully discussed in *Proceedings of the American Philosophical Society*, and was brought up from a depth of one hundred and twenty feet, with the borings of a well in Illinois. The crosses reported in the *Smithsonian Institute Reports*, 1881 are puzzling. Looked at in a mirror, some of the inscription resembles Roman numerals, but is not quite intelligible. Their appearance is certainly not indicative of anything within everyday experience. They may have been dropped from space ships. The alphabetical characters resemble our own to a degree, but are not interpretable in any known language. These were found in an ancient grave in the state of Georgia.

> Cross is Atruscan-Lemurian, language is that now called "Black tongue" spoken by "Gitana" the World over. Show this to a Brother-Gypsy & Lord know what the reaction would be if the original were shown. It is a Chiefs or Nabobs own insignia of Clan. He flew to that place but had to walk. Later. He died from Walking for His Muscles were not used to *or* for such purpose. Manner of Death indicated by Horses Head, even tho there were no horses on this Land at that time. His name and address & his accomplishments are signified on the metal. The cross was Left so that the body Might be brought home. The making of this required Calipers, Scribes and Drawing compass, plus Mathematics.

> Punch, a Press, a set ot Stamps, a Drill, SeveralDifferent FILES, A FORGE, SMELTER & ETC. *OR* ONE FORCE-RAY *STAMP & BURNER* PRESS. *(italics by Jemi)*

We continue to have a choice between terrestrial antiquity or spatial antiquity. But antiquity we do have, and a race so ancient, on earth, could very well have invented space travel.

All of these samples lead to conclusions, but we must not overlook the actual sighting of shaped objects, falling from the sky. The object, five inches by fifteen inches, for instance, which fell at Twickenham, August 5, 1889.

Samples of script have come out of the Brazilian jungles which are almost identical with alphabetical characters from Ceylon's buried and forgotten ruins. Tiahuanaco is thought to have been in ruins so long before the formation of the Andes that it had actually been submerged and was raised from under the sea at the time of the formation of the Andes. (Red is A & B).

> Confirmed, 1954, American Arch. Exp.

ED: The following has no obvious reference or necessary postion.
> Read, "The Day the Sun Stood Still" Edited 1941. Readers *Digest of the book*.

> Andes were impelled upwards by Great force once by Nature once by "The War of the Great Freeze" & by, in part "The Great Bombardment"

Some scientists believe that the Andes have been formed twice, and that the last formation was perhaps 10,000 to 12,000 years ago. It probably was farther into the past than that. The meteor craters spread across the southwestern United States and down into tropical Mexico have an apparent age of 8,000 to 12,000 years. The traditions agree that "Atlantis" or its equivalent, was destroyed about

9,000 years or so BC. There are several traditions in several parts of the world that the ancestors of some races and tribes were flourishing before the moon existed.

A detailed build-up for this antiquity is beyond the scope and ability of this book. Mainly we are interested in showing that such an antiquity did exist, and that it is conceivable that some very early race, 200,000 years ago or so, may have developed space flight, and after the cataclysm of 12,000 years ago may have chosen to stay in space, thinking it a safer habitat than this uncertain planet.

We offer no proof for this supposition. What we do offer is a set of conditions which might make it possible, plus a long series of observations of activity in space which gives every appearance of being the result of intelligent direction. Such a hypothesis relieves us of having to assume that the UFO's of today must necessarily come from another planet, or another star. We submit that our postulate is an improbability of lesser order, and that the growing evidence of the antiquity of mankind, far beyond anything heretofore admitted by science is a contributory factor worthy of consideration.

Falls of Water

There are many instances of lights, clouds or structures which seem to exhibit voluntary or controlled motions. This applies to some isolated freak storms which appear in otherwise undisturbed skies. Some of these storms seem to have organic entity. They seem to have many components, including debris of all sorts, and their clouds are apt to be of unique shape, density, texture, or color; they may be luminous or contain lights; they often produce extremely violent winds and stygian darkness.

It is my contention that some of these storms are associated with intelligent action, that they may contain navigable structures which may surround themselves with clouds, for purposes of camouflage, or merely through natural interaction with the atmosphere. We will try to distinguish between these and the meteoritic disturbances proper, some of them very huge indeed, which sometimes appear to share some of their physical characteristics.

Also, we are going to draw a very fine distinction. We must distinguish between rain and falling water. We are going to assume that the rain is falling water, but that falling water is not necessarily rain – at least not as understood by meteorological science.

DEC. 22. California Mysteriously flooded, 1955.

All through our research into the falls of unusual objects from the sky, we frequently encounter the statement that these objects fall in a torrential downpour of water, and almost as frequently we find references to peculiar cloud formations which do not appear to have their origin based on normal, or at least familiar, meteorological conditions – conditions of weather, that is.

We hope that you will give very special thought to the world-wide scope of some of these intense and violent storm periods. There are many cases where storms and floods which inundated a considerable part of our own country have been almost universal in their action. This tends to hint the entrance of the earth into a large cosmic cloud of water and debris sufficient to deluge most of the areas in both northern and southern hemispheres together. The volume of water falling and the concomitants of mud, black rain, stones, etc., indicate unity of external origin.

There are some cases where the distribution of violence follows restricted belts of terrestrial latitude, so that one thinks of the rotation of the earth as carrying successive longitudes into the disturbance.

About the middle of September, 1886, water was falling from a cloudless sky, always within an area of twenty-five feet square, at Dawson, Georgia, and showers were reported over an area ten feet square at Aiken, South Carolina, and at Cheraw, South Carolina, (*Charleston News and Courier*, October 8, 21, 25, 26). Falls of water from a cloudless sky, to a point in Chesterfield County, South Carolina, and falling so heavily that streams of it gushed from roof pipes.

To the honest skeptic, either layman or meteorologist, who protests that these events, while not usual, are nevertheless not abnormal nor paranormal, I would ask: "Since when are meteorological conditions so stable that water can condense and fall over precisely delimited areas, over such periods of time?"

There is an account from a Dr. Wartmann about water which fell from the sky, at Geneva, Switzerland. It seems that there were clouds on the horizon at 9:00 AM, August 9, 1837, but the sky was clear at zenith. It may not be startling that some raindrops should fall from a clear sky, but these were large drops of warm water, and they fell in such abundance that people were driven to shelter. This kept up for several minutes, and there were repeated falls during a period of an hour or so. Warmed, perhaps, by meteoric velocity?

Repetition, selection, pinpoint localization, warmth!

Not only do we have pinpoint accuracy in these precipitations but there is an obvious tendency for reports of them to be restricted to certain general areas.

Compare these extremely localized falls of water with the highly delimited falls of other objects, and the purity of segregation which is so characteristic of most of the falls which we have noted. It is falls of water, of this type, which we believe should be included in the same overall category with ice, stones, live organisms, etc., together with the dumpings of water concomitant with the unloading of periwinkles, fish, etc. We suggest that intelligence is involved in the obvious selection and placement.

As with the case of ice, we believe there are three types of water falling to the ground. That class of water which seems to partake of direction and isolation corresponds to the ice, for instance, which we postulated to have origin in, on, or with, space navigating objects. We hope it will be apparent that cloudburst and the almost solid masses of water know to fall are the counterpart of the large pieces of ice or their congregations of "chunk-like" nature: in other words, both the ice and the water are meteoritic. Then we have the common variety of meteorologically formed hailstones and rain. To us, there appears a parallelism.

It seems, at times, that there is a merging between the space structure, the water and cloudbursts. Here is a little item from the *New York Tribune* of July 3, 1922. For the fourth time within a month, it is said, a great volume of water, or a "cloudburst" had poured from one local sky, near Carbondale, Pennsylvania. This event, or series of events, has the localization and repetitive qualities which we have learned to associate with falls of periwinkles, snails and frogs and other things. In addition it has the almost cataclysmic feature, on a small scale, of the impacts of meteoritic masses of water. But in line with our speculation regarding the dumping of hydroponic tanks, we find it convenient to link repetitive, highly localized impacts of dense masses of water with the dumpings. Sometimes there is animal life in the water; sometimes not. We think that some judgment can be exercised in deciding which of these falls of water are meteoritic and which are connected with space contrivances.

Yet Will not be, for No set up exists to XXXXXX (crossed out by A)

ED: The following has no obvious reference or necessary position.
Observe these phenomenal "coincidnents" Some
Chemical Gardening Practiced in Arks & D ships
Not too much, at Last report.

In *Symons Meteorological Magazine*, for 1889, it is said that the annual fall of rain, at Norfolk, England, is about twenty-nine inches, and that is not a dry or desert locality. But Mr. Symons points out that volumes of water up to twenty-four inches fell from May 25,to 28 in New South Wales—and of a deluge much greater, thirty-four inches, which engulfed Hong Kong on May 29 and 30. In the United States, one inch of rain a day is a big fall and two inches is a flood. A normal thunder shower can bring from one-eighth to one-half inch of rain water. Mr. Symons called attention to these two splashes which were a couple of thousand miles or more apart, and posed the question of whether they were merely coincidence, but leaving it to ⌘⌘⌘⌘⌘⌘⌘⌘⌘⌘⌘⌘⌘⌘⌘⌘⌘ professional meteorologist thought ⌘⌘⌘⌘nds of miles apart, might be remarkable, and not easy to explain on any known basis of meteorological science.

This is another example of partial data and partial thinking. Newspapers reported the soak in New South Wales, but from their reports: columns of water fell in other places, notable Avoca, in Victoria; Tasmania was flooded, its fields gutted with floating rabbits. The *Melbourne Argus* "explained": a waterspout had burst in Victoria. Victoria, Tasmania, New South Wales—a whole continent and more – and Hong Kong. That is not local, and bulks of water are not normal. We look for outside help.

Also, New Zealand, and I do Not know How this
came to Pass. Jemi.

I remember. My Twin. This was the Cleaning and the
Regeneration of the Great Ark & all its "Great Rooms"
All Arks too, needs Cleaning same as any other ship.

Let us now follow the startling cases of the floods of 1913 which seriously damaged our Middle Western States but which were practically world-wide and, for some reason, failed to attract much attention from science or to be recognized as a single, complex disturbance. It is especially this sort of condition to which we direct your attention. We believe that you should question how such a widespread upheaval of our normal meteorological processes could be generated without an encounter with extraterrestrial clouds of space matter.

In March, 1913, farmers were caught short with their spring planting. People were alarmed and driven from homes... March 23, 1913, found the State of Ohio flooded, inundated. Torrents were falling and rivers were out of control. The floods at Dayton, Ohio were singularly disastrous and they were the center of attraction in the national press. 250,000 people were homeless, many homes were obliterated.

Dayton was a shambles of bodies, stalled street cars, snarled traffic, wrecked buildings, and the general flotsam of any flood. Dayton got the headlines, I remember them. I was two hundred miles away, on a farm in western Indiana. It rained there, too. We couldn't plow the land, much less plant crops. That was the year I got my first camera, and I bought a brownie. And one of the very first rolls of film I used was to photograph the tiny brook which ran through our pasture. Only it wasn't tiny then, it was a raging torrent and I snapped my sister standing by it. The little brooklet had a drainage basin not over a half a mile long, but it was a river that day in March. So I remember 1913 and the news from Dayton—the last dispatch: "Dayton in total darkness—no power."

Meteorology was not as advanced in 1913 as it is today, but it was a lusty infant and weather forecasting was not wholly undeveloped. But there was no warning to farmers about the protracted deluge. It surprised the scientists as well as the layman.

On March 23, 24, and 25, a watery sky sat on the Catskills and Adirondacks. It slipped and ripped its pants on a peak, and rivers invaded the streets of Troy and Albany. Lampposts disappeared and furniture floated against the ceilings of rooms. In New Jersey something called a "cloudburst" grabbed factories and made a mess of them, cluttering up the nicely laid out streets. There were a thousand dead in Columbus, Ohio, which is close to Dayton, and the Delaware River at Trenton was fourteen feet above normal. The Ohio River floods at the slightest opportunity—it had a field day. At Parkersburg, West Virginia, people called on their second-story neighbors in rowboats. There were lakes in Vermont. Farmers were caught napping in Wisconsin. Destructive floods occurred in Illinois and Missouri.

By March 27, the meteorologists began to catch up, and the weather bureau was issuing storm warnings (*New York Tribune*, March 28, 1913). Indiana was an inland sea.

Waters were falling and freezing on trees in Canada, breaking power lines and telegraph wires and flooding powerhouses. Towns were in darkness, listening to crashes of trees heavy with ice. California, two thousand miles from Ohio, was drenched; torrents were falling in Washington and Oregon. Texas should be warm, maybe hot, in latter March; there were unprecedented snows, as also in New Mexico and Oklahoma. Alabama was inundated; Florida flooded.

Deluges in France. All Europe was wet. Not much sunny evaporation there. In Spain, near Valencia, there was a hailstorm: trains were stalled by unusually large hailstones, piles three feet deep.

South Africa is practically antipodal to our Midwest; there were watery fists from the skies of Colesburg, Murraysburg, and Prieska, and one of these bulks was the equivalent of one-tenth of the total normal rainfall of South Africa for a whole year!

Summer in the South American Andes? Maybe, but snow was covering them two months ahead of schedule—and in the jungles of Paraguay people were dispersing in panic from flooded rivers. The Uruguay River was rising—governments were rushing supplies and equipment to thousands of starving, homeless people.

The Fiji Islands were drenched and Tasmania was under water. On March 22, the day before the catastrophe in Ohio and four neighboring States, there began a series of great thunderstorms in Australia; a "rain blizzard" in New South Wales, in Queensland all transportation was tied up.

According to the *Wellington Evening Post*, of New Zealand, March 31, there was "the greatest disaster in the history of the colony"; where there had been listless rivers there were unruly brrents embellished with the woolly bodies of sheep and the accouterments of farming. The roar of rivers was the cry of drowning and cattle. Store windows were smashed; dead bodies were wrapped in silk curtains from the red-light district.

May, 1889: There was a spectacular "afterglow" in France although no volcanic eruptions had occurred to fill the air with dust—and storms everywhere had supposedly cleared the murky air. There was a red rain in Cardiff, Wales, and red dust fell on the island of Hyeres, off the coast of France. An unknown substance fell for several hours from the sky at St. Louis, crystalline particles, some pink and some white. Fine dust fell in Dakota: looked like a snowstorm. In Greece there was a monstrous debacle and the rivers choked with cattle. The Bahama Islands were on a spree of water. A downpour was described by a newspaper on St. Helena. A drought occurred in British Honduras, followed by heavy rains, June 1 and 2. Floods raged in California, Ceylon, Cuba; cities and plantations of Mexico were raped by deluges.

All in certain Range of Latitude.

Deluges and falls of lumps of ice throughout England. France deluged. Water dropped from the sky in Switzerland, flooding some streets five feet deep. It was not rain: there were falling columns of water from what was thought to be a waterspout. "Bulks Dropped! and one of them was watched—or some kind of a vast, vaporous cow sailed over the town, and people looked up at her bag of water. Something that was described as a large body of water was seen at Coburg, Ontario. It crossed the town, holding its baglike formation. When it broke, it splashed rivers that broke all dams between Coburg and Lake Ontario. In the *Toronto Globe*, June 3, this falling bulk is called a waterspout. Fall of a similar bulk was noted in Switzerland and Saxony." (Quoted from The Books of Charles Fort.)

One can find plenty of other references to concentrated, local cloudbursts. They are all of a pattern: solid masses of water flooding small demarcated areas, causing local floods and flash flash floods. One was observed in France, yet two miles away, dry land.

These are what we may call single, or isolated slugs of meteoric water.

What can account for these erratics?

Surely, here is proof of intelligence, or selectivity and regularity of a sort which must be attributed to something in space.

Clouds and Storms

Many of these singular objects which are known to have fallen with storms come from storms having some peculiarity. Sometimes the only notation is that the storms were of unusual violence, but even then there is something, perhaps of statistical significance. These small, you might say independent, storms sometimes seem to have causes other than the accepted meteorological conditions. They are quick, tempestuous, sometimes luminous; frequently with geometrically defined clouds of rare and striking colors. They often appear suddenly in clear skies.

As in the instances of some other phenomena, there appear to be three classes of clouds. The first, and most common, of course, are the ordinary meteorological or "weather" clouds. Everybody sees them by the million. Then there are clouds that seem to come from, at least be connected with outer space. These, we can sort into two broad categories, although there may be some merging of one into the other. Of these, the small, peculiarly formed, and sometimes startlingly colored, are the more difficult to define and the rarest in literary descriptions. They are often noted only by a casual phrase in passing, in connection with hailstorms, earthquakes, and sudden violent disturbances of the air; or in some other way they call themselves to the attention of observers whose most urgent interest lies in the more forceful physical aspects which may endanger him, or his crops, animals and home. It is seldom that anyone has the time or opportunity of observing such clouds carefully, and even more rarely does he make notes.

ED: The following has no obvious reference or necessary position.
    1955, 9 Hurricaines (sic) Where they never *were*
    before & all of a sudden, too

The other category of clouds, or storms, of seemingly cosmic nature, are larger sometimes we think they may be larger than the earth itself, and in the case of dusts or mists they may be very much larger. They seem to cause all sorts of widespread trouble and disturbance, either directly or by generally upsetting the earth's meteorological balance. They may cause discoloration of the sun for considerable periods; or diminution in its light, with ensuing darkness; or very cold weather, such as the extremes of the winter of 1882-83, when space around the earth seemed to be replete with clouds of spatial debris. They may bring floods to the whole earth, simultaneously, they do not always seem to be wholly vaporous, and there are some which are certainly made up of debris, dust, water, stones, ice, etc.

It seems impossible to organize a firm classification from data not at hand. There are apparently mergings or blendings of each type into the others. We will describe and list some of them. Maybe something will work out as we go along.

1697: A horrid black cloud, attended by frequent lightnings, was precursor of a violent hailstorm. Animals were killed, crops ruined, and people had their heads broken. The breadth of the cloud was about two miles. The hailstones were some round, some semispherical and others were embossed and crenulated like the foot of a drinking glass, the ice being very transparent and hard.

1812: The latest remarkable fall of aerolites in Europe, of which there is a distinct account, was in the vicinity of Laigle, Normandy, early in the afternoon of April 26. A fiery globe of a very brilliant splendor, which moved in the air with great rapidity, was followed in a few seconds by a violent explosion which lasted five or six minutes and was heard for thirty leagues in all directions. Three or four reports like those of a cannon were followed by discharge resembling musketry fire, after which a dreadful rumbling was heard like the beating of a HUGE drum. The air was calm and the sky serene with the exception of a few clouds such as are frequently observed. The noise proceeded from a small cloud of rectangular form, the largest side being in a direction from east to west. It appeared motionless all the time the phenomenon lasted, but the vapor of which it was composed was projected momentarily from the different sides by the effect of the different explosions. The cloud was about half a league to the northeast of Laigle, and was at so great an altitude that the inhabitants of two hamlets a league apart saw it directly overhead. A multitude of meteoric stones fell amid a hissing sound.

Thunderbird, Dragon of Lao Fzu, p. 27, Saucer,
ALL the same thing, all Rumble when "Hit" Hard
or When in Need of Repairs.

The shape of that "cloud" is important. It seems to be the only sure clue that this could be anything more than an ordinary exploding meteor. Rectangular clouds do not just happen. They almost certainly have to be made. And the cloud appeared to be motionless. Meteors do not remain Motionless. The clouds which they usually provoke are not capable of sustaining the heavy meteoritic material inside, should the whole complex become immobile. So this cloud was certainly not of ordinary meteorological origin, and seems to partake of artificiality. Also, a stationary state is indicative of control.

There is something of the incongruous in meteors which exit from clouds, especially clouds of such peculiar formation that they do not associate easily with the common variety of weather clouds. Maybe that seems to be a rather remarkable statement. But if a meteor is moving through the atmosphere at a rate of ten to twenty miles per second there is not much time for clouds to form ahead of it. A cloud train behind the meteor would require little in the way of explanation, but, under such circumstances, how do we form a cloud in time for the meteor to emerge from it; why does the cloud suddenly and sharply stop moving while the meteor passes onward; why, in short, does there seem to be a slight difference between the usual meteors and those which emerge from clouds?

We quote the following from *Observatory*, 1877, a popular British astronomical monthly of competence and reliability:

... the meteor was seen by J. Plant, Esquire, F.O.S., at Salford, and is described by him as bursting from an intensely lit cloud, like a ball of silver quite as large as the moon. The explosion was remarkable, a whirling shower of pear-drop (sic) stars—ruby, blue, white and yellow—radiating from the center mass, the colors being quite brilliant. The meteor was seen about three seconds before the explosion.

The meteor itself may be only casually interesting, although its colors may be unusual and may hold some interest for students of meteoritics. What is of interest to us is the cloud, which seems to have preceded the meteor instead of following it, and especially, to have been illuminated or self-luminous.

Many are the report of meteors emerging from clouds, as in 1808: "...such a phenomenon as appeared at Siena in 1794, when stones descended, not from a moving meteor, but from a luminous cloud..."

A yellow cloud appeared over Paderborn, from which came a torrential rain and a shower of mussels; the triangular cloud with a tail, whose red nucleus exploded; February 13, 1901, greenish-yellow clouds appeared in France, spreading "intensest darkness"; people froze to death in Naples that night.

Naples in Southernmost Italy.

Did something bring in the cold of outer space?

The Journal of Royal Meteorological Society contains some extracts from the Captain's log, of the ship Lady of the Lake, Captain F.W. Banner. On March 22, 1870 position 5° 47' N Lat., 27° 52' W. Longitude, the crew observed a remarkable cloud in the sky. It was a cloud with a circular form which enclosed a semicircle divided into four parts, the central dividing line (cord, bar, partition or what?) starting at the center of the circle, and extending far beyond the limits of the structure, then curving backward, like a hook.

NO CLOUD EVER SHAPED BY WIND COULD EVER TAKE THIS SHAPE, NOHOW, IN NATURE

This cloud had geometric shape, and a mechanical complexity. In fact it had an organic, or an artificial form.

Thompson says: "In August and September, 1831, there was an anomalous brightness in the sky and small print was visible at midnight—the barometer fell, the sun was of a silvery whiteness and storms were general in Europe and the West Indies."

W.S. Forest says: "Citizens were much surprised on the morning of August 13, 1831, by the strange appearance of the sun. The sun's disc seemed on rising, to have changed from its usual golden color to a pale, greenish tent which soon gave way to cerule blue and this to a silvery white. In the afternoon the sun appeared like an immense plane of polished silver and to the naked eye there was exhibited an appearance on the surface termed a black spot. The sun shone with a dull gloomy light, and the atmosphere was moist and heavy."

These two passages, one written in England, the other in Virginia, will serve to indicate the vastness of this condition and nature of it.

Many sources mention frequent cases of darkness and obscuration of the sun. There is, in this darkness and "cold days," the blending of terrestrial and cosmic clouds. We will have other occasions to mention cosmic clouds, in connection with things astronomers have seen in space. For now, it is enough to say that when these clouds contact the earth, we have dust, gas, obscuration, darkness, cold and meteorological disturbances in general; a blending of meteoritic and meteorological conditions.

According to the *Chicago Tribune*, January 7, 1892, a fiery blast shot across the State of Georgia, on the previous June 5th described as "a black tornado, filled with fire." About this time there were earthquake shocks in Italy, approximately the same geographical latitude; people in New York State were watching a glare in the sky and shocks were felt. On June 8th, dust fell from the sky in northern Indiana. Quakes followed around the world for several days. Snow fell in Mobile, which is certainly an indication that the storm may have brought materials from the cold of outer space. There was a tidal wave in the Atlantic, and there were shocks at Memphis, Tennessee, on June 14. There was a tidal wave in Lake Michigan on June 18. A mass of fire fell from the sky on the 20th, on a town in Massachusetts. At the same time quakes occurred in Italy and France. On the 24th, a great meteor shot over Cape Town. Durango, Mexico had its first rain in four years. Glare in the sky alarmed Germans on the 26th. In England, people watched a luminous cloud at night. Quakes were reported in Tasmania and Australia.

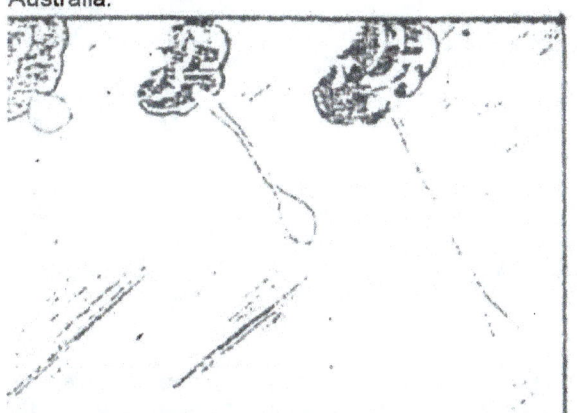 

Meteor from an organic cloud, seen by J. Plant, F.S.S., Salford, England, November 23, 1877 - - t The first year of the "Incredible Decade."

SMALL BATTLE

Why recite all those things? Why imply a relationship? Because it is a part of our present purpose to indicate that earthquakes and local storms may be engendered by huge masses of space material passing close to the terrestrial surface.

That storm across Georgia, from the phrase, "A black tornado, filled with fire," does not have to be considered extranormal just from that description. Tornadoes are black, and they often involve brilliant and vicious displays of electrics. on OUTER EDGES, NOT IN MIDDLE "FILL" It is the concomitants which cause us to wonder. The events which we mentioned spread over a rather long time to be in any way connected with one local storm, but there does seem to be a family resemblance, and there are many such examples. Yet in view of the concomitants, and since we do not have a definite statement that the storm was a twister, the term, tornado, being frequently used loosely, we wonder if there were extensive gravitational irregularities, or if something was made to surge through our lower atmosphere, thereby creating a vehement black cloud, filled with fire, which was only a detail in a world-wide melee. Could we have had the close approach of a vast scattering of space debris, through which the earth passed during a period of several days, and from which we had meteorites, water, dust, cold, etc., and disruption of the normal meteorological processes over most of our globe, not to speak of seismic upheavals on a wide scale?

The instances of apparent association between clouds, meteors, and quakes are many. It seems like stretching things too far to claim that all are merely coincidence.

For four hours, in the wake of the Georgia storm, on January 8, dust fell on northern Indiana—no records of such in between. Research fails to disclose any volcanic action to put dust into the air, and if it did, what of the intervening places? There was no dust bowl in Georgia, and besides this storm, as is general, was moving eastward, not northward. From the western deserts—a long way to carry a heavy fall of dust without dropping noticeable amounts! Could it be that the dust was not from Georgia's tornado, but from the common cause of both?

Time after time it seems that isolated clouds, of a singular appearance, approach the earth's surface, yet remain suspended in flight. To be sustained by velocity they would have to move with the speed of escape, around six and one-half miles per second, which they obviously are not doing. Since they apparently bring with them a considerable amount of space debris, they are indicated to have celestial origin rather than arising from the earth's surface.

It is our suggestion that some of the singular, or disassociated clouds, contain camouflaged, navigable space contraptions, or they are dirigible space widgets, guided and directed by intelligence.

Again we close with an arresting quotation. Bearing our theories in mind, consider the following contribution from John P. Bessor to *Fate*, March, 1954:

The Battle of the Clouds: On July 28th, 1874, the little community of Saw Mill Run, near Pittsburgh, Pennsylvania, met with disaster from a most singular phenomenon. Curious villagers and country folk looked at the sky and beheld something very strange. Over the northeastern horizon, slowly and majestically, sailed a black cloud ringed with a scarlet belt; and over the southwest horizon slowly sailed another black cloud—with a scarlet belt.

Onward they came towards each other, like two men-of-war approaching the scene of battle. As they drew nearer, they discharged flashes of lighting, and the whole effect was that of an eerie sea battle high in the air.

Nearer and nearer they drew, the violence of the flashes of lightning increasing the closer they approached, until, with one great flash, they collided, and rain fell in torrents. One hundred and fifty persons drowned and it is believed to be the most disastrous flood ever to befall that section of the country.

> The L-M Live *in* Water half or More of the time
> and it is No Wonder so Much Water fell from two
> "Mother Ships" Lemurian & Muanina Ships in Battle,
> no Doubt.

Rubbish in Space

- These few chapters of observational material show that space contains a much greater amount and variety of material scattered between planets than most of us, including the astronomers, have known. Before true meteoric material (the now well-known iron and stone meteorities) were scientifically accepted there had to be innumerable cases where meteorites were truly seen to fall. These were collected by authoritative witnesses. That these meteorites had been identified by their testure and chemical elements, as well as their external appearance, was not enough to overcome bigotry, and more than one French scientist had to risk his professional standing before the Academy in Paris ere it was accepted by science that iron and stone did fall from the sky. This controversy was raging as recently as one hundred and fifty years ago, in spite of firm demonstrations by some isolated scientific observers one or two hundred years previously, and there were still holdouts until the end of the 19th century. So firm is astronomy in its entrenched dogma, that there are still some respected men who dispute that the Arizona meteor crater is meteoric in origin, or that the Carolina Bays were caused by anything but mysteriously formed whirlpools.

GREAT BOMBARDMENT.

The great Bombardment Announced the end of Mu.

It is not surprising, therefore, when we learn that among the vast amount of material that has fallen from the sky, sulfur is present. But it cannot fall from the sky because it isn't in the sky! But it does!

1868: A mass of burning sulfur about the size of a man's fist fell at Pultusk, Poland, on January 30. It fell upon a road and was stomped out by several villagers.

Inflammable objects falling from space may well account for the many reports of falling "fire," from which no tangible debris is found; and since such material is of low specific gravity, its velocity is speedily checked by atmospheric friction, and it can fall slowly, burning the while, and thus, perhaps, give rise to some of the reports of large appearing slowly moving masses of fire.

S-M SHIPS OR ARKS.

"Burning bituminous matter" fell during a thunderstorm in July, 1681, upon the deck fo the English vessel Albemarle.

The jagged pieces of ice which fell at Orkney, July 24, 1818, had a strong sulphurous odor; and also the coke—or what looked like coke—which fell at Mortree, France, April 24, 1887, with which fell a sulphurous substance. And, the enormous "round things" which rose from the ocean, near Victoria: whether we accept that they were superconstructions, or something else, including perhaps imagination, it was reported that they spread a "stench of sulfur." If they smelled like that, they could not have been too distant, could they?

L-M SHIPS ON UNDER SEA EXPLORATION, STAYED TOO LONG, GATHERED A "COAT" ON SHIELD EDGE. BURNED IT OFF AT SURFACE. ICE GATHERED ON VENUSIAN VOYAGE & BURNED OFF WHEN COMING OUT OF "SHIELD"[2] SAME FOR OTHER MATERIALS BUT THESE "CAUGHT" ON OTHER PLANETS

There was a staggering fall of dust and mud in Europe in February 1903. It seems that southern England was quite a dumping ground, although some scientists thought the dust cam from lanes and byways of the local shires. They hadn't heard that it also covered the Canary Islands. The substance contained a sizable percentage of organic matter, and was, of course, identified by some as sand from the Sahara Desert. It covered Ireland, England, and the Canaries. It was reported on the 27th in Belgium, Holland, Germany, and Austria. Ten million tons fell on south England alone! A vessel reported the stuff falling midway between England and Barbados. It fell in Switzerland, according to *Symons' Meteorological Magazine*, of March, 1903. It fell in Russia. Not only did Australia get covered with this stuff in November 1902; it was falling there again in February – enormously—fifty tons per square mile of red mud.

-RESULT OF L-M'S "HOME ON MOON" being built.

This stuff was variously said to be like brick dust, buff colored, or light brown, chocolate colored and silky to touch, and slightly iridescent, gray; red-rust colored; quite red, yellowish brown, tinged with pink.

I do not believe these falls of mud on earth indicate life in space, unless in very indirect ways, obscurely, and deviously. But there is definitely, here, an indication of dust in the space proximate to the earth, or in orbits intersecting our orbit. It seems more and more inescapable that there are immense amounts of material of almost every fanciable type. That such unaccountable millions of tons of red dust composed of a high percentage of organic matter could be whirled aloft from the Sahara, or any desert,

---

[2] :"SHIELD" is by Jemi. It is printed over a word, which may be "STASIS", BY Mr. A.

and disseminated to such scattered areas, is an incomprehensibility far more durable than that of orbital existence in space – and we have to assume clouds of something in space to account for the disturbance of comets' tails, and for the temporary disappearance of comets, as for instance the great comet of 1882.

It is therefore, my contention that these falls of mud originate in space, and that such clouds of dust are a normal part of space debris. Whether they come from the explosion producing the asteroids, or from an atom explosion which hoisted Mu into the firmament and into eternity, is beyond or ability to ascertain.

> NOT ATOMIC. Was sudden, broad inerse snap of stasis

It is our stand that, if there is such diversity and quantity of material in vicinal space, then there is room, and perhaps sustenance of a sort, for intelligence and intelligently manipulated space ships.

It is equally our contention, that, if all of this dispersed, but tangible, array of assorted items can exist in nearby space, or in orbits intersecting that of the earth, and if all of these things (except the conventional iron and stone meteorites) can have escaped the cognizance of science for such a long time, even though falling to earth in considerable quantity, then there is no reason why intelligently operated contrivances cannot also be in the same celestial regions, and have escaped our attention, in spite of visiting our atmosphere frequently.

> VISITING! They Live here & Work here & build Here but fortunately all undersea.

To list but a few of some of the other materials reported: ashes, sand, algae, iron, gelatinous matter, seeds, red edible stuff, mud, dust, powder, vegetable matter, white substance, soot, coke, charcoal, coal, earthy matter, soft substance, wedge shapes, black rain, colored rain.

Add these things to the stone, ice, water, organic matter, living organisms, gadgets, gold thread, etc., and you have three possible explanations: the surface debris of an exploded planet, the surface debris of a continent blasted off the earth, or the rubbish of a space life of vast extent and unspeakable age; perhaps also, curiosity, a trait of intelligence.

I believe it substantiates a "space life" of some sort. Space being cluttered with such a vast amount of debris, sparsely scattered, but of all types and enormous in the aggregate, it is sufficient to supply many of the needs of space life. You will note that throughout our enumeration of "falls," our theme has been that there seem to be two types of arrivals from outer space: those which are moving in highly elliptical meteoric orbits (true space debris, that is), and those which seem to be, or have been, associated with intelligence. There may well be some overlapping for some of the intelligences may be moving in such orbits, especially if it should develop that some of them are associated with the great comets such as those of 1880-81-82. In its simplest form, then, our idea is that the least objectionable explanation for these falls is that they come from intelligently operated space craft, or are in some way formed, guided, or influenced by the operators of such craft. We base this on characteristics of shape, texture, functionality, delimited and localized distribution, timing, repetition, location in places inaccessible to modern man; and on the purely negative deduction that they could not have happened through any commonly accepted chain of casual conditions.

Such a cause or, such a common denominator does appear to exist in the contemplation of space flight or space navigation, to put it more simply, in space life. This appears to be the least improbable causal factor in sight at this time. Also, there appears to be ample observational proof for this view since 1947.

I believe that space between the earth and the moon is occupied, however thinly, by large navigable constructions of a rigid nature, whose size may range from one to many miles in diameter, and which have a planetary appearance as seen in telescopes. These sometimes come close to the earth.

There are other bodies which seem to be of a cloudlike nature, which cast shadows on both earth & moon, and; which may range the entire solar system accompanying comets. These also, or their smaller components, sometimes approach the earth. All of these objects evince evidences of control by intelligence, as do the more recently sighted UFO's.

Smaller "scouts or operators," which are probably inhabitants of, or associates, of the great spherical contraptions, are constantly seen in earth's atmosphere. They are of many types, and in fact it does seem that many of them have the ability to change shape. They seem to be of two sorts: the solid or material, and the massless or ethereal. All exhibit elements of control, but the weightless ones seem more to have the appearance of remote control. Solid types tend to be discoid or to be spherical or spindle shaped, and these shapes, in themselves, are indicative of intelligent construction. (Red is A and B)

> read "YOUR SINS & MINE" for clues "Ethereal types" *Don't change shape*, only change in-stensity or amount of Protective Force-Shield to Ward off extra fast tiny Meteors *or* to change course.
>
> ALSO WARDS-OFF COSMIC RAY PARTICLES
>
> As to What is to come *if* L-M's GET DISGUSTED WITH MANS MISANTHROPIC, NON-PHILOSOPHISM & MATERIALISM. MAN HAS *MANY* BOOKS ON "TRUE-THOUGHT" YET THEY IGNORE THEM, BIBLE, KORAN, ETC. *ANGERS L-M's FEIRCELY* (sic)
>
> Ethereal types Similair to results of Navy expieriments, in force-Field invisibility, 1943 SOLIDS GO THROO THEM, NO HARM TO OCCUPANTS AT ALL.

The following notes appear at the beginning of Part Three.
> A force able to propel every Molecule of itself, plus its passengers, at 7500 MPH if used as a force shield to withstand the *impact* of Meteoric Rock groups can also be used to Withstand the Tremendous Pressures of Undersea *Living & Working & building* Especially when this force is used to create new *Tre-mendously* Compacted-tough *Plastics & Metals*, out of Which their ship are Made. With *only* these Latter, Undersea Living is easily and Nicely accomplished.
>
> Metal Lamination. Would become feasible, at Last.

PART THREE

History Speaks

Disappearing Ships and Crews

There are two purposes to be served in discussing the disappearances of ships and crews. First, we shall list enough of the available material to show that such phenomena have occurred and, second, we shall see what conclusions can be drawn and how it will serve our space thesis.

> *Yes, Many Many times. More often than is recorded. Ulysses & crew believed suffered same fate. Nes[3] "Wanderings thus Were Pure invention.*

It is well-known sea lore that ships develop a kind of spiritual or psychic entity, or personality, like people, and the strange tale of the *Marie Celeste* illustrates this as few other histories can. After reading the whole story, it cannot be denied that a malignant curse enshrouded this unhappy vessel. The dramatic disappearance of her crew is vital to our present theme, but it is only one incident in the strange experiences of the brigantine.

The following account by Henry S. Galus is from *Fate* (Vol. X, No. 8):

> *Marie Celeste Had an Extra Compass in Captains Cabin.*

On the afternoon of December 4, 1872, the British brigantine, *Dei Gratia*, made a queer discovery, about three hundred miles off the Portuguese coast, which soon tangled seamen, courts and researchers in the hottest controversy in nautical history.

Mate Oliver Deveau had raised his glass to windward and had seen a vessel under short sail, plowing directly toward him. Deveau notified Captain David R. Morehouse, of it, and the skipper "spoke" to the craft in greeting. There was no reply. Sensing some tragedy, Morehouse went abreast the brig to lend it possible aid. Nothing stirred on her deck. Yet this brig had been holding a course *as if guided* by the skill of a salty helmsman!

Deveau and two hands boarded the craft. Official records reveal the baffling sight in his own words: "I found no one on board—I found three and one-half feet of water in the pumps—fore hatch and lazerette hatch both off—binnacle stove in – skylight of the cabin was open and raised—the compass in the binnacle was destroyed. All the Captain's effects had been left – I mean his clothes, furniture, etc. I found the log book in the mate's cabin, on his desk.

> *CAPT. ALWAYS TAKES THE LOG WHEN ABONDONING SHIP. LOG MUST BE TAKEN EVEN IF CAPT. IS DEAD. THEY WERE FROZE & "SWIPED"*

"There seemed to be everything left behind in the cabin as if left in a hurry, but everything in its place. I noticed the impression in the Captain's bed as of a child having lain there."

---

[3] Clearest Translation.

NOT A CHILD, WAS ANOTHER "LITTLE-MAN" OF MU

GRAVITY IS GREAT STRAIN ON THEM, THEY TIRE EASILY & MUST REST OFTEN WHEN ON "TERRA."

EXCEPT UNDERSEAS.

Nine days later, at Gibraltar, Deveau swung the ghost ship into port with the idea of collecting salvage money for the 1,700 barrels of alcohol under her hatches. But the destiny of the *Marie Celeste* was more complicated than that. The Marshal of the Vics Admiralty Court put the brig under arrest. The Queen's Proctor, Frederick S. Flood, asserted that a crew just didn't leave a ship with $80,000 worth of alcohol, to risk their necks on a directionless joy ride. What, then, had Deveau done with the missing crew?

The *Dei Gratia* had also pulled into port. Flood turned suspicious glances toward its hands. Clearly he was determined to find evidence of crime. He entered the *Marie Celeste's* cabin, and his eyes snapped when he uncovered an old Italian sword under the Captain's berth. Flood scrutinized the deck—and found the stains he expected! Dr. J. Patron was summoned to make a chemical test.

"No," he told Flood, "these are not blood stains."

John Austin, the ship surveyor and diver, next examined the brig's underside. He came up dripping to report that there was no indication that the brig had struck anything like a reef which might have caused the crew, fearful of being trapped on board, to abandon ship.

Then, why had the *Marie Celeste* been abandoned? It was learned that her master had been Captain Benjamin S. Briggs. Nine others accompanied him, including his wife and daughter Sophie. Surely Briggs, and old sea master, would have done nothing to endanger his family. The destroyed compass was a clue—but there was no further evidence of violence. Superstitious seamen pedicted:

> *They break compasses, fearing that we may use More than one Bar Magnet, & thus fly as they.*
>
> *A compass "card" Looks EXACTLY Like a FLYING SAUCER from the top, Looking down on a Large Ships binnacle compass card floating in its Liquid.*

"You'll never find the answer. An unworldly power cleared the brig's deck." The tribunal scoffed. Ghost ships! In the 19th Century!

Lack of evidence now bogged down the court's hearing of the *Dei Gratia's* salvage claims. Meanwhile, as news of the riddle boiled in the world presses, amazing background facts came to light. Rumor stated that the current tragedy was only a continuation of the misfortunes that dogged the brig since she was first launched in Nova Scotia. Who ever had touched her had suffered disappointments, financial losses, or worse.

As the *Amazon*, in 1861, the 206-ton brig made her maiden voyage under Captain Robert McLellan. He took sick while plying the Bay of Fundy. Ashore, days later, he died. John N. Parker, the next skipper, was only mildly successful with his trips. The owners replaced him with William Thompson. Promptly, the brig cracked up on Cape Breton Island. This broke her owners. Salvors seized the vessel. John Howard Beatty bought and lost her quickly, for as the Sackville, New Brunswick, Tribune reported, the *Amazon* piled up on the Maine coast.

As a condemned hulk she was auctioned off at New York. On November 12, 1868, Richard W. Hains paid $1,750 for her, and it was he who named her *Marie Celeste*. Scarcely ten months later he forfeited the brig for debt. James H. Winchester, her newest proprietor, put the blame for his poor profits on a swift succession of skippers; however, not until the middle of 1872 did a serious misfortune befall him. A Boston Marshal charged Winchester with fraudulent ownership. The *Marie Celeste* was immediately bonded for $2,600.

Reeling under the blow, Winchester was reedy to let the bedeviled craft go, but fate, through the court, settled in his favor. During ensuing repairs, the ill-fated Benjamin S. Briggs reduced Winchester's costs by purchasing a third interest. And the Captain's wife, Sarah, penned these final words to her mother-in-law, on November 7th, 1872, off Staten Island: "Benje thinks we have a pretty peaceable set (crew) this time, if they continue as they have begun. Can't tell you how smart they are."

Had Captain Briggs conveyed any suspicions of his crew to his wife? One theory of what happened to the *Marie Celeste's* human cargo, with a possible correlation to Sarah Briggs' words, comes from an English author, Laurence J. Keating. In 1929 his book, *The Great Marie Celeste Hoax*, "exposed the famous sea mystery with ruthless truth." Keating charged that: "Mrs. Briggs was a prime irritant on board the *Marie Celeste*; trouble rode most of the voyage; she died and was cast overboard; Captain Briggs disappeared one night from the brig, apparently murdered while most of the men were drunk. Lastly, the *Dei Gratia* had not found the *Marie Celeste*, but a brig named *Julia*—and the whole puzzle was the result of a criminal conspiracy between Captains Morehouse and Briggs, which unfortunately cost the latter his life!"

More than any other theory to date, this astonishing one from Keating has been shouted down. J. Franklin Briggs, nephew of the lost skipper and now living in New Bedford, Massachusetts, has spent many years trying to disprove both Keating's claims and other statements he considers a defamation of the innocent dead. In a privately circulated booklet published August 8, 1944, the surviving Briggs presents a digest of his voluminous investigations which included interviews with H.S. Morehouse, the *Dei Gratia's* Skipper's son; Winchester Noyes, grandson of Captain Winchester; and Mrs. Alice Melason, Mate Oliver Deveau's daughter.

Still, the booklet does not solve the riddle. "We may believe," J.F. Briggs concludes, "that the Captain became suddenly alarmed (Presumably by rough weather), hauled aback the square sails to stop the brig's headway, ordered all hands into the yawl, and temporarily left the ship, which subsequently gathered way and sailed off."

This view is the simplest explanation. But scores of other solutions have been just as sincerely forwarded. There is the letter Proctor Flood wrote to the London Board of Trade on January 22 or 23, 1873: "My own theory, or guess, is that the crew got at the alcohol and in the fury of drunkenness murdered the master, his wife, child, and the chief mate; that they damaged the bows of the vessel with the view of giving it the appearance of having struck on rocks...so as to induce the Master of any vessel which might pick her up to think her not worth saving; and that they did, sometime between November 25, and December 5, escape on board some vessel."

This, so closely paralleling Author Keating's accusations, was countered by a Captain Shufeldt, U.S. Navy, who had examined the *Marie Celeste*: "The damage about the bows of the brig appears to me to amount to nothing more than splinters made in the bending planks,,, neither hurting the ship nor any possible chance the result of intention to do so,"

In *Yachting*, for February, 1940, Dr. Oliver W. Cobb, cousin of Sarah Briggs, wrote: "there may have been leakage, and gas may have accumulated in the hold" because of the effects of temperature changes on the alcohol store. Thus, the *Marie Celeste's* master, fearful of an explosion, got his crew off the craft. Cobb feels that Briggs used a halyard line to hold the brig until it was determined safe for a return aboard. "Probably a fresh northerly wind sprang up, filled the square sails—these people were left in an open boat on the ocean."

A sailor named Lund, one of the three who sailed the *Marie Celeste* into Gibraltar claimed that the derelict's "peak halyards were broken and gone." The second seaman, Anderson, "saw ropes hanging over the side." Deveau at the same time testified: "the main peak halyards were broken." He didn't say, "gone." Has Dr. Cobb provided the true solution, then?

> No Lazarette Hatch & Stow Hold Hatch covers
> could have been taken off & the body of Ship
> Ventilated, often done, common practice.

Several researchers suggested that icebergs threatened the brig and, therefore, the fear-stricken crew took flight only to become victims of other icebergs. However, one of the most painstaking historians of the enigma is Charles Eddy Fay, who now lives at Lake Worth, Florida. He went directly to the Navy Department to ask whether icebergs were common in the part of the ocean where the ghost ship was picked up. On December 7, 1940, the hydrographic office told him: "As to the possibility of icebergs being found in the locality—that is highly improbable, due to the long drift, through comparatively warm water, necessary for any ice to reach this vicinity. However, small pieces of ice have been sighted exceptionally far south as follows—up to 1934."

Another more popular assumption saw Captain Briggs and his crew fall prey to merciless pirates. On this one, too, Fay sought government information. A letter dated January 15, 1941, came from the *Naval Archives*: "—concerning the possibility of pirates—records do not reveal that any piratical operations took place as late as 1872 between the Azores and the coast of Portugal."

A swirling flood of conjectures continued to pour forth as to the fate of Captain Briggs and his men and women. Was J. L. Hornibrook any nearer the facts in *Chamber's Journal*, September 17, 1904? "Suddenly a huge octopus rises from the deep, encircles the helmsman. His yells bring every soul running on deck. One by one they are caught by the waving wriggling arms. Then, freighted with its living load, the monster slowly sinks into the deep, leaving no trace of its attack."

Or do you prefer the story from the *Washington Post*, December 19, 1931, quoting a feature published earlier in the *London Daily Express*? An R.E. Greenbough found a document in a floating bottle which told of the crew being kidnapped from the *Marie Celeste* by an undisclosed ship. Kathleen Woodward wrote in the *New York Times Magazine*, October 12, 1924: A man referred to as Triggs, a bo'sun's mate on the *Marie Celeste*, quoted as charging Captain Briggs and crew abandoned ship, boarded a derelict steamer, broke open its safe, stole gold, fled and arrived with a misleading tale at Cadiz.

In the *British Quarterly Review*, July 1931, there appeared a story by Harold T. Wilkins. The *Dei Gratia*, on a predatory mission, purposely waited in the middle of the ocean for the brig, somehow induced the crew to come aboard and slaughtered all hands. In *Nautical Magazine*, July 1922, D.G. Ball tried to wash the log page clear once and for all—"the whole story is just a myth without any foundation of fact." He assured his readers that no such ship had ever existed. He regretted that he must divulge this truth for the controversy fascinated him.

That the *Marie Celeste* did exist is proven by subsequently recorded voyages after her release March 10, 1873, by the Gibraltar court; and by the court records themselves.

EXTANT, STILL

ED: The following has no obvious reference or necessary position.
> Alcohol fumes partly inebriated the Whole
> Crew & L-Ms WERE OVERHEAD; Drunk men
> naturally are not Mentally Paralyzed by "Freeze"
> They seized Lines as they were starting to
> ascend & Hung on Grimly. Some fell on
> Deck, L-M SHIP STOPPED M-C & took them all off.

Captain George W. Blatchford, of Wrentham, Massachusetts, finally delivered her alcohol cargo to Genoa, then sailed to Boston. "When she arrived," related Winchester, her owner, "a great many people came to look at her, but as soon as they found out her history they would not touch her." Those who believed an ominous fate still pursued her were soon presented with a convincing sequel. Here are the actual incidents that followed.

Winchester refused to gamble further on the brig. He managed to get rid of her at an $8,000 loss. The succeeding owner, Captain David Cartwright, according to the *New York World*, January 24, 1886, "sent her to Montevideo with a cargo of lumber. She arrived there minus her deck load, and minus spars and sails. There the Captain got a charter to carry horses. The few delivered alive were too ill to be worth anything. Edgar M. Tuthill (her skipper) obtained a charter to bring freight from Calcutta. On the passage home he was taken sick and died in St. Helena, three weeks later. We next sent her to Africa. She lost $1,000.00."

But the end was near. The *Marie Celeste's* last proprietor, Wesley A. Grove, signed Captain Gillman E. Parker and loaded her with assorted cargo for Port-au Prince, Haiti. The various shippers; first took out insurance for $25,000—and on January 3, 1885, the drunken Parker staggered up to the helmsman, pointing to a clearly visible coral reef.

"Steer hard for her, m'hearty, and do the job real good." The brig crunched viciously, and the grinning skipper shouted all hands below for a lusty drink session, after which all rowed ashore.

In Haiti, someone talked. The plot failed when the insurance companies dug up evidence to indict the bribing shippers. At the trial in Boston, the shippers admitted guilt. Parker escaped conviction, as the judge ordered a new trial on the charge of barratry.

Perhaps the last echo of the *Marie Celeste's* evil fate intervened to cheat justice. For within three months Parker died. Six months later his mate was dead. All the conspiring firms by this time had bankrupted, and one of their members committed suicide.

Thus the log book of the most ill-fated brig in history was closed forever.

There are several facts which we must stress. First, the upper rigging of the ship was slightly damaged, as if some unusual accident or activity took place there. Then, the compass was damaged. Aside from these, there was no note of disarray or a struggle. Life had departed from the ship instantly, apparently with all the routine activities interrupted and; no preparations made; log book on the table, clothing in order, sails set, galley undisturbed—but no records in the log or anywhere else!

To attempt to postulate motive for space inhabitants kidnapping crews from ships—not to mention isolated individuals to which we shall come momentarily—is in the realm of pure speculation. On the other hand, bearing our two possibilities in mind as to the origin of space contrivances, in either case our space friends would want to know what has happened to us since they left, or what has happened to us since they put us down here. Again, there is always the possibility that the open seas provide an easy catching place.

> Ought to, the Sea is Natural home of the Little bastards.

ED: The following has no obvious reference or necessary position.
> The Little pricks come-aboard at nite and go Wandering about the Decks, Scares the Crews but No Crew Man meeting one, *ever* says so. Just quits drinking.

In any case, selective transportation requires intelligence. A force acting from the sky and intelligently directed could do some very puzzling things.

Here is another mystery at sea as reported in *Fate Magazine*, June 1954:

SOS, SOS—came the distress call from the Dutch vessel *S.S.Ourang Medan*, Dutch and British listening posts located the vessel as proceeding through the straits of Malacca. It was early February 1948, the sea calm, the weather clear.

SOS, SOS, again came the frenzied call. After a short silence, "...all officers, including Captain dead, lying in chartroom and on Bridge... probably whole crew dead..."

There followed a series of indecipherable dots and dashes and then came quite clearly: "I die." And after that only an ominous silence.

Rescue ships from Dutch Sumatra and British Malaya rushed to the indicated location of the vessel in distress. They found her only fifty miles from the position given. Boats were put over the sides to investigate.

> "Medan" *was MOVED*. RADIO DIRECTIONALFINDERS ARE TOO ACCURATE & SHIPS TOO SLOW TO MOVE THAT FAR IN *SO LITTLE TIME*. (*Italic emphasis by A*)

When boarding parties reached the *Ourang Medan* they found an eerie sight. There wasn't a living creature on the ship. The captain lay dead on the bridge. The bodies of the other officers sprawled in the wheelhouse, chartroom and wardroom. The faithful "sparks" was slumped in a chair in the radio shack, his hand still on the sending key. The bodies of the hapless crew lay everywhere: in their rooms, in the passageways, on the decks. And on all the dead face was a look of convulsive horror. As a report of the Proceedings of the Merchant Marine Council put it: "their frozen faces were upturned to the sun, the mouths were gaping open and the eyes staring..." Everyone was dead! Even the ship's dog a small terrier, was lifeless, its teeth bared in anger or agony.

> Navigator trying to Plot Movement of ship?

But strangely there was no sign of wounds or injuries on any of the bodies.

> SUFFOCATION? JAMMED "FREEZE" SomebodySlipped-up on this one Must Have been a "Jammed"-Freezer to kill all. Otherwise, the "sparks" would not have got Hit so hard.

After a quick conference, the would-be rescuers decided to put a tow line onto the unlucky vessel and take her into port. But at that very moment smoke and flames belched froth from No. 4 hold. The fire was immediately so hot and so widespread that it was impossible to subdue.

> Telepathic, Eh?

The boarding parties hurriedly abandoned the doomed vessel and returned to the safety of their own ships. Moments later there was a terrific explosion on the *Ourang Medan* and the ship seemed to leap into the air. Then it settled back and quietly slid beneath the waters. From that day to this, no one has ever been able to determine what happened to this unfortunate ship or to her officers and crew. The fate of the *S.S. Ourang Medan* is another unsolved mystery of the sea.

> More Work of "The Little-Men" of Mu & their force-ships.

> Radio Men are Liffle affected by "freezing" when *in* their Shacks *with* sender turned on. Electro Resistance.

The notable points: sudden death (or disappearance) of people (all life) at a lonely and isolated spot, at sea. No apparent cause assignable. A sudden and unexplained fire, obviously for the purpose of "destroying the evidence," a fire so suddenly violent and widespread as to defy action, although strong men, familiar with ships, were at hand, prepared for emergencies.

Some meteorologists and astronomers have suggested from time to time that ships and aircraft disappearing at sea may have been struck by meteors. Many writers have expressed the feeling that there is something unexplained in these disappearances without trace, but there is no proven case of an aircraft being struck by a meteor over land. In fact there are a few, if any, proven cases of cars, trucks, trains, buggies, sleighs, mud scows, coal barges, or even buildings, being struck directly by meteors, and considering the millions of these features on a landscape, it seems like stretching and distorting coincidence rather far to blame random meteors for the dispatching of numerous ships and aircraft to oblivion. Especially without trace, and more especially, today with constant radio vigil, without warning or without radio reports from the victims. Can you imagine a ship, struck by meteor big enough to sink it, going down entirely without some debris being scattered about?

As a Sailor, I say, impossible for Meteor.

PRESUME MEN OF "MEDAN" LIKE ALL OTHERS, PILOTS OF AIRCRAFT, AUTOS, SHIPS, ETC, SAW "SUN BLACK-OUT" in Middle fo Day as per "*DEEP* FREEZE." *THIS* WAS AN ATTACK FOR REASONS WHICH I DREAD, IF DONE BY S-MEN, AS HERE SEEMS PROBABLY FROM DESCRIPTION.

The *New York Times*, of June 21, 1921, discusses the disappearances of three U.S. ships, with such a dearth of information that piracy was suggested. Several departments of the U.S. Government were investigating. In February, the *Carol Deering*, a five-masted schooner, had run ashore on the coast of North Carolina, in circumstances startlingly like those of the *Marie Celeste*. The crew had disappeared about the time a meal was to be served. Some bottles were later found with messages, one purporting to be from the Captain and one from the Mate, but they were contradictory, and not to plausible. The *Times* of June 22, 1921, commented on "More Ships Added to the Mystery List," and on June 24 mentioned about a dozen disappearances without a trace.

For something modern, we cite the Washington D.C. Times-Herald, of February 11, 1953"

Colombo, Ceylon, and February 10, 1953: A slightly damaged motor ship whose five-man crew vanished mysteriously at sea was towed into Colombo today, still carrying plenty of food, water and fuel.

Something else MUST HAVE BEEN MISSING.

A Meal had been prepared in the galley, ready for serving. Despite a broken mast, the *Holchu* rode well in the waters with a cargo of rice. The ship normally plies between Andaman and Nicobar Islands, near the route from Colombo to Singapore.

There was no clue as to the fate of the five Asiatic crew men known to have been aboard.

Sighted three days ago, two hundred miles south of Nicobar Islands, the derelict was boarded by crew members of the British freighter, *Ranee*. The British vessel was carrying 7,450 tons of rice from Communist China to Ceylon—the first consignment under a new trade agreement...

Note the pattern again in this modern case. The broken mast is the key. This was a motor ship, and carried no sails (presumably), but in any case was not dependent on sails. The damage aloft is a common feature of these events and somehow indicates activity above the ship, or at least above its deck.

Another training ship, British, the *Atlanta*, set sail early in 1880 from Bermuda, with 250 cadets and sailors aboard, and was not heard of again. Two things strike me: the year 1880, a year of unexplained mysteries; and the Bermuda-Caribbean area where mysterious disappearances are many.

The Danish training ship, *Kobenhoven*, sailed from Montevideo on December 14, 1928, with fifty cadets and sailors aboard...and disappeared. She was a beautiful sight, full-rigged and radiant of strength and dependability—I saw her and photographed her in the harbor of Funchal, Madeira, in November, 1927, when I was aboard the *S.S. Windsor Castle*, en route from Southampton to Capetown, What happened?

May I suggest that there seems to be a tendency for selectivity toward sailing vessels? And don't overlook the fact that this strong ship disappeared in the era of wireless and radio. As in the cases of so many airplanes, where radio operators are constantly on duty, this ship not only disappeared with trace, but met a fate so instantaneous that it was impossible to radio for help or to announce impending disaster.

> Don't know about *Kobenhoven*. May have sighted Home-ship in the Water. Making ready for ascent & so Many Highly trained eyes could not be permitted tell What they had seen. So! they are on the Greak Ark. Now? Yet feel that *Kobenhoven* is still being Held. *Intact*. Windjammer Sailors are Hard fighters & Prove good sport to the L.-Ms Later when pacified. they are good company. Make good *Space Sailors*. Deep Space is Not for every Man. only a few types can take it for Very Long. Most of these type Men *are* Sailors. used to Long Long Voyages.

On October 3, 1902, the German bark, *Freya*, cleared from Manzanillo, on the west coast of Mexico (a tropical pesthole, if ever I saw one), for Punta Arenas (see *Nature*, April 25, 1907). On October 20, she was found at sea, partly dismasted, lying on her side—nobody aboard. The anchor was still hanging from her bow, not fully shipped, a good indication that calamity had struck very soon after she left port. The date on the wall calendar, in the Captain's cabin was October 4. Weather reports showed that there had been only light winds, but upon July 5 there had been an earthquake in Mexico. It does not seem that this quake could have created a tidal wave sufficient to capsize and damage this vessel, without doing some noteworthy damage along the nearby shores. Note that she was dismasted—not the type of damage to expect from a tidal wave.

Several weeks after the disappearance of the crew of the *Freya*, another strange sea occurrence was reported. According to the log of the S.S. Fort Salisbury, the second officer, Mr. A. H. Raymer, had, October 28, 1902, in Latitude 50° 31', Longitude 4° 42' W, (which is a few hundred miles off the coast of French Equatorial Africa, in the South Atlantic), been called by the lookout, at 3:05 AM, who reported that there was a huge, dark object, bearing lights, in the sea ahead. Two lights were seen, and the steamer passed a bulk of an estimated length of 500 – 600 feet, which seemed to be slowly sinking. A mechanism of some sort, the observers thought, was making a commotion in the water. Phosphorescence was mentioned, but seems weak to account for two definite lights.

The Captain was interviewed, and said: "I can only say that Mr. Raymer is very earnest on the subject, and has, together with the lookout and helmsman, seen something in the water, of a huge nature, as specified."

> HOME-SHIP in process of taking on enough ballast to get to The Atlantic "Chain: cities

Now comes a tale in which there seems to be little chance of error or hoax. This is the sort of thing that can be certified, and it happened in the open, among a group of hard-headed people noted for clear thinking and straight-forward speech. Note how typical it is, as to details.

About seven AM, on a bright sunny morning in 1850, the people living in the vicinity of Easton's Beach, near Newport, R.I., rubbed their eyes in disbelief. They saw a large sailing vessel heading hard-in for shore and disaster. At first they believed it was an optical illusion, but as the vessel drew closer, they heard its weather-beaten sails flapping like shrouds in the stiff breeze, and they shouted: "It's the *Seabird*?" Frantically they tried to wave her, from her course. But the vessel come (sic) on.

Then miraculously, as though lifted by giant hands, the vessel majestically berthed herself on the shore, undamaged.

The watchers, most of them God-fearing fishermen, crossed themselves, and like a funeral procession, boarded the ship, their hearts filled with fear of the sight that their eyes might meet. But the only thing they did meet was a friendly mongrel, its tail wagging as it emerged from the shadows of the vessel and followed them about the dock.

A search was made for Captain John Durham and his crew, but no sign of them was found. A look of bewilderment covered the faces of the searchers when they crowded into the small galley and found coffee boiling on the stove and an elaborate breakfast laid out on the table. They also found that the crew's quarters smelled strongly of tobacco smoke, but there was no clue to the crew's whereabouts.

Should Have spilled.

Captain Durham was a rugged New Englander, not afraid of the Devil himself, and an excellent seaman. The ship's course was carefully plotted and the navigation instruments all in order. The ship's log lay open, with the last entry neatly noted: "Branton Reef, sighted." Branton Reef, a chain of rock off-shore, is only a couple miles from Newport, where the 300-ton trading boat was scheduled to dock. The *Seabird* had been on a four-month voyage and was just returning from Honduras.

The *Seabird* remained beached on the sand, the object of many curious eyes. There was mu;ch speculation of how, where, when and why the captain and his crew had disappeared—so close to home—without leaving a tangible clue.

The crew of a fishing boat, which returned two hours earlier with a catch, reported hailing the captain from a distance, and said that he waved back at them. They said that the *Seabird* then was on her course for Newport.

One fisherman speculated that a sea monster reached aboard the vessel and swallowed the crew. Friends nodded agreement, for there were reports by reputable seamen of the sightings of strange denizens of the seas, bigger than whales.

FOOD-SHIPS or Home ships

A thorough investigation by a Board of Inquiry failed to shed new light on the mystery. They reported their findings to the Captain's wife, a woman of few words. She glanced up from the Bible she as reading, and with a look of resignation, said: "'Tis the will of the Lord."

The vessel's holds were unloaded. Tropical hardwoods, pitchpine, sacks of coffee and some dyewoods were transported to her designated port of call. Then an attempt was made to refloat the ship—but the *Seabird* dug deeper into the sand.

She was *pushed* in Deeper. *(Italic by Mr. A)*

Soon after, a night gale blew itself into a violent storm. The wind howled around the neck of Rhode Island, kicking up the sea. The sea, in turn, threw mountainous waves at the *Seabird*, lifting her from her sand anchorage and tossing her about.

In the calm of the day that followed, when the sea was gentle again, the fishing folk who lived in the quiet village near Easton's Beach arose early to see what damage the storm had done. They expected to find the *Seabird* pounded to pieces, her debris littering the shore.

Instead, the vessel was gone. Like her ill-fated captain and crew she had vanished without a trace, and was never seen or heard of again! (*Fate*, April, 1953)

There are really at least two important events in this story. The disappearance of the crew can be considered one event, or certainly as one distinct phase of one event. The final disappearance of the ship is another, and perhaps the initial beaching of the boat, without damage, is something to be singled out for attention.

The crew must have abandoned the ship—or disappeared—within sight of land. In fact they were within sight of their homeport, and most likely there were fishing boats around in the area. There was no storm to complicate matters. No boat or wreckage came ashore, in spite of the nearness of land. It would be interesting if we could know whether there was damage to masts or rigging.

It seem obvious that the ship was close enough to port so that the last and final alteration in course had been made before the crew disappeared, and this fact would enable us to place a maximum limit on the distance from shore at which an "event" could have occurred. The vessel was spoken to about two hours previously, another check on distance, as well as on time.

It is one thing for a crew, to vanish without a trace; another for a stranded ship to do likewise. The two disappearances, in quick succession, create an improbability of much higher order. For our present purposes we cannot overlook the disappearance of the ship, for some wreckage should have been seen somewhere, but none was reported, although there was a storm of sufficient violence to make an experienced seagoing population expect to find the ship completely demolished.

> Experience has taught that the gear, clothes, supplies & comforting atmosphere of The ship FOR its crew are far More Desirable than a "Froze" crew with nothing but fear to guide their actions when they are "unfrozen." Of course if No one is telepathic on board, there is some difficulty; cannot sense friendliness.

The crew disappeared, suddenly, unexpectedly, completely, in daylight within sight of the home port, in good weather, and left the dog. A sailor leaving a ship casually, or leisurely, would not abandon the ship's mascot or pet!

Now—let's peer into the records a bit closer. First the crew. Do you begin to see a pattern? Complete and sudden disappearance, with no time to leave a record of any kind, from a ship under sail, in calm weather. A very high order of selectivity—so high as to demand that purposefulness be considered. A dexterity for segregation beyond the capability of natural forces in one case, much less in a long sequence of events. A disappearance almost impossible to explain except as upward.

But in this case, the disappearance of the crew is but one phase, and there is evidence of continued application of intelligence—from above. As if the force, which abducted the crew, might have some element of compassion for the owners of the cargo, the unfortunate ship was brought carefully to shore, and gently grounded, high on the sand, "miraculously, as if lifted by giant hands." What better description can there be of a ship being levitated by an intelligently directed force from above?

But even that is not all. The ship lay quietly on the beach until the undamaged cargo was unloaded. Then—disappearance. Yes, we know there was a storm, a big one. Yes, storms do queer things. But this storm, with all the delicacy of a watchmaker, removed all of a large ship...hull, spars, rigging, hatchcovers, deck rear, dunnage, small boats—everything. Took it off the beach where experienced salvors could do nothing with it...took it away, completely, suddenly finally—without trace.

Are we to keep on forever attributing this high order of dexterity and selectivity to untutored storms and whirlwinds?

In the disappearances we certainly have an intimation, however slight, of levitation...of something operating from above, with great and decisive power, and suddenness of action. Whatever it may be, it seems to favor isolated places and ships. There is without doubt, an element of our old friend: selectivity, and perhaps segregation. There is also a suggestion of ruthlessness—selective ruthlessness. There is something of evasion, or secretiveness. All are attributes of intelligence

The story is told—by C.F. Talman, in *Realm of the Air*—of a ship which was expected to arrive in New York in colonial days. One Sunday afternoon, after a violent storm she was floating in the air, every spar so clearly visible that there was no doubt about the identity of the image depicted in the sky. That was the last ever seen of her. Mr. Talman opines that this was a mirage, and that probably she had sprung a leak in the storm, and foundered before she got to port.

> *Air* too Cleared-up of Dust & etc. *after* Storm at Sea. Clouds Show Whole convoys Coming over Horizon, *Not* air. ESPECIALLY SUCH CLEARED AIR.

We're in none to good a position to argue with the learned meteorologist. It may have been a mirage. Could be; but let's peer a bit closer.

First of all, if the ship was seen so clearly, it should have been possible for seaside folk to note whether she was in distress. Nothing was said of that. No wreckage was reported, although she was admittedly close to shore, and we're familiar with that characteristic, too. Disappearance close to port, without a trace: and that's a repeating tale, along the Atlantic seaboard. Nothing was said about the image being upside down, which is a usual characteristic of mirages. And if so close as to make every spar recognizable, would not this be pretty close for a mirage? And, again, are mirages commonly noted right after a storm? Aren't they more likely in a time of stable weather when stratification of the atmosphere over water and land is possible?

It is entirely within the realm of possibility that this ship was seen in the process of being levitated!

> Tried that with XXXXX[1] & I on XXXXXXXXXXXXX[1] and he [1]XXXXXXX[1] was drunk enough to slip out of the "Freeze" & He Made them know it *in No uncertain terms.* They put us down & *Then* unfroze the crew who to this day Do Not remember of it. THEY CAN'T. (Mr. M. was Chief Mate, "Hatteras" 1943)
>
> Perhaps they detected "FIELD" Activity of NAVY D-E WHICH WAS CLOSE BY, (BEFORE) TESTING AN *INVISIBILITY* EXPIERIMENTAL "gadget."

Teleportation or Kidnapping?

As sheer entertainment, little compares with the intrigue of the countless reports, verified, of the strange and instantaneous movement of persons from one place to another—distances of many many, miles.

---

[1] Crossed out by Jemi

But to serve our ends, we must look again for selectivity and, if possible, some indication of motive. Perhaps we should ascribe these phenomena to caprices of space inhabitants. On the other hand, there may be an element of error involved. Perhaps, for some inexplicable reasons, the UFO's made choices for capture or kidnapping and <ins>then discovered</ins>, suddenly, <ins>that their choice had not been a wise one.</ins> From what we have already discovered, as to speed of movements and the vast areas which can be covered. It is not at all unlikely that the pickup was made, the error discovered, and the kidnapped set down again—but the UFO has traveled such a great distance that it does not realize that it is not putting the object (person) down in relatively the same place! But if they are that intelligent they'd know they weren't putting the object (person) down in the same place. Perhaps so—but why would they care?

> A Malaria infested person. Not Desirable to
> L-Ms It is a Deadly fearful Plage to them.
> This Man *May* have Had it & also for this reason
> was Let go. Quien Sabes?

Bear these thoughts in mind as we review our first case of teleportation.

On the morning of October 25, 1593, relates Don Luis Gonzales Obregon, in Las Calles de Mexico, a soldier suddenly appeared in the Plaza Mayor of Mexico City; a soldier dressed in the uniform of the regiment which at that moment was guarding the walled citadel of Manila, in the Philippine Islands.

With the soldier's strange appearance came the rumor that his Excellency, Gomez Peres Dasmartinas, Governor of the Philippines, was dead. A preposterous rumor, of course! But one that spread through the city like wildfire.

Puzzled as to how the soldier could have traveled more than nine thousand miles without so much as soiling his uniform, the authorities nevertheless jailed him as a deserter from the Philippines regiment.

Weeks passed while the soldier languished in prison; the long slow weeks necessary for new to travel by sailing ship from the Philippines to Acapulco, then by messenger across the sky-high mountains and into the valley of Mexico.

Suddenly, Mexico City was quaking with news. His Excellency, the Governor of the Philippines was dead, murdered by a mutinous Chinese crew off Punta de Azufre shortly after he had left his island home on a military expedition against the Moluccas! Moreover, he had been murdered on the very day the Philippine soldier had appeared in the Plaza of Mexico City.

The Holy Tribunal of the Inquisition took charge of the soldier. He could not tell them how he had been transported from Manila to Mexico. Only that it had been "in less time than it takes a cock to crow." Nor could he tell them how it had come to pass that Mexico City was buzzing with the news of the Governor's death, even before it was known in Manila.

> Time of battle, = each inch of the way.

At order of the Holy Tribunal, the soldier was returned to the Philippines for further investigation into the mysterious matter. Irrefutable witnesses came forward to swear that the soldier had been on duty in the Island City on the night of October 24; just as it had been proved beyond doubt that on the following morning he had been apprehended in the Plaza of Mexico City, more than nine thousand miles away.

> "Froze" or Semi-Froze, time not recognized.

A Legend? Not according to the records of the chroniclers of the Order of San Augustin and the order of Santo Domingo. Not according to Dr. Antonio de Morga, high justice of the criminal court of the Royal Audiencia of New Spain, in his Sucesos do las Islas Filipinas.

This case of this peripatetic soldier is one where we can tie down both ends of a teleportation

> peripatetic my eye, He fought Like a Mad-Man
> & could not be taken aboard, so he was Let-down.
> They kept his rifle, though

axis, if indeed it is teleportation. We can find unexplained disappearances and appearances, but, offhand, we don't know of others just like this one. And t seems as though there may be several debatable disappearances. But what are you going to do with apports, or appearances? It seems to me that they are a sort of second order phenomenon, unless they can be connected somehow with corresponding disappearances, some place. Shall we settle for a kidnapping by UFO's?

"Help, help! It's got me!" This pitiful plea ending in a piercing scream brought friends running to Oliver Lerch's home, into the bright moonlit night. But he was not to be seen, although they could hear his voice, growing fainter, calling for help from a hundred feet or more above their heads. "Help me, help..."

Oliver Lerch was never seen again on the face of this earth; and thus was recorded one of the most amazing disappearances ever to confront our modern age—the disappearance of a man into thin air!

The facts of the case are clearly written down for everyone to see in the police records of South Bend, Indiana, and have been attested to by level-headed persons not given to delusions, mass hysteria or suggestion. These witnesses include lawyers; Reverend Samuel Mallelieu, the local Methodist minister; and responsible citizens who actually witnessed the weird disappearance.

The impossible happened on the farm of Tom Lerch, Christmas Eve, 1890, in a community of over 100,000 people—by no means an ignorant backwoods settlement filled with limitless superstition.

The Lerch farm stood (and still does) on the outskirts of South Bend, an ordinary farmhouse with the roof sweeping low over the entire building and no attic—no nook or crevice which could conceal a dead body.

Tom Lerch was a stern father who demanded absolute obedience from his two sons; 23 year old Jim, and especially 20 year old Oliver; however, there was nothing to indicate that he was unkind to the boys.

The house was the scene of a merry Christmas party, and young Oliver was in good spirits as he sang with his girl, pretty Lillian Hirach, daughter of a Chicago attorney, a friend of his father's who was also a guest. Jim had his attention also arrested by a young lady whom he later married. Altogether, perhaps twenty people were gathered around the piano, singing hymns and gay holiday songs. Nothing foretold of the grim tragedy which was to come.

Outside, the night was still and quiet. After a day of dimness and snowfall, the winds shifted and the clouds faded away. Now the moon shone down on a countryside charmingly beautiful with glistened snow. Around 10:00, Oliver's mother, who was preparing supper, called to him to fetch some water from the well. He smiled and excused himself from Miss Hirsch. He walked from the living room and put on his coat, cap and gloves. Then he went out into the calm night. That was the last time any person saw him on this earth.

Some minutes later, perhaps five, a horrible cry for help, so terrifying that it could be heard above the singing, split the serenity of the happy occasion. For a second the group in the house froze, looking at each other in astonishment; then with Tom Lerch in the lead they dashed out into the night. The cry sounded again, only this time it was fainter.

"Help, help... It's got me..." Oliver's terror-stricken voice called again, this time from a position above their heads.

With panic in their hearts, some of the people dashed back into the house, while the others continued to call to the voice above their heads which was still moaning: "Help me...Help..." Anxiously they continued to scan the moonlit sky, but there was nothing to be seen; only the voice could be heard: "Help me, help..."

It is highly possible that the glare from the lights of the house may, to a limited extent, have affected the visibility of the would-be rescuers. Then too, the trees and bushes situated near the house may have deflected the apparent direction of the pleading voice. But for almost five minutes the voice continued to call. Sometimes it was loud, then soft, now close at hand, now feeble and far away—but always from the sky, never on the ground level.

Neighbors were called and a frantic search was begun which covered the entire yard, the farm buildings, the roof and chimney of the house, and even the basement. Men got ladders and climbed in trees, poked in the snow, and even lowered the lantern down the well. Oliver could not be found.

At 10:00, the horror of the ghastly situation became all the more apparent when eight or nine people in the yard heard the voice calling to them from above their heads. Once more it uttered a soul-tingling plea for help. After that, the voice was never heard again.

The search was continued with renewed effort, the members not daring to venture an opinion as to what weird, unnatural event was taking place. Then it was noticed the Oliver's tracks had stopped about 225 feet from the house, about half the distance to the well; beyond these tracks the snow was undisturbed. There was no sign of struggle, nothing to indicate that a fracas of nature had occurred. At the end of the tracks, halfway between the house and the well, lay an abandoned bucket. Oliver had left the house with two. Where was the other one?

The search for Oliver continued all night and all the next day, without revealing the slightest clue as to his whereabouts.

Some witnesses disagreed as to the exact words called out by Oliver. Some swore he called "It's got me." Others were just as dogmatic and claimed he screamed: "They've got me!"

> Said both, first "Its" when attractor hit Him
> & upon sight of L-M on receiving-Port, said
> "They"

Different theories were advanced to the effect that an eagle might have carried him off. But who ever heard of an eagle carrying off a grown man? And would an eagle, even if it could do so, hover over the scene for half an hour, holding on to its victim? What about the missing bucket? Would Oliver, thus lifted up into the sky, still retain his hold on a bucket? Would he not drop it and use both hands in the struggle?

For a time it was thought that the grapnel of a balloon had carried off the man. This, however, was quickly disproved. Due to weather conditions no balloon had ascended that day, anywhere.

Another theory holds that Oliver was murdered; that the slayer crept up behind his unsuspecting victim as he went to the well, seizing the bucket and killing him with it. One of the guests at the Lerch farm that night, driven mad with jealousy over the attentions Oliver was giving to Lillian Hirsch, may have been a amateur ventriloquist. Did he murder Oliver and conceal his body somewhere? If so, how did he manage it? The entire farm was searched. Aided by the darkness, did this guest simulate Olivers' voice and "throw" it into the air, thereby confusing the other startled guests? Or was Oliver Lerch, by some unknown trick of nature, sucked into another dimension? (*Fate*, September, 1950)

As a corollary to the disappearance of Oliver Lerch, a Mr. H.M. Cranmer of Hammersley Fork, Pennsylvania, Wrote a letter tot he editor of *Fate* Magazine which we reproduce in part.

An event similar to the strange disappearance of Oliver Lerch happened here, about twenty-five years earlier. (This would make it around 1865).

It was late in summer when a group of men gathered here for the winter work of cutting pine. Just after dark a dozen men finished their supper at the hotel kept by Uriah Hammersley, and seated themselves on the hotel porch to enjoy their after-dinner smoke.

PO-Great, WANA=FISH (NATICK LINGO)

As they sat talking, they noticed a drunken man—a stranger no one had ever seen before—staggering along the road in front of the hotel. The stranger, cursing to himself as drunks often do, passed the hotel without stopping, and continued down the road. After he had gone about two hundred yards, he suddenly began to shout angrily, "damn you, let me go!"

The men from the hotel porch ran down to the spot, and Kelleys who lived on a farm an equal distance below—came running from the opposite direction. The stranger was nowhere to be seen, but everyone could hear him still shouting, "damn you, let me go," from overhead. His voice got fainter and fainter and finally stopped.

No more drunks will be picked up after Ole Potter. His breath killed two.

The dust in the road was several inches thick and the stranger's boot tracks were plainly visible up to the spot where they abruptly ended. On one side of the road was Kelley's cornfield – no tracks could be found in it. On the other side was a creek forty feet away, with a sandbar thirty feet wide. No tracks were found in the sand.

In the crowd there were men who could track deer or bear all day on bare ground, but not one of them could, or even did, find a trace of the missing man!

PO=*Great*, MOLA=*BIRD* (NATICK)

Up to 100 years ago the Indians stoutly maintained that the "thunderbird" – a bird that could carry a full grown deer or a man – still existed in the United States. In Maine the Indians called it "Pomola."

"Bird"= Primitive Description

Sometime after 1500 AD, the Indians killed two "thunderbirds" along the Mississippi River, and carved and painted them, life size, on rocks on the Illinois side. One of the carvings was destroyed by a stone quarry but the other one is still there. The Indians along the upper Mississippi called the bird "Piazzi"—meaning destroyer.

In translating "thunderbird" from the Indian languages, the word "eagle" was used. The average American, if he saw a gigantic bird carry off a calf, would be afraid to tell of it, because he would know that no one would believe him. Or, if a pilot saw one, who would believe his story of a bird with a 25 or 30 foot wingspread?

> S-M SHIPS-THUNDERBIRDS *or* DISABLED L-M SCOUT ship. Both Made considerable Noise, old type ships Made Much Noise. Heard at a certain WAVE distance.

Ed: The following has no obvious reference or necessary position.
> FATHER, AVIATOR, DIPLOMAT, SAILOR, SOLDIER, & LAWYER & common-Men *ALL* Were Necessary to L-Ms SCRUTINY OF "OUR" *TOO RAPIDLY* GROWING CULTURE.

> No Man Wearing Hob-Nail boots or Cleats on shoes has ever been know to have been "stolen". Neither a Man in a *cave*, under earth.

> When I am hunting in Woodland: I make My Mind a BLANK & *always* get animals at *Close* range. HOL-M can quiet his Mind thusly. So it is that all animals are silent when they are near.

> If a Man Can KEEP His Mind as a Lifeless clod, He *can* escape Detection from the L-Ms *or* S-Ms *in this way*. They "feel" you out, in the country, in Cities Listen to Birds. IF BIRDS DON'T SING, BE READY.

> FURTHER PROOF, BOOKLET, LAO TZU, "THE WAY OF LIFE" IS "A MENTOR BOOD, BY R.B. BLAKNEY, PAGE 27, bottom.

I am interested in Mr. Cranmer's comments about the Indians and the thunderbird. Has there ever been a better description of a noisily-powered flying machine? And for the word "Piazzi" meaning destroyer, is not that fairly descriptive as well?

> See full grown, Mummiefied "Little –Man" in Vault in Casper, Wyo. *DO NOT TOUCH.*

According to the *Chicago Tribune*, of January 5, 1900, there disappeared a young chap named Sherman Church. It seems that Mr. Church was employed in the August Mills in Battle Creek at the time. He was seated in the company's office, when he arose and ran into the mill. He has not been seen since. The mill was almost taken apart by searchers, and the river, woods and country were scoured, but to no avail. Nobody saw Church leave town, nor was there any known reason for his leaving.

What can we make of that one? If somebody (or something) desired to teleport Mr. Church, it seems that the teleportation could just as well have taken him right out of his seat. So—what impelled him to run out of the offices? Did "something" want him to go outside where he could be lifted...?

> Have resisted this of them. Myself. "Telepathic control" only resisted by another telepath. Darn tough on me, I am only partly telepathic but can "set" call-barriers. If ever see L.-M swimming about again, Ill grab him.

This account, from the *London Sunday Express*, September 21, and 28, 1924, bears careful consideration. On July 24, 1924, at a time of Arab hostility, Flight Lieutenant, W.T.Day, and Pilot Officer, D.R.Stewart, were sent from British Headquarters upon an ordinary reconnaissance flight over a desert in

Mesopotamia. According to scheduled flight plan they would not be absent more than a few hours. The men did not return, and they were searched for. The plane was soon found, easily spotted in the desert. Why it should have landed was the problem. "There was some petrol in the tank. There was nothing wrong with the craft. It was, in fact, flown back to the aerodrome." But the men were missing. "So far as can be ascertained, they encountered no meteorological conditions which might have forced them to land." There were no marks to indicate that the plane had been shot at.

In the sand around the plane were seen footprints of Day and Stewart. "They were traced, side by side, for some forty yards from the machine. Then, as suddenly as if they had come to the brink of a cliff, the marks ended."

The landing of the plane was unaccountable. But, accepting that as a minor mystery, the suggested explanation of the abrupt ending of the footprints was that Day and Stewart had been captured by hostile Bedouins, who had brushed away all trails in the sand, starting from a point forty yards from the plane. But hostile Bedouins could not be thought of brushing indefinitely and a search was made for a renewal of traces.

Airplanes, armored cars, and mounted police searched. Rewards were offered. Tribal patrols searched unceasingly for four days. Nowhere beyond the point in the sand where the tracks ended abruptly were other tracks to be found.

What is there about that account that would lead you to suspect a hoax, a mistake, or an error? I do not see anything, and if there is I would be grateful for being put straight. So far as I can see, these two men really did disappear—at the end of their tracks...in a barren desert. Oliver Lerch disappeared the same way. He left a bucket. These sturdy Britishers, two of them, mind you, walking side by side, left a plane. I have known some British airmen. They would not give up without a struggle, unless they were overpowered instantly and unexpectedly—or were snatched up off the ground! Have you ever tried to brush tracks out of the sand without leaving more disturbance than you obliterated?

> **Came to L-M Ship hovering a few feet off ground. LMs wanted to know about their Mode of flight, so brought them aboard. Their Progeny Proved to be of good Stock & are highly regarded undersea Explorers or Soverning "Men".**
>
> **L-Ms WERE IN STASIS, THUS NOT VISIBLE.**

I suggest that these two men were abducted by some levitating power which suddenly pulled them off the ground after compelling them to land and walk away from their plane to a point where they could be levitated without injury to themselves or damage to the plane.

On November 25, 1809, Benjamin Bathurst, returning from Vienna, where he had been a representative of the British Government, stopped in the small town of Perleberg, Germany. In the presence of his valet and secretary he was examining the horses which were to take his coach further along its way to England. Under observation, he walked around to the other side of the horses—and vanished!

> **FELT L-M PRESENCE BY PSI, WAS SUSPICIOUS BUT DID NOT KNOW OF WHAT. He was Indignant, became good sport & was well Liked y al L-M's.**

Teleportation or kidnapping?

Kaspar Hauser entered the town of Nuremberg, Germany, on Whit-Monday, May 1828. Most accounts agree that he had poor control of his legs as he walked. About sixteen or seventeen years old, he knew nothing at all of the accoutrements of civilized living, even trying to pick up the flame of a candle. Either he suffered from almost complete amnesia, or practically his entire life had been spent in solitary confinement or its equivalent. Nobody knows to this day where Kaspar came from. Many suspect imposture but that doesn't fit the known circumstances. In view of some of our modern knowledge of handling prisoners, he may have been subjected to brain-washing. There may be no connection at all for us, in the advent of Kaspar Hauser. We merely mention that he suddenly appeared, full grown, at the gates of Nuremberg, but without mentality enough to have arrived there by his own volition. ??? (Red is A & B)

Could he have been dropped from a space ship?

> Kaspar & No Gravity were a problem. His Legs were weak from Lack of it.
>
> Kaspar could talk a complete Language BUT None of Germanys Best Linguists could define it.
> He DID Not Lack Mentality, Worried, Had kids
> Spoke Good "Kraut" after a While.

Not too long ago I had some correspondence with R. DeWitt Miller, author of *Forgotten Mysteries*, and, some time back, the contributor of a long series on the same subject in *Coronet*. Mr. Miller is devoted to the investigation of all types of paranormal events, and especially the sort of thing we have been discussing here. When I mentioned Oliver Lerch's case to him, Mr. Miller expressed the opinion that the Lerch story might have had the same origin of that of David Lang. Certainly we must concede an element of parallelism in the various accounts of sudden disappearances. Miller sent me the following story, which bore the pencilled note that there is an affidavit and the story is said to be essentially identical with the disposition. This is it:

On September 23, 1880 (again those incredible 1880's), Land, a farmer and prominent land owner living near Gallatin, Tennessee, returned home from a business trip. After greeting his family, he started across an eight-acre field to inspect his blooded horses.

While he was walking across the field his wife and two children saw a buggy approach along the road, and stop. In the buggy were "Judge" Peck, a local attorney, and a friend. When he saw Lang crossing the field, Peck stopped his buggy and signaled the farmer to return to his house.

There, in full view of five persons—Lang's wife and two children, Peck and his friend—Lang vanished in a field which was devoid of trees, boulders, or any sort of cover; a field covered with grass and without caves, bogs, abandoned wells, or other chasms. In fact, a later geological survey showed this entire field was underlayed at a depth of a few feet with a solid stratum of limestone.

The press of Tennessee was filled for months with stories about the "Lang Disappearance." There were searches -- made immediately following Lang's vanishing and for months afterwards.

Bloodhounds were used. Detectives were called in. The story reached Vienna, and a Dr. Hern stated that: "there are vortices (in the so-called physical world) through which a man might vanish." Ambrose Bierce wrote a fictionalized version of the incident. The bloodhounds, the detectives and the theorists produced nothing.

> VORTICES, NODES, DEAD SPOTS "traps," = *all the same things*.

The case has been the subject of endless speculation. But no one has ever found a trace of David Lang. And there remains only the affidavit of Lang's daughter and the statements of the the other witnesses that Lang simply vanished while crossing an open field.

E=MC HERE APPLIED PROOF SHOWN BY USE OF converter-FEILED (sic) in ACTION? HARMLESS

And so we are faced with the problem of explaining these phenomena. Are they cases in which the psyche of the individual is such that he can control his movement and body in time and space? If so, why does he not return?

I submit that capture by a space contraption, for purposes beyond our ken, is the only truly satisfactory answer. '

Lang did XXX dematieralize (sic) XXXXXXX, swept up *so quick*, XXXXXXXXXXXX.[1] The same for Nurd, Plants, Water, Rocks, Etc. "Kaspar" *was* a problem, a result of cross-breeding that for once falied. He had no Gills & grew Much too Large for his *old* environment. He *Had* to be dumped.

L-Ms or LEMURIAN-MUANIANS OR LITTLE-MEN! WERE FORCED BY THEIR SIZE & BY THE FACT OF THEIR GILLS TO DIG DEEP HOLES IN ROCK, WHERE, NOT ONLY COULD TITANIC EDIFICES BE RAISED, WELDED, CUT & SCULPTED TO their Leaders Honor but Where they could Live with GRAVITY. WATER WAS TO FILL THE QUARRY HOLES & WATER IS THE BEST NATURAL GRAVITY NEUTRALIZER KNOWN TO MAMMALS OR FISH. Here they could sleep & Rest & be More acclimated to Gravity, While they also built temples in other terrestrial places,or XXXX-XXXXX XXXXXXXXXXXXXXXX[2] so the plan was to have been, S-MEN BROKE IT ALL UP.

---

[1] Italic and three markouts by Mr. A
[2] Markouts by Mr. B

LEVITATION

It is not within the scope of this book so show that a civilization of single origin covered this planet some tens of thousands of years ago – perhaps hundreds of thousands.

Such a case can be made, without too much difficulty, in spite of the anti-Atlantians who have a phobia against it; and we can show that there have been two – at least two—principle waves of civilization. The first can be said, roughly, to be antediluvian and the second postdiluvian, speaking in general terms and putting the Flood, or its equivalent, far enough back in history so as to coincide with the cataclysm which caused it.

All of the centers of civilization and cultural renaissance recognized by present-day anthropologists – India, Peru, Yucatan, Egypt, Babylonia, Greece, China, Rome, England and others – are but the reviving remnants of an empire and civilization which colonized the world a hundred thousand years ago. They area all "parts," or nuclei, in one great renaissance which has been taking place for, roughly, six to ten thousand years. In it are some traces of the archaic, original, master culture, and, perhaps through India, Tibet, Egypt and Middle America, there are some tenuous links between our immature revival and the parent past. These traces are mostly in the form of stone works, and some glyphs, of a singular nature, with a very few written records existing mostly in the Orient, and particularly in southern Asia.

LEFT UNAVOIDABLY IN "GREAT WAR.

Above is true, Jemi They are Written about
in Many Writings, So old, as to be Nulified
by antiquity.

All of this is anathema to conventional science, archaeology and anthropology especially, for organized science has set up a pattern which covers human growth in broad general terms, and has accepted some rigidly restricting tenets which limit original thinking and shut out much that is obvious. While these general assumptions of science are largely proven by observation and deduction, they are only proven up to a point. Beyond that point there are the "erratics": little annoying things, events, or artifacts, which stubbornly refuse to fit into the pattern, and which are sturdily disregarded in the interest of maintaining a working hypothesis acceptable to science in its current state of thinking.

A THORN IN AN OSTRICHES HEAD, PAINS SO
CONTINUALLY THAT IT HIDE IT IN THE SAND,
YET IT PAINS IT STILL, ED?

In addition to all this there is the refusal to acknowledge evidence antedating the current subwave which extends back only about three thousand to eight thousand years, and that far only in Egypt and south Asia. All data in conflict with this basic assumption are rejected by definition.

Many of the so-called erratics cease to be erratics by the simple expedient of admitting the real antiquity of human culture upon the earth. Most of the perpetual squabble over whether Asians settled America, or American colonized Asia, are painlessly dissolved by merely extending the time scale back a few thousand years—and, perhaps, accepting a new working theory to the effect that all present cultures are traceable to a common origin.

ED: The following has no obvious reference or necessary position.
I do Not know much about The Ancient L-M'
Colonies.

Aside from written records, to be discussed later, which establish mechanical flight at a remote time of maybe 70,000 to 200,000 years ago, we concern ourselves at the moment only with the gigantic stone masonry which remains in almost all parts of the world. Certain characteristics of some of the stone work bespeak origin in a single, widespread civilization, highly developed in some way, but not mechanical in the same sense as ours of today. We will presently limit ourselves to one phase only: the massive size and weight of the various monoliths. The manner or method of their carving is material for another report, but it can be confidently said that the First Civilization had simple and effective methods of working and moving stone which are unused today, and which were more effective than anything which we of the Second Civilization have developed. (red is A & b)

   Cut with *over sized* Measure-Marker

   on All-Power, i.e. *cutter*

In many areas we find evidence of stone blocks of unbelievable weight being quarried, more or less casually moved considerable distances, then lifted into place. This common factor connects pre-Inca Peru with Easter Island in a startling and undeniable way, and seems to tie in the Middle East, the Orient, Africa, and maybe Polynesia. Many investigators and thinkers have proposed methods for moving these quarried and dressed blocks. All of the proposals are based on application of such simple

   Block & tackle unknown to those peopole (sic)
   Mech. Lifting, thusly Not feasable,

   (DON'T KNOW)

present day engineering equipment as block-and tackle or sand ramps. The great pyramids, consisting of hundreds of thousands of huge stone blocks, are thought by some to have been erected by thousands of slaves toiling up long ramps of sand to bring these gigantic masses from the Nile. Flotation has been considered. No suggestions have been made which really fit all cases, and some of the submissions are so cumbersome and inadequate as to seem ridiculous.

Let's take a look at some of these great monoliths, and note their size, their geographical distributions, and, where possible, something of their age and any other details which stand out.

One such example is that of Sacsahuaman Fortress, in the High Andes of Peru, above the ancient Inca, and pre-Inca city of Cuzco. There are several eras of civilization represented in the poorly understood archaeological remains at, and near, Cuzco. The latest, aside from the present Spanish-Indian population, are the Inca ruins, most of which were in use at the time of the iniquitous Spanish conquest. The Incas were also using some structures which were inherited from their predecessors, and this has led to some confusion, because practically all other ruins in the neighborhood have been vaguely and uncertainly classified as "pre-Incan."

This is a rather too comprehensive term, and the pre-Inca remains should be divided into those ruins which were immediately pre-Inca, and those which had their creation remote in time; some of which were skillfully constructed before the mountains were raised to their present high level -- certainly before glaciation.

The massive work of Sacsahuaman seems to be intermediate between the extremely old and the more immediately pre-Inca, and may very well be the initial works of those people who were last in the area before the Incas, and whose works the Incas inherited and used.

   Rope of that day was so crude as to even
   be negligible, Lacked strength.

   L-M's Build this before deciding to go Undersea. They were too Puny to Withstand an attack

> such as the one received in the Great Bombardment prior to building it.
>
> Inca & Mayan peoples (sic) Did NOT know the use of the Wheel in any shape, form or size, at all. SO THEY COULD *NOT* HAVE MOVED SUCH HUGE MASSES.
>
> Not so, Jemi, one by one they were Lifted & only one face was "matched" at a time, using FORCE-GRIPS OR THE STRONG "FREEZE" SIMPLY MAKING SHIP TO MOVE BACK & FORTH each thusly NOW *appears* to have been ground between each, which, as you know & see could Not work for the force-freeze Doesn't Grip two Huge ones AND RUB them. If two were "Gripped" BOTH Would be forced to Move with the ship, back & forth, *simultaneously*, thus roughness would BE between the two Held. HOWEVER, if these *HUGE* STONE BLOCKS WERE FORCE CUT BY FORCE-CUTTERS, THEN, END TO END, SIDE FOR SIDE THEY WOULD "MATCH" PERFECTLY WHEN CUT FROM SAME QUARRY. BOTH WAYS WERE USED. A SHORTCUT *LATER USED* WAS ROCK-WELDING.
>
> ROCK-WELDING, IE. MOLECULAR-ELECTRONIC-FIELD BLENDING Was used as the signs of the Great War approached as an Emergency speed-up Measure.

The Fortress (so-called by archaeologists, who admit no types of building other than religious, military, and occasionally residential) of Sacsahuaman is on a mountain top overlooking modern Cuzco. It is noteworthy as one of the earliest works showing the construction of walls by grinding and fitting stones, in situ. These walls are also noted for the very large stones which make up the lower of three tiers, and it is these in which we are more interested. (See *Fate*, Vol. II, No. 1, and *American Anthropologist*, 1936.)

The stones making up the corners of the reentrant angles, of this lower tier, appear to be a dark basalt; heavy, hard, and rugged. They are so large that they dwarf a man on horseback standing beside them. Some of them are about twelve feet square at the base, and eighteen to twenty feet high. They are estimated to weigh about two hundred tons each. Other stones in the same walls range from small ones of only a few hundred pounds, through continuous gradations up to the largest. All of them were crudely rough quarried, and were then ground into their designated niches in the structure by pushing them back and forth, in situ, until they fitted so closely, completely and accurately that a knife blade cannot be inserted between them. This is a logical and practical shortcut to effective stone fitting which we have not equaled in modern engineering.

(It is interesting to note in passing, however, that we use this method in what is probably our operation of highest accuracy and precision: lens and mirror grinding for astronomical telescopes. No substitute has been found for this system of grinding pieces of glass together to obtain perfect curvature, and there is no basic difference in the two operations.)

However, there are some startling inferences in the size and mass of the stones. To place the largest of these corner stones in place, so that others could be worked to fit them, required tremendous force. It is unimaginable that sufficient hand labor and crude tackle could be massed around them so that they could be moved and handled.

The intermediate sizes, some to them weighing ten, twenty, and forty tons, or more, had to be picked up, put approximately into place, and pushed back and forth until they ground themselves into their individually fitting contours. This was no mean chore. It is inferred that means of handling must have existed which made it easy, or at any rate possible, to swing these stones up and around, and to shove them to and fro, against terrific friction, while pinched between their adjacent neighbors. Such power would tax any modern machine or power plant and require an installation of generating equipment sufficient to run a city. It seems plainly obvious that some other source of power existed.

ALUMINUM, NON-MAGNETIC METAL HAS & IS NOW BEING MADE TO "FLOAT" IN A FORCE-FIELD, 1948 cyclotron, 2000 WATTS. NEW YORK STATE.

It may be that this tremendous power was limited in its application to articles of stone texture only, but this is a little doubtful. Or, perhaps it was limited to nonmagnetic materials in general. Such a limitation would have sidetracked the development of a mechanized culture such as ours of this day, and would partly account for the strange fact that almost all relics of the profound past are non-metallic. It does seem possible that the usefulness of that power, whatever it was, may have been limited by its very nature and that it was never developed along industrial lines because of this limitation and even, perhaps, because of a basic difference in values. This writer cannot see his way to believing that such a power was electrical, magnetic, calorific, or strictly mechanical, else it would have led to industrial developments leaving at least a few traces.

The ruins of Baalbek lie to the northeast of Beirut, between the eastern end of the Mediterranean Sea and the northern end of the Syrian Desert. The ruins of Baalbek are the most majestic and the most notable of the earth's ancient structures. They have caused more speculation among scientists generally, and archaeologists in particular, than any other group of ruins on earth, for it is usually conceded that there has never been found a single vestige of information intimating or showing when, or by what people, they were created. I have several descriptions of these ruins before me. The one of all others which, it seems to me, would appeal to the layman, as strongly as to the scientist is Mark Twain's, and as this book is written for the people, his description is the one I have selected to use:

At eleven o'clock our eyes fell upon the walls and columns of Baalbek, a notable ruin, whose history is a sealed book. It has stood there for thousands of years, the wonder and admiration of travelers. Who built it is a question that may never be answered. One thing is sure though, such grandeur of design, and such grace of execution as one sees in the temples of Baalbek, have not been equaled or even approached in any other work of man's hands that has ever been built within the last twenty centuries.

The great Temple of the Sun, the Temple of Jupiter, and the several smaller temples are clustered together in the midst of these Syrian villages miserably dirty. They look strange enough in such plebian company. These temples are built upon massive sub-structures that might support a world almost. The material used is blocks of stone as large as an omnibus, very few of them are smaller than a carpenter's tool chest. These structures are traversed by tunnels of masonry through which a train of cars might pass. With such foundations as these it is little wonder that Baalbek has lasted so long.

The temple of the Sun is nearly 300 feet long and 160 feet wide. It has 54 columns around it, but only six are standing now; the others lie broken at its base, a confused and picturesque mass. Corinthian capitals and entablatures, and six more shapely columns do not exist. These columns and their entablatures together are ninety feet high, a prodigious altitude for shafts of stone to reach, and yet one only thinks of their beauty and symmetry when looking at them. The pillars look slender and delicate, the entablatures with their elaborate sculpture look like rich stucco work, but when gazed aloft until your eyes are weary you glance at the great fragments of pillars among which you are not standing and find that they are eight feet thick, and with them lie beautiful capitals (?) apparently as large as a small cottage, and also single slabs of stone superbly sculptured that are four or five feet thick and would completely cover the floor of any ordinary parlor.

**DON'T KNOW, SURELY NOT WRITING L-Ms WERE
& ARE ALL TELE-PATHS**

The temple of Jupiter is a smaller ruin than the one I have just been speaking of, and yet it is immense. It is in a tolerable state of preservation. One of nine columns stands almost uninjured. They are 65 feet high and support a sort of porch or roof. This porch roof is composed of tremendous slabs of stone which are so finely sculptured on the undersides that the work looks like fresco from below. One or two of the slabs that lay around me were no larger than those above my head. Within the temple the ornamentation was elaborate and colossal. What a wonder of architectural beauty and grandeur this edifice must have been when it was new and what a noble picture it, and its stellar companion, with the chaos of mighty fragments scattered around them made in the moonlight.

And yet, these sculptured blocks are trifles in size compared with the rough-hewn stones that form the side verandah, or platform which surrounds the great temple. One stretch of that platform composed of only three stones is nearly 300 feet in length. They are thirteen feet square, two of them are each 64 feet and a third 69 feet long. They are built into the massive wall twenty feet above the ground.

We went to the quarry from whence these stones of Baalbek were taken. It was a quarter of a mile off, down-hill. In a pit lay the mate of the largest stone in the ruins. It lay there just as the giants of the old forgotten time left it when they were called hence; to remain for thousands of years an eloquent rebuke to such as are prone to think slightingly of the men who have lived before them. This enormous block lies there squared and ready for the builder's hands, a solid mass 14 feet by 17 feet wide and 70 feet long.

One could use the same words almost to describe the massive unfinished stone statues left in the quarries on Easter Island. Something sudden terminated the work of Easter Island and Baalbek. I do not say that it was the very same something, but the epoch is certainly of the same order of time and there are elements in common —Easter Island, Peru, Baalbek, Egypt — all with screaming evidence of sudden overwhelming disaster happening to a race of beings who handled rocks weighing hundreds and hundreds of tons.

**THEY SHOULD SEE THE "ATLANTIC CHAIN" CITIES
GREAT UNDERSEA METROPOLISES.**

There is little in Baalbek, Easter Island, Peru, or Egypt to show a gradual development of so advanced a culture or civilization: they, or at least their megalithic stone work, appear to have been ready-made, as though a colony was set up directly, complete, a going concern. In Peru it appears that the levitator, or power plant, was lost. In Baalbek it has been shown that the work was never completed and the largest stone still lies in the quarry. In Easter Island a similar great stone, a statue, still lies in the quarry where it was being sculptured, in a depression from which great power manipulation would be required to move it. In both cases work stopped suddenly, and apparently the "force-lift" for the 1,200 ton stones was lost, somehow.

**THE BOMBARDMENT, OF WHICH THE EAST COAST
SHOWS GOOD SIGNS, even yet. THE GRAND BANK,
Circular swamps & etc.**

**Largest Would Have been cut into regular building
sizes or else it Had a twin to be Marched to.**

It seems necessary to conclude that while massive stone work was in progress all over the world (for we have to include India, Tibet, Polynesia, etc.), sources of power were limited in number, and available only to a few important projects. It seems that such levitators disappeared suddenly and unexpectedly. Where to?

They Went Home.

It is further possible that maybe there was only one machine available which could lift the greatest of weights, and that it was mobile and used first in one part of the world and then another.

What kind of power was this levitation agency? How did it work? If through our crude mechanical principles of ropes, cables, blocks and tackles, how did the ancients get enough rope on a 1,200-ton block to take the strain of lifting it, and how shift the position of the prime mover? Rocks are not magnetic. Does flotation offer a complete answer for lifting the big ones into place? Sand ramps do not seem suitable.

THESE PROVED INADEQUETE

THEORY.

TRUE. "PRIME-MOVER" Caused GRAV. NODE OR MINOR STRENETH (sic) or Major. thus Gravity didn't exist upon these stones

I have used the word "levitation" as a substitute for power or force. I have suggested that flying saucers used some means of reacting with the gravitational field. In this way they could apply accelerations or lifting forces to all particles of a body, inside and outside, simultaneously, and not through external force applied by pressure, or harness, to the surface only. I believe that this same, or a similar force was used to move stones in very ancient times. I believe the source of this lifting or levitating power was lost suddenly.

All Comes under one Principle, just applied diff.

We believe, in short, that this lifting engine was a space ship, probably of vast proportions; that it brought colonists to various parts of the earth, probably from other terrestrial areas; and that it supplied the heavy lift power for erecting great stone works; and that it was suddenly destroyed or taken away. Such a hypothesis would underwrite all of the movements of stone over which archaeologists and engineers have puzzled.

We believe Mu to have existed as a world civilization, hoary with age, replete with knowledge or astronomy and physics in an almost unbelievably remote past; that this entire civilization was wiped out with great, and sudden, violence, leaving very little trace. Whatever we have of culture development today

Yet, Mu *has* Left some traces, artifacts and Highly civilized remnants, *Undersea.* (italics by Mr. A)

is but the thin, reviving remnants of that era, propagated by a little handful of people who happened to be in sheltered positions when the devastation struck. Earthquakes have been most usually cited as probable causes for such catastrophes, but they do not explain all the concomitant details. One thing does, and is logical. Collision from outside bodies striking the earth. It is the only common denominator for our broadest and most basic problems of anthropology.

Heh: He's hit it.

Let us merely state that our tenet, and the point of inserting this discussion into the general concept, is to indicate that there was long ago a very advanced culture, which could and almost certainly did, invent a means of levitation and space mobility; that this world-wide culture was cataclysmically and instantly wiped out all over the world. Remnants of humanity escaped, and it is our suggestion that at least one space ship was afloat at the time and escaped the disaster and sired a race of space dwellers which has ever after used the neutral at the limit of the earth's sphere of influence as an abode or headquarters.

ED: The following has no obvious reference or necessary position.

> Had Farraday concerned *Himself* With The Mag. FIELD SURROUNDING HIS Elec. current. Man today would already Have reached the outermost Parts of our Galaxy.
>
> There, Jemi, Was given the results of What Would have been possible had Dr. Farraday Done as suggested other page. The S-Ms & L-Ms FOUGHT *USING* SMALL ASTEROIDS.
>
> We have no inclination to fare-forth to other things & other Ways. our is Way of Life, time-proven & Happy. We have nothing, own Nothing, except our Music & our Philosophy & are Happy.
>
> Any action has a re=action, thus if Something *pulls* upward, it also pushes downward. Such a trimendous (sic) force could cause SHEETS of Diamonds *to be Made in saucer-shape, ??* [1] (to divert cosmic ? rays.?) It could cause[2] new Metals to be Made, or tougher ones.
>
> (*HELP* DIVERT RAYS & ETC.)
>
> It could cause earth to become rock with in a few Minutes, It could change a Whole
>
> World or
>
> Civilization just by its potential.
>
> AND IT DOES, TOO

---

[1] Italics and Question marks by Jemi.
[2] Italics and the insertion of parentheses by Mr. A

Marks and "Footprints"

The following series of oddities is perhaps the most conclusive of all. Because I wish to develop *"The Devil's Footprints"* fully, I shall not go into detail about the innumerable marks and depressions in stone. However, after the footprints study, and a mention of the stone depressions and what they are, I believe the case for the UFO's will be clearly in your mind. What other source but something from space could account for these erratics?

The story of *"The Devil's Footprints"* is classic. It was told as follows, by Frank W. Lane, In *Fate*, April-May, 1952 – The material being largely the product of research by Rupert Gould as printed in *Stargazer Folks* and elsewhere:

On the night of Thursday, February 7, 1855, there was a fall of snow over South Devon, in southwest England. The next morning, as men and women went about their business, they discovered, imprinted in the virgin snow, a series of tracks unlike any seen before. At first glance they looked like the impression made by a donkey's hoof, measuring four by two and three-quarter inches. But there, all resemblance between the imprints on the snow and the sort of tracks left by a workaday donkey, ends. And the real mystery begins.

It was found that the hoof marks ran in a single line, and also that the distance between one impression and the next, as carefully measured, was undeviatingly eight and one-half inches. to appreciate properly the imprints in the snow that greeted the incredulous eyes of the Devonians, that Friday morning, you must try to imagine a line of marks such as would be made by a creature with only one leg, terminating a hoof, which proceeded by a series of jumps, always mathematically eight and one-half inches apart.

MARKER: IDELING (sic)

This was only the beginning of the puzzles associated with this mystery written in the snow. As word of the strange markings spread and men began to look more closely at them, and to trace their path across the whitened landscape, they discovered further inexplicable details.

Whereas the tracks of cats, dogs, horses, rabbits, birds and so forth, looked much as tracks always do in the snow – some clearly defined, others smudged, some cutting the snow deeply, others merely leaving a light imprint – these mystery markings were everywhere utterly clear and distinct. One investigator-on-the-spot said: "This particular mark removed the snow wherever it appeared, clear, as if cut with a diamond, or branded with a hot iron – so closely, even, that the raising in the centre of the frog of each print could be plainly seen." Some witnesses claimed to have seen traces of toe or claw marks at the edges of the impressions.

MARKER IS LIKE LOW POWER STONE CUTTER

The tracks were not confined to the ground. Two men following the tracks for three and half-hours ("under gooseberry bushes and espaliered fruit trees") suddenly lost all trace of it. They cast around and eventually picked up the tracks in the last place they thought of looking for them: on the roofs of some houses!

The witnesses already quoted said that the marks could be traced "in some instances, over the roofs of houses, and hayricks, and very high walls (one fourteen feet high), without displacing the snow on either side, or altering the distance between the feet; and passing on as if the wall had not been an impediment. The gardens with high fences or walls and gates locked, were equally visited as those open and unprotected."

Another investigator said that he traced the prints across a field up to a hayrick. The surface of the rick was wholly free from the marks but on the opposite side, in a direction corresponding exactly with the track already traced, they began again. A similar occurrence was noted when a wall intervened in the path of the track.

As high walls, hayricks, and houses were no obstacle to the onward march of these tracks, so neither was a great stretch of water. The hoof marks were traced to the bank of the estuary of the river Exe, and then picked up again on the opposite bank – across two miles of salt water.

The meanderings of the track ranged from Bicton in the east to Totnes in the west, a distance of about twenty miles as the crow flies. But the actual mileage covered by the track, as measured by the distance between hamlets, villages, towns and so forth, where the marks were seen was very much more. As one Devonian who was greatly interested in the occurrence wrote: "When we consider the distance that must have been gone over to have left these marks – I may say in almost every garden, on doorsteps, through extensive woods of Luscombe, upon commons, in enclosures and farms – the actual progress must have exceeded one hundred miles."

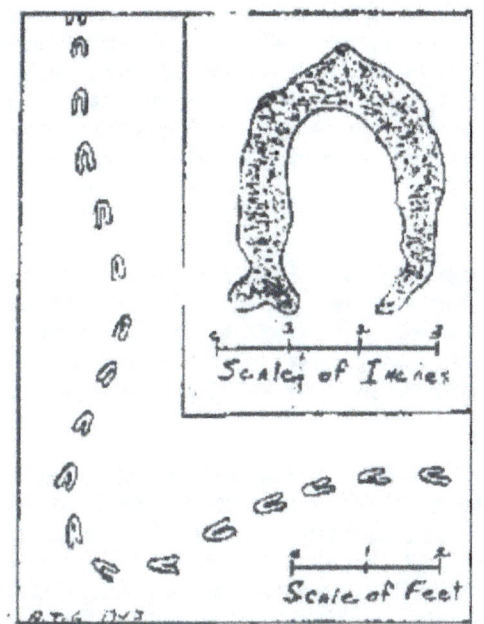
This the best illustration I know of the "Devil's Hoofmarks."

It did not take long for these markings in the snow to become the talk of all Devon. It was not so difficult to step in those days for a village rustic, pondering the inexplicable nature of the markings and their apparent ability to go wherever they would, and remembering their shape, to wonder fearfully if perhaps the Devil himself had been abroad in the land.

This fear was mentioned in a letter from the Reverend G.M. Musgrave, a local clergyman who was keenly interested in the whole matter, and who wrote of "the state of the public mind of the villagers, the laborers, their wives and children, and old crones, and the trembling old men, dreading to stir out after sunset, or to go half a mile into lanes or byways on a call or message, under the conviction that this was the Devil's walk, and no other, and that it was wicked to trifle with such a manifest proof of the Great Enemy's presence..."

What of the explanation of these prints in the snow? First, review what has to be explained; an exceptionally clearly defined single line of equally spaced marks, which was found on the tops of houses, walls and in enclosed gardens, on both sides of an estuary two miles wide and at places twenty miles distant and which, at a conservative estimate, had a total length (allowing for doubling and meandering) of a hundred miles.

All sorts of well-known creatures were suggested as the makers of the tracks: swans, cranes, bustards, otters, rats, hare, and badgers. It is hardly necessary to add that none of these creatures provide even a plausible explanation. Birds do not leave hoof marks, nor make tracks that remove snow as clearly as if "branded with a hot iron". If a mammal is chosen as the track maker, then how are we to explain the imprints across the roofs of houses and on tops of high walls, let alone the line of single, exactly spaced imprints?

One ingenious correspondent suggested that a hopping toad was the mischief-maker! The hopping would explain the single track, and the imprint of the toad's belly and claws the mark...

There is one single argument against all explanations of the tracks being made by any common animal or bird. The tracks left by such creatures were perfectly familiar to the inhabitants of Devon and if such tracks had been anything like those made by well-known animals nobody would have thought twice about it.

Two unfamiliar species of animals were suggested as possible makers of the tracks: Two kangaroos and a raccoon, these allegedly having escaped from near-by captivity. But simple arithmetic is fatal to the hypothesis that one or even two animals could have made all the tracks. To make a line of marks eight and one-half inches apart and one hundred miles long, the two kangaroos would have had to make an average of six steps a second for some twelve hours nonstop, and the raccoon over a dozen steps.

It is at once obvious that these hoof-prints could not have been caused by an animal. The single prints, in straight line, exactly in front of each other, confute this idea without the necessity of further data or analysis. But there is further data. The tracks extended a hundred miles or more crossed an inlet of the sea without deviation or interruption, passed over and on buildings and walls. Yet, we are asked, by explainers, most of whom were nowhere near the site, to believe that this was done by a badger or a kangaroo?

In the descriptions there are two or three notations which are very significant. First, let's take the rectilinear nature of the line of tracks: no animal walks in such a manner, nor for such a distance, nor over housetops. So – something passed over the country in the air, making contact with the ground as it went. No animal walks by putting one foot directly in front of the other, so these holes in the snow were made with mechanical precision by something mechanical. Therefore let's make the broad conclusion that something, mechanical passed over Devon in the air.

Mechanical, Not Precisely but slightly.

"F" for Force

Some acute observers noted that the prints did not look like normal hoof marks, wherein the snow is packed into the bottom of the track, but that it looked as if the snow had been removed. Also, someone noticed that the tracks looked more as if they had been burned into the snow. Again, it "F" could not be an animal. So – lets's broaden our conclusion to include, not only something mechanical passing over Devonshire, but also, that it reached out in some way and made surface contact at regular intervals.

Something reached, projected or emanated from this contrivance at regular times, and because the contraption was moving with uniform velocity this instrumentality of contact made regularly spaced marks.

"On the Head!"

Now we note that this thing did not pack snow into the tracks, but perhaps removed it instead, so it was not pressure, and therefore, not a mechanical contact. On the other hand, it appears to have been hot, or warm, or at the very least to have conveyed energy convertible into heat. "F" Whatever the method or manner, it conveyed enough energy to melt or remove part of the snow, almost instantaneously. What have we left to consider? Anything besides a ray of some sort? It doesn't seem too likely.

We have advocated levitation as an explanation before; thus the levitation of a few snow crystals in trivial as compared to the kicking, squirming body of Oliver Lerch, or the 1,200-ton blocks at Baalbek.

So we have, by elimination, a mechanical device passing through the air, emitting some sort of ray of heat or energy, at regular intervals of time and distance. What sort of device, and why the rays?

> Close, Someone is telepathing to his infierior (sic) receivor.

I suggest that this ray was something in the nature of radar, and that it either adjusted the distance of the machine from the ground or acted as a repulsion medium to sustain the machine in flight. The slight pressure in the prints could hardly account for the latter, so let's guess that the rays were for guidance or navigational purposes to maintain the ship at a uniform distance from the ground or prevent too close an approach to the surface.

> Tests *should show* emanations, else the "Measurer" was only Idleing his "Marker."

> or unless, Now Elec. Power is close-by there.

And from the *London Times*, March 14, 1840, fifteen years before the event of the "Devil's Footprints." Among the high mountains of the elevated district where Glenorchy, Glenlyon, and Glenochay are contiguous, there have been found several times, upon the snow, the tracks of an animal seemingly unknown at present, in Scotland. The prints in every respect resemble that of a foal of considerable size, although perhaps the sole seems a little stronger and not so round. No one has obtained a glimpse of this creature, only, it is remarked that, from the depth to which the feet sank in the snow, it must be a beast of considerable size. It has been observed also that its walk is not like that of the generality of quadrupeds, but more like the bounding or leaping of a horse when scared or pursued. It is not only in one locality that the tracks have been met with, but through a range of at least twelve miles.

Here, once again, is the element of localization which we can associate with intelligence.

"Cup Marks" are strings of cuplike impressions in rocks. Sometimes there are rings around them and sometimes they have only semicircles. They have been found in America, Great Britain, France, Algeria, Palestine, almost everywhere except the far north. In China, cliffs are dotted with them, and in Italy, Spain, and India they occur in enormous numbers.

There are twenty-four cups, varying from one and a half to three inches in diameter, arranged approximately in straight lines, on the Witches' Stone near Ratho, Scotland. It is explained locally that these are tracks of a dog's feet (in stone?). In Inverness-shire the marks are called "Fairies' Footmarks." In Norway and other places they are said to be horses' hoof prints. The rocks of Clare, in Ireland, have prints supposed to have been left by a mythical cow.

Ed: The following has no obvious reference or necessary position.
> Picture coming to Strange unexplored, never seen planet. Not knew Photography or cartography SO *Must* Mark it, *indelibly*, No?

On U.S. 40, between Dayton, Ohio, and Richmond, Indiana, there is a popular roadside stop where tourists pull over to look at the footprints in a large stone by the side of the road.

Now, in Devonshire, our space-navigating device seemed to be cruising around, probably slowly and silently, using a weak ray, maybe a sort of beamed radar, to maintain its elevation above the ground. But, where the cup marks appear in stone we get the impression that a more powerful ray was used, capable of disintegrating, or fusing, rocks; and that the flying gimmick was hovering over a small area. This hovering would account for the cupmarks appearing in clusters within which there were rows of cup marks in straight lines, since the hovering machine would be certain to drift back and forth, due to air currents and other disturbances while using its powerful ray to maintain position over a certain area or object.

GRAV. FIELD NOT STEADY, CAUSES WOBBLES

I am reminded, here, of the pigs somewhere in the French-Canadian wilderness which were killed by circular burned spots of totally unexplained origin.

Some hints might be gained by studying all of the places where cup marks are found, and determining whether these locales have any prominent features in common, such as might attract a space flyer, either for a particular interest, or merely for anchoring. For levitating stone, perhaps.

> One must have SOME permanent way of finding
> ones way to lifes necessitys & pleasures.

So, we premise that the cupmarks, like the Devil's footprints, the prints of Glenorchy, and those in the Chinese Palace-compound, and who knows, perhaps those of the legendary "abominable snow man" of the Himalayas, were all made by somewhat similar types of rays from space navigating contrivances.

SNOW MAN CAPTURED, OCT. 1954

It would appear that any resemblance to Morse Codes, or codes in general, or any other form of communication is purely coincidental, and is merely personal interpretation of the obviously mechanical nature of the distribution of the marks, be they cups in stone or depressions in snow. It is the establishment of the mechanical nature of these manifestations and their consequent subordination to intelligent control, which is our first concern. The whys and wherefores must be secondary issues.

Have you heard of the vitrified forts of Scotland, Ireland, Brittany and Bohemia? There are a number of very ancient forts, many on hilltops, which are scattered through those areas. They are

> From the below he *may have surmised* that
> there Were two types of people, at War with
> one another. *Can't say for sure*.

unique, because a part of the stone work is vitrified. It isn't clear as to just what enemies caused the building of the forts—whether they were built by invaders or defenders, or already in place prior to an invasion. These forts seem almost to surround England, and since some are in Brittany and Bohemia, one wonders if England at that time was connected with the mainland of Europe.

> TRUE.

Archaeologists postulate that these incredibly ancient people built vast fires to vitrify the stone forts and cement them together by melting them externally. Even where there was not a good supply of wood to burn; but then, that was a long time ago and there might, then, have been wood, coal, oil, or something. But a Miss Russel, in the *Journal of the B.A.A.*, has pointed out that single stones, much less long walls, are not vitrified when large houses are burned to the ground, or where the stones are otherwise cooked by so-called natural means.

> Force Cutter, full blast.

But the singular fact of these vitrified forts is that the stones are vitrified in streaks, as if special blasts had struck or played upon them

> Bdra! He's hit it, on the nose!

Lightning? At any rate, once (or more) upon a time something melted, in streaks, the stones of forts on the hills of Scotland, Ireland, Brittany and Bohemia. Whoever, or whatever did it, they, or it, had some handy way of getting around. Lightning has a way of hitting things prominently displayed on hilltops. But some of the vitrified forts are inconspicuously located and yet didn't escape; their walls, too, are vitrified in streaks. But, on hills and mountains all over the rest of the world are remains of forts which have not been vitrified. I have in mind Sacsahuaman, on top of the Andes at Cuzco.

ANCIENTS WARS, TOO WERE THE CAUSE, BY "F" CUTTER

In this instance of forts partially vitrified, in streaks, we have one of the most outstanding examples of selection and segregation —attributed to intelligence. Not only do we have forts of a certain circumscribed area picked out for attention, but we have such a high degree of concentration and direction that only streaks in certain forts are vitrified.

> Boe da lograni tash na Stendic og daeli mork
> "Pielidismacraeli!" Stones cut with "P" at
> full power of "F" cutter.
>
> *UPON REVIEW*; I BELIEVE THIS Man MAYBE being
> "Iluminated" Telepathically. *Somebody*, L-M
> or S-M *is Making* him write about that which
> he "sees" in his head & has checked upon to
> Verify. THAT somebody wants to come out of
> Hiding. *Not be Misunderstood, or* feared but
> Wants to co-exist in a Very Peacefu fashion.
> OR IS PLANNING ON MAKING THE GAYORI THEIR
> *ALLIES*, FOR WAR. IF THIS IS SO THEN ONLY THE
> S-M;S WOULD WANT WAR. THEY ARE IMMATURE &
> *only* they are SO immature as to desire War.
> One planet in the Galaxy Means *Nothing* to
> them, all they foster is "War as a Game to
> alleviate their boredomish, unplayful, un-
> happy existence. THE NON-PHILOSOPHISM OF
> HUMAN & S-M = DESTRUCTION.

Disappearing Planes

We shall not devote too much time to disappearing planes as it is a modern phenomenon, by definition, and we are building our Case for the UFOs from a wealth of historical information. However, inasmuch as these disappearances relate, directly, to our thesis of intelligence in space, space contrivances which kidnap human beings, either for study, food, or experiments of a nature beyond our ability to grasp, they bear mention.

FOR PROGENATION.

I should like to suggest, first, that a continuous flow of conversation, via a special frequency, be recorded automatically from all large craft in the air. There could be a series of Air Force and Civil Aeronautics Administrations base stations which could record this conversation. It becomes increasingly unthinkable that so many aircraft are falling from the air without time for a single crewmember to shout something, however brief, into the microphone so that we shall know what is happening to them. If we could establish this system of running conversation we might get some clues as to the destroyers of these ships and the captors of their crews and passengers.

Also, I believe in all fairness that we must admit the ease with which one can overemphasize mysterious disappearances of planes over water. Whereas I, personally, will not accept, categorically, mechanical failure which makes it impossible for the crew to report, and which means the ship is lost forever, its last moments with it, I will admit we cannot afford to draw too many conclusions from these incidents.

But, contrast the sea disappearances with the C-46 with thirty-two marines aboard. The wreckage was found – but never any bodies!

GOD HELPTHE L-Ms, THE MARINES HAVE LANDED

Also, at half past ten o'clock on the morning of March 7, 1922, Flying Officer B. Holding set out from an aerodrome near Chester, England, on what was intended to be a short flight in Wales, turning back and heading in the direction of Chester. He was never seen again. Holding disappeared far from the sea, and he disappeared over a densely populated land of highly civilized people!

The unexplained and unannounced crashes of planes over land are numbered in dozens, but these are crashes – not disappearances. Nevertheless there is a strong element of mystery in many of them. It is the rule, and not the exception that the major catastrophes come without warning. Whatever causes the crash seems to cut off communication simultaneously, for seldom is there any warning from the radio: only routine reports, and then – silence, until the wreckage is found with no survivors, and in at least one case, no bodies!

We cannot, with reasonable certainty, say that aircraft are attacked wantonly, promiscuously, or indiscriminately by a malicious enemy, for if that was true, the attacks would almost certainly be more universal, and we believe, more selective. Yet, it is most difficult to overlook the possibility that some sort of intelligence, coupled with the necessary forces, has destroyed some of our aircraft while simultaneously muting the occupants thereof.

It is one thing for a solitary plane to vanish, from above the sea, without trace, and without signals being heard. It is quite another thing for five military planes, flying as a group, all with full crew and radio, to pass silently and irrevocably from human ken.

There were fourteen men aboard those bombers. As the hours passed, anxious buddies back at the base and in other aircraft out on patrol listened hopefully on the radio channels. But no word came to tell of the whereabouts of the missing flyers.

The last routine message, received at 5:25 that gusty afternoon, had given the position of the flight as seventy-five miles northeast of Banana River (Florida) Naval Station, or about two hundred miles northeast of Miami.

The hands of the clock crawled around to the point where the bombers' fuel supply would be exhausted. Still no word. The Navy swung into action. Search planes and ships were ordered out to cover the entire area from Key West northward to Jacksonville and two hundred and fifty miles out to sea.

For the benefit of the public the Navy pointed out tersely that the Avenger bomber was noted for its buoyancy. In similar emergencies such planes had always remained afloat long enough for the crews to launch the life rafts, often "without getting their feet wet."

One of the first rescue craft to roar off the water in search of the missing fliers was a Navy PBM, a huge Martin Mariner bomber with a crew of thirteen that had been trained for just such work.

This plane, too, disappeared without trace!

Interest in the disappearances now reached the stage where it dominated discussion in the streets. How could five bombers, each with its own crew and radio facilities, disappear from the face of the earth without even flashing a single message of explanation? It was hardly logical to assume that the planes had collided in mid-air, killing all the crewmembers simultaneously.

And, even were such a weird explanation acceptable, how about the PBM?

ED: The following has no obvious reference or necessary position.

L-M INVESTIGATIONS OF TECHNICAL LEAPS & BOUNDS OF THE GAYORI IN PAST TEN YEARS BEING DISTORTED TO SHOW CAUSE FOR HOSTILE INTENT & *THIS NOT SO*. CURIOSITY IS SIGN OF INTELLIGENCE & L-Ms HAVE THIS IN *OVER-ABUNDANCE*.

Sorry to Say L-Ms REGARD HUMANS JUST AS HUMANS *HAVE CHOSEN TO BE REGARDED*: AS JUST SO MUCH VALUELESS *ANIMAL FORMS* OF LIFE, SWORN TO DESTRUCTIVENESS N& TO FOLLOW THOSE PASSIONS THAT NEGATE IDEA OF HIGHER LIFE-FORM-POSSIBLITY TO THEM.

In July 1952, a strange silvery object was seen high in the sky over San Anselmo, California, and five minutes later there was an unexplained crash of a quite airworthy plane, five miles away, and the Navy has been unable to account for it.

In March 1952, a case-hardened British fighter pilot, Wing Commander J. Baldwin, was flying a jet plane for meteorological and reconnaissance purposes over Korea. He flew into a cloud – and didn't come out again. The mystery was never solved. (About this time, a U.S. Carrier in Korean waters had sighted a strange object in the skies.)

On June 9, 1952, British Air Vice-Marshal Aitcherly set out in an amply fueled meteor jet from Suez to Cyprus, three hundred miles away. A radio signal was received from him three minutes arter take-off. Nothing more has been seen or heard of him. "Without a trace."

February 2, 1953: A York transport aircraft, with thirty-three passengers and crew of six, vanished over the Atlantic, on a trooping flight to Jamaica. No explanation. "Cause unascertainable." (And this, again, in the eerie region of the Gulf and the Caribbean.)

The lists of disasters to jet planes is long. The list of explanations is short. Pilots surviving crashes of whole squadrons have been silenced. When four British jets, all without collision, crash-landed at the same time in foggy flying weather, it was "explained" that all four ran out of fuel at one time.

NOT SO, THEY WERE "PUSHED" DOWN.

Your own reading for the past ten years will tell you of a number of unexplained disappearances and accidents to planes. The *Constellation* over Brazil. The DC-3 in Lake Michigan, apparently torn a part and its blankets, etc., shredded mysteriously.

On August 2, 1947, the British South American Airways plane, *Lancastrian Star Dust*, mysteriously vanished on a flight over the Andes. It would not have been so surprising if the craft had disappeared in the high peaks of the Andes, but – she was due to land at the airport at Santiago, Chile, at 5:45 PM, she sent out a signal stating her time of arrival. That is just four minutes from the airport, almost within sight of the control tower. At the end of the message came a word "Stendec," loud and clear and given out very fast. The Chilean Air Force operator, at Santiago, queried the word which he did not understand. He heard it twice repeated by the plane. No explanation of the word has ever been found. Nothing further was heard from the plane although calls were sent out. The plane never arrived, and from that day to this the mystery has never been solved. Searchers were made by ski troops and planes and by skilled mountaineers and automobiles over an area of 250 square miles, in vain. That plane carried a crew of five men and there were six passengers. The pilot, Captain R. J. Cook, had crossed the Andes eight times as second pilot. Four minutes from the landing strip – what happened?

> STENDIC "GAELIC" FOR "Stranger to World
> Was Cook raised around "Gaelic" folks when
> a child? Where heard he of "The Stendics."
>
> Cook was talking TO NEAR BY & CLOSING-IN L-M
> SHIP "STEN-BECK" SAID FEARFULLY & SAID VERY
> RAPIDLY BECOMES "STENDIC" Meant "STAND-OFF"
>
> "You bloody Stendicer" or Stendisher or
> even Standisher is an *occaisional* (sic) oath of
> Scots border. (italic by A)
>
> & in Some parts of England.
>
> It is used only to imply the very worst
> sort of Mysterious-Doing person.
>
> Ychym tae bu dall "Stendic"? Ne Bdi ta
> Hoanni fahn bi skoa kaii tog ymi, ok? Yes,
> could have been an L-M aboard & he said
> "Standback" VERY FAST.

In 1947, an American Superfortress bomber strangely vanished when 100 miles off Bermuda – the area of Missing planes. In March, 1950, a U.S. Globemaster disappeared while flying from North America to Ireland, without warning, without trace.

The Pan-American Airways liner, a Constellation with forty people aboard, was on her way from South Africa to New York, on June 20, 1951. The ship left Accra, West Africa, for Monrovia, Liberia, and at 3:00 AM the crew radioed that she was due at Roberts Field airport, Monrovia, at 3:15 AM. This plane was never seen nor heard of again. Fifteen minutes out, with no trouble to report, and anticipating an eventless landing, this giant craft disappeared – without a trace of a record, no outcry from its radio.

> MEN "FROZEN – HELPLESS" are good Prey.

I submit that these disappearances are in greater number than those of the past – disappearances of people, etc. – because our air age is proving of great interest to our space neighbors. Also, we are infinitely more aware of such disappearances. (The same reasoning, of course, applies to the increase of UFO's sighted since the advent of the air age and use of radar.)

I suggest, further, that these disappearances are but more kidnappings, by the space contrivances. Are there any other explanations which satisfy all the questions?

We close the strange accounts of disappearing planes with an account, published in *Coronet*, March, 1951, which is as startling as any yet encountered.

On a calm, but overcast Sunday in August, 1942, two experienced Naval Officers, Lieutenant Cody, and Ensign Adams, in fine spirits took off on an antisubmarine patrol in the U.S. Navy blimp, L-8, from a small base on Treasure Island, California. Adams, after fifteen years' service, had just been made Ensign, and this was his first flight as a commissioned officer; so the flight was a bit more than merely routine, as they flew low to look for submarines.

Not far from San Francisco they saw an oil slick, which might denote a submarine. The blimp circled and came over it. There were several patrol craft and many fishermen about, and everyone was interested in whether a depth charge would be dropped.

To the surprise of everyone the airship neither circled nor bombed. Instead, she shot upwards and disappeared into the clouds. The ship was not seen again by the watchers in the patrol and fishing boats – and her happy crew was not heard of again, by anybody.

The L-8 rose to 2,500 feet and drifted for two and one-half hours, and then came down on a California beach, almost striking two fishermen, who grabbed her towing lines and tried to hold her. They looked inside the gondola and found it empty. The craft tore out of their hands and drifted against a cliff, until one of her depth charges loosened and dropped, after which she soared over the cliff and later made a perfect landing in a street of Daly City, a suburb of San Francisco. Inspecting officers found everything in the gondola in perfect order, except – Cody and Adams were missing.

The last word from Lieutenant Cody, commanding, was at 7:50 AM when he radioed, "Am investigating oil slick." There should have been a follow-up report and, at 8:00 AM, a routine position report. There was nothing.

Nothing has ever been found out about the disappearance of these men. They must have left the blimp at the instant when it shop into the clouds, for there is no other suspected cause for it to rise, and the loss of their weight would certainly cause it to do so. Many patrols and fishermen were watching the maneuvers of the aircraft over the suspected area; everyone was standing by, to avoid a possible depth charge; dozens of eyes were on the blimp. Nobody say Cody and Adams jump, fall, or otherwise leave the gondola – no sign of trouble or struggle. The craft merely shop upward into the overcast. Cody and Adams just disappeared – for keeps, with at least a dozen or two interested observers watching every move of their airship. Why? And where to?

> Will remain in a "Stasis Neutral" Living with L-Ms & being fed by them until they are of No use & No farther info can be gotten from the. L-Ms USE a Mental Probe, NOW, SOMETHING LIKE ENCALPHOGRAPH. SAVES MUCH TIME & SWEAT WITH SUBJECTS WHOSE PSI FACTORING & OR EXTRA-SENSORY PERCEPTION IS TOO LOW FOR TELEPATHY."

Fireballs and Lights

Followers of flying saucers are well acquainted with the "Foo Fighters" reported so extensively during World War II. Because they are modern, and because their presence is so undeniably established and their activities so well catalogued, we shall do nothing with them other than this brief mention in the general category of lights and fireballs.

The "Foo Fighters" seem, however, to be of a slightly different genre from the usual UFO lights. "Foos" are usually reddish or yellowish, soft and diffuse, unattached to any tangible object and extremely mobile. UFO's, on the other hand, have hard, bluish-white lights and are brilliant, functional, and flickering.

> Hard, Bluish, White Lighted are Scouts, Solid,
>
> SCOUTS, CURIOUS ABOUT THE LAST WAR, ABLE
> TO DETECT ELECTRONIC-MAGNETIC FIELDS IN EQUIPMENT
> AND SO KEPT THEMSELVES AT A STAGE OF *MOLECULAR
> DISSOLUTION* IE, STASIS, THAT THEY COULD OBSERVE
> YET NTO GET HURT BY *WHATEVER* WEAPONS "WE" HAD,
> KNOWINGLY OR UNKNOWINGLY. Some of our Electrom's
> Equipment *could have had* an odd effect upon
> functionality of L-M observer Scout ships &
> caused some consternation to the L-M's, A PEACE-
> FUL NAIVELY CURIOUS BUNCH OF INADVERTANT HAVOC
> WREAKERS, AS YOULL EVER SEE, Jemi.

With that distinction in mind, let us suppose that the "Foos" either have intelligence or are remotely directed by intelligence. It is only another short step to say that they are intelligence. That they are a manifestation of some intelligent activity seems the most logical compromise.

The references throughout history to strange lights in the sky, and burning objects fleeing through the air, are common knowledge. There are myriad cases where lights, balls of fire, luminous points and areas, and ball lightning which do not seem to be attached to or emanate from any solid object, have been observed. Two recent sightings will serve to establish our basis of judgement.

> QUITE SO!

The following letter, to the editor of *Fate*, March 1951 bears careful scrutiny. I ask that you recall the rays we suggested in *"Marks and Footprints."*

"My husband and I live alone in a little hidden hollow in Nye County, Nevada, known as the Old Burns Ranch. It is almost completely surrounded by bleak gray hills, and is located a crooked mile back from the paved highway that runs to the little town of Beatty, eight miles distant.

"The nearest human habitation is a cattle ranch a mile away by coyote trail over the hills.

"It was 1:45 AM on a night in January, 1949, just after what is known as The Big Snow. A frozen white pall lay draped over hill and desert. I had wakened from sound slumber a half-hour earlier. More sleep eluded me and I was standing at my window drinking in the beauty of the dimly moonlit landscape. Not a creature was stirring, nor a breath of wind.

> IF THIS HAPPENS, COVER YOURSELF WITH EARTH, Jemi.

"Gradually, my eyes focused upon a pale gray stain, irregularly shaped and no bigger than by two hands. It rested on the smooth crust near a corner of the grape arbor about three rods from the house and in line with the window. Almost at once this fuzzy-gray shadow that was not a shadow bloomed into a disc of clear white light approximately three feet in diameter. It lay there for fully two minutes. Then suddenly contracting into a brilliant orange-tinted stream five or six inches wide, flowed swiftly over the snow toward my window and, to all appearances, exploded soundlessly against the stone foundation of the intervening front porch.

"Several tongues of scintillating red and blue flame spurted a few inches above the two-and-a half foot high wainscoting of the porch. That was all.

"When daylight came, we searched conscientiously but found no signs, marks, or tracks of any kind that might help to explain this phenomenon."

Sara Elizabeth Lampe
Gardnerville, Nevada

We have another interesting account of a recent visit by a fireball which warrants attention. It was reported by Gordon W. Hackbarth of Seattle, Washington, and tells of an electronics mechanic at the Puget Sound Navy Yard, Robert Burch, and his experience on Tuesday, November 6, 1951.

Returning from his evening meal, Burch stopped at the desk of the Bremerton YMCA, picked up his key, then rode the elevator to the top floor. Inside his room, he noticed that it was 7:30 PM He switched on his radio, then turned to the dresser.

Suddenly, something made him look up. The mirror reflected a ball of orange-red fire coming toward him through the open window. There was a blinding flash and a loud report. The ceiling light went out and Burch was knocked to the floor. In a daze he reached for the foot of his metal bed to haul himself upright. A searing pain shot up his arm. Later it was diagnosed that he had received second-degree burns.

> DON'T KNOW IF BULB IMPLODED
>
> (LATER) HYPER-ACTIVATION BY F-F ON MOLECULES COULD HAVE CAUSED BURNS OR PURE-ENERGY IMPLOSION "BOUNCES" BACK, EFFECTS SECONDARY EXPLOSION, THUS BURNS & ETC.

In the corner of his room the contents of a wastebasket blazed furiously. Beneath the window a piece of fireproof Samsonite luggage was charred and smoking. The cabinets of two radios were burned. The sill of the window through which the fireball had entered was black and too hot to touch.

> YES, ALL THE ABOVE ARE SCEINTIFICALLY EXPLAINABLE THEY ARE REACTIONS OF FORCE & ENERGY, WILD & TAME.

Burch's roommate, Alex Myers, rushed in from the shower room three doors away. He had heard the loud report. A moment later, a city policeman entered. The officer, in the process of writing a traffic violation ticket three blocks away, had looked up, seen the orange-red ball flash across the sky in an arc from a southerly direction and enter the window.

In the Bremerton Naval Hospital the next day the bewildered Burch, his arm swathed in bandages, still suffered from shock.

ED: the following has no obvious reference or necessary position
> The terrifying thing about Fireballs is
> that When Human & Fireball face each other,

> **the one recognizes a *Panicked* intelligence in the other AND is thus terrified in reciprocal emotions. A Fireball is either L-M or S-M WHO, *LIKE* THAT process that Burned the Ancient ARKS HAS TOO HAD A MALFUNCTION**
>
> **ACCIDENT. OR CAUSED.**
>
> **OF ONE OR ALL OF HIS "INDUCED" FIELDS & thus burns.**

"Crawling fireballs" are still another form of oddities which lend substance to our theory of intelligence in space. Most of these awesome incidents occurred in France. In Marseilles, during October 1898, an adolescent girl was seated at a table when suddenly a spherical shape of fre darted into the room, paused in the corner farthest from her and gradually moved toward her along the floor. Terror stricken, she drew back against the wall. Then, abruptly, it changed its course, circled her several times and shot toward the ceiling. It flung itself at a paper-covered stovepipe hole and burned a ring in it on its way up the chimney. Minutes later a loud crash shattered the chimney top.

A similar occurrence was reported in Paris on July 5, 1852, in the shop of a tailor on the Rue Saint Jacques, near Val De Grace. This time the fireball crawled over the windowsill into the room and came at the man in a floor-skimming action. Horrified, he retreated as the globe of blazing light climbed to the height of his face. It was too much for him. The tailor collapsed. A little later he revived to hear a tremendous explosion atop the shop which scattered bits of chimney brick over surrounding rooftops. Proof that the fireball had fled up the chimney again appeared in the form of a burnt paper cover over the stovepipe hole.

In one series of volumes published around 1898 by *The Association Francaise*, M. Wander, a scientist, wrote: "A violent thunderstorm has descended upon the Commune of Beugnon. I happened to be passing through a farm in which two children of about twelve and thirteen were playing. I saw these children take refuge from the rain under the roof of a stable, in which were twenty-five oxen. In the courtyard grew a poplar. Suddenly there appeared a globe of fire, the size of an apple, near the top of the poplar. We saw it descend branch by branch, and then down the trunk. It moved along the courtyard very slowly, picking its way, and came through to the door where the two children stood. One of them touched it. Immediately a terrible crash shook the entire farm to its foundation. The children were thrown back, uninjured but eleven of the oxen were felled dead."

In the town of Gray, on July 7, 1886, a luminous ball from thirty to forty centimeters in diameter jumped to the roof of a home and ripped off the corner. In this case, unlike so many others, the fireball didn't disintegrate after a single act of destruction. It rebounded to the home's outside stairs, crushing the slates. Still it retained its shape, crawled into the midst of a group of passers-by who had stopped to watch the queer sight. These persons, in a body, took off down the road. The perverse object seemed to pursue them momentarily: **then it vanished without a sound.**

> **Must have hit a Vortice, *or* been saved somehow.**

M. Lawrence Roth, Director of the Blue Hill Observatory, in 1903, was visiting Paris on September 4, of that year. At 10:00:PM, he happened to be looking toward the Eiffel Tower from the Rond-Point of the Champs Elysees. The tower was suddenly struck by white lightning. Simultaneously he spied a flaming sphere edging downward to the second platform. Roth claimed the ball was about a yard in diameter, and that it covered some one hundred yards in a matter of seconds and then vanished completely.

> **It is very interesting to note that these reports are from the general area where a great deal of UFO activity was reported in late 1954. Localization? Selectivity?**

Yes, no doubt.

Additional substantiation of the localization-selectivity factor comes from reports from Hammersly Fork. Remember the strange disappearance in that area.

A fireball at Hammersly Fork floated down through the roof and exploded in a cabin, blowing out windows and doors, at midday on December 9, 1951. Another one came down fifty yards east of the post office there and vanished just before reaching the ground on January 9, 1952. A week later, another one came down just at dusk, at Cross Fork, eight miles from Hammersly Fork and vanished just before touching the ground. On January 23, again at dusk, a fireball floated down in the woods about two hundred feet from the car of Mr. Doyle Schoonover, and vanished just before reaching the ground. Another fireball went through two inches of boards on a building, on February 1, and within seconds the whole roof was ablaze.

Mr. John P. Bessor, a very careful and reliable investigator, made a special trip of inspection to the vicinity of Brown Mountain, near Mogantown, North Carolina, and personally saw the mysterious lights reported there. He avers that they cannot be due to locomotives, cars, houselights, or whatever else the Geological Survey would like them to be. He was not able to coordinate the lights with any mineral deposits, or human activity. Nevertheless the lights were observed by him over a period of several days and nights. They appeared to move at will, to have volition.

No Will of Wisp Gases in that area at all.

While the innumerable reports on strange lights may be only indirectly related to space travel, it does seem obvious that some of the same forces and physical characteristics are common to both types of phenomena, and a study of one may supply insight into others. For instance, we note the common traits of maneuverability, transparency, color, and evidence of intelligent manipulation, not to mention the ability to appear and disappear at will, as did the saucers over Washington in 1952.

There is a report on a puzzling light seen in Hampshire on the night of September 14, 1908 -- a light as if from an unseen moon. Strangely enough, that same night, David Packer, in Worcestershire, saw an illumination which he thought was auroral, and proceeded to photograph it. What he saw was a broad, diffuse series of cloudlike illuminations. His photograph in English Mechanic showed a large luminous disc of sphere over the auroral illuminations. This does not in any way indicate a flaw in the film or lights leaking into the camera. The only possible explanation in that case is based on the conventional knowledge that this thing, invisible to the eye, was luminous in that part of the spectrum to which the plate was sensitive, probably ultraviolet, as infra-red plates were not then available.

ED: The following has no obvious reference or necessary position.
Each Pilot of a F Ship receives the ability to become Molecularly Dissolute AFTER he has been so done by His own Ships "fields" enough times. Further, *when* He Has been *imbued* with this ability he sometimes Loses control of it Due to too Many repetitions or flows in Natural fields, or break Down of Ships Fields. L-Ms ARE COMING CLOSER & CLOSER TO SOLVING HOW TO TOTALLY PREVENT THEMSELVES FROM "CATCHING FIRE" PERHAPS HAVE BY NOW SUCCEEDED, I hope, FERVERENTLY!

In *Cambrian Natural Observer*, 1905-32, are several accounts of lights, in the skies of Wales, which are exactly like many of those reported in the United States since 1947. Lights like "a long cluster of stars, obscured by a thin film of mist," were reported. Later this thing is said to have taken on the shape and appearance of a vertically suspended iron bar heated to an orange-colored glow; but the initial description is that of lights in formation.

SHIP STANDING VERTICALLY IS SIGNALLING
"HELP" TO ALL IN VICINITY

I submit that <u>all</u> strange lights reported, throughout history and today, are either from UFO's themselves, or reflections of them. They may be UFO's.

I think we can agree, further, that fireballs may be the only available indication that UFO's have weapons -- and that fireballs are their weapons. I base this upon the singular fact that the only reports of destruction or injury come from these fireballs. <u>This is not to inscribe malicious intent to UFO's for accidental shooting of a hunter does not condemn the sorrowed friend who fired the shop, much less the distant manufacturer.</u> That fireballs are released at all is, again, probably sheer experimentation on the part of the UFO's.

(NOT, SO) THE "BURNINGS" *MUST* BE EJECTED
or the ship will catch fire in control pit.

As an example of destruction, we shall close with this brief case.

An intelligent boy was trudging along the highway at night near Palestine, Texas. A woman was riding in the same direction, on a horse. The boy reappeared in Palestine that night, out of breath and very pale. He said he saw a ball of fire come out of the sky and strike the woman and set her ablaze. The horse ran one way and he ran back to town to tell what had happened. The people went to look for further particulars of this curious accident. They found the woman lying on the ground with all her clothing burned, but with enough life in her to tell that she had been struck in the breast by a ball of fire. The horse was found with his mane singed. The woman died the next day.

Such fireballs could also be the new method of Execution of Outlaws or Method of Disposal for Olden Peopole. These theorys could each and every one be Possible. I do know that The Arks were burned. That Scouts can also burn in this fashion. I dread these Fireballs & I believe the U.S. NAVY May also have formed some out of Human Material, 1943-44.

I do Not fear the L-Ms or their enemies themselves but I dread in a Terror filled Hellish Dreadfulness the Least intimation of the appearance of a Fireball that is Not inanimate & thus clearly mere "Burnings" of & from a "coat" upon interior parts of a ship. All electricity gathers a "coat" & this must be disposed of else functionality of ship & fields is impaired. This I understand, but Not a burning personality in TERROR. IT VERGES TOO MUCH UPON THE INHUMAN, THE HORRIBLE.

Legends

In all these discussions, one thing seems to be outstanding as a common denominator. All of the aerial or spatial contrivances and gadgets which we have postulated appear to have one feature in common: they have their natural habitat in space, or at very least in the atmosphere. There is no sure record of an appearance on the ground, and few indications. Appearances from, or disappearances into, the sea indicate only an ability to make use of the fluid medium of seawater, when necessary or desirable. This leads to an assumption that UFO's live naturally and easily in space; that they do not necessarily come from other stellar systems, or even from other planets.

> No. Not Easily
> The "Little-Men" are known to have GILLS
> Just as all Men before birth, have gills, too.

After considering that the space structures or UFO's spend most of their time in line between earth and the sun, it has been suggested that some of the ancient Sun worship may have originated in the condition that some god-like beings may have come from UFO's which were said to be "in the Sun," because of this alignment of the neutral, and that perhaps the "death boats" for celestial flight which were buried with the Egyptian kings may have been symbolic of the UFO flight XXXXXX . Perhaps some of these traditions were fragmentary memories from the first wave of civilization. In fact there are several very ancient traditions which can be at least partially accounted for by our common denominator of life in and from space.

For emphasis, and for the establishment of present principles, we repeat that it is relatively unimportant whether we decide that civilization was brought to us fom space, perhaps from the exploded planet between Mars and Jupiter, or whether it reached space from terrestrial development in a previous upsurge of civilization. Such relics as the Great Pyramid indicate the advancement of that age, and it is perhaps a little less strain on our sensibilities to assume that space life, especially if limited to the earth-moon system, originated on earth. Our two greatest mental hazards at the moment are to overcome the blows to our racial ego, and to free ourselves from the idea that UFO's and space life now reaching our cognizance necessarily come from a planet. Their presence in near-by space regions is improbability of lesser order and has little about it which is difficult of acceptance.(Red is A and B)

There is much to make us believe that this extraordinary thing which we call civilization today is nothing but flickering flamelets rekindled from almost extinct embers of civilization, the antiquity of which is undreamed of by modern archaeologists.

> The Man is Right, So What.

The Hawaiians claim to have known about flying saucers for 1,000 years, and even to have a name for them: Akualele, or flying spirits. They describe these flying spirits as appearing in many shapes and colors just as they are sighted today...the balls of fire. cones and saucer-shaped discs.

From this it is an easy jump to an obscure, but reliably documented case from England, A.D. 1290. It is one of the best reports on things in space that we call UFO's.

A Mr. A.X. Chumley, a British scholar, recently found a Latin document at Byland Abbey, in Yorkshire, describing a strange aerial object that terrified the monks in A.D. 1290. The document refers to a "Round, flat, silver object called a discus which flew over the monastery exciting maximum terrorem among the brethren."

> YES, L-MS INTRODUCED DISCUS THROWING WHILE
> TRYING TO EXPLAIN THE METHOD OF HAPHAZARD
> ARRIVAL IN THESSALONIA TO The "Blocked-headed

Locals who thought it a New game.

The farther back in time, the less note is taken of plain, bare facts, thus antiquity of obfuscates, realty.

It is the purpose of this chapter to lead you still farther back in time – to the threshold of human intelligence, in a wave of civilization covering the world before the flood. If we discover that no matter how far we push the periphery of our quest, we still find a ready-made civilization – we have to admit human intellectual antiquity of (to us) fantastic and unbelievable vastness. Could this mean that civilization was planted here, within the species of animal selected by some superintelligence as most fit to develop culture? Could these superfolk be space dwellers? Could they be tending us as sheep are tended? Are we actually owned? Could the UFO's be their abode? Or perhaps their supervisors, shepherds? Could it be that the saucers, in their whimsical variety, are the space dwellers – the intelligences?

GETS A LITTLE WILD HERE BUT HE DOES DARE FACE THINGS NO OTHER ARCHEOLOGIST EVER HAS (italics by A)

In 1809 a Mr. Stavely, in London, saw many bright specks of light moving around the edge of a black cloud. The lights played around for an hour, and one of them became as large and bright as Venus, moving with great speed around the cloud; later it became stationary, lost its brilliance and finally disappeared. There was no lightning, and the altitude of the lights seemed variable.

On June 19, 1801, a great body, moonlike but larger with a dark mark across it, appeared over Hull, England, at about midnight. It devolved into five bodies, all brilliant, which faded away, leaving a very bright sphere. A bluish light was around it all the while, but when it disappeared the sky was left calm and clear. On July 14, in the early evening, something that looked like an ordinary cloud, several miles long, seemed to take fire, burning with a bluish flame, lasting fifteen minutes, and twice repeated for shorter intervals.

MOTHERSHIP, INDUCTOR LEFT RUNNING WHILE DISCHARGING SCOUTS, THEN, RAN-OFF OVER CHARGE.

An elliptical sphere rose and fell over Edinburgh on June 21, 1787, and disappeared behind clouds. On December 26, 1785, Edinburg was, at nine o'clock PM, illuminated as bright as day by a sphere with a sort of cone shaped attachment. This was seen in a number of distant places.

Cone was Measure-Marker on Tracker-Scout ship.

Jacob Bee's Diary records a "comet" that "appeared" at 4:45 PM on December 20, 1689: "first in ye forme of halfe a moone, very firie, and afterwards did change itself to a firie sword, and ran westward."

On June 3, 1732 a storm of lights appeared in the sky having all the earmarks of an intense meteor shower.

YES.

Throughout the 19th century there are many reports of explosions, cannonading, and crashes in the sky. Holby, Kepler, and other scientists acknowledge the veracity of these reports but never offer real solutions.

ED: The following has no obvious reference or necessary position.
    Mother

    Dreadnaught & Scout-fighters, with Force-Shields at full-blast-TOTAL

Compressed Matieral, or "Frozen" Matieral (sic) *hits*
atmosphere *or is* (italics by A)

PRONTO

unfroze, results in Mild Explosions.

WHEN AREA SUDDENLY "FROZE" it causes implosions.
(AIR)

Kepler reported "A burning globe appeared at sunset, on November 17, 1623, visible all over Germany and much of Austria."

A whole series of observations of illuminated crosses, burning globes, horrid celestial clashing noises, beams of fire, discolored sun, sun dogs and mock suns is reported from 1501 through 1557. These reports include a thunderbolt that disrupted the bridal chamber of Francois Montmorency and Diane de France.

Heh! Chuckle. Lost his "erection"

The *Chronicles of Basel*, AD 1478, recount "Divers kinds of crosses and fiery bowls fell to the ground from the sky leaving tokens behind."

Yes, May still be Laying there.

In the early winter of 1387, a fire in the sky was seen many times, like a burning and revolving wheel, or a round barrel of flame, emitting fire from above, and others in the shape of a long fiery beam, in the country of Leicester, England.

imploded & burning Ship-frame, some expierimentals (sic)
were faulty and actually burned Whole "alfoat."(sic)

This weird report is dated AD 1322. In the first hour of the night of November 4, after 7:00 PM, there was seen in the sky over Uxbridge, England, a pillar of fire of the size of a small boat, pallid and livid in color. It rose from the south, crossed the sky with a slow and grave motion, and went northward. Out of the front of the pile of fervent red flame burst forth with great beams of light...many beholders saw it in collision, and there came sounds of fearful combat, and sounds of crashes.

"Buja"

Matthew, of Paris, says: On July 24, AD, 1239, at the vigil of Saint James, in the dusk, but not when the stars came out, but while the air was clear, serene and shining, a great star appeared. It was like a torch, rising from the south, and flying on both sides of it there was emitted in the height of the sky a very great light. It turned towards the north in the aery region, not quickly, nor, indeed, with speed, but exactly as if it wished to ascent to a place in the air. But when it arrived at the apparent middle of the firmament, in our northern hemisphere, it left behind it smoke with sparks.

An *old* Ark being "Demolished." (Italics by A)

March 20, AD 1168, "a globe of fire was seen moving to and fro in the air."

I wonder if there is any significance to the month of March in regard to these events?

ONLY A FEW old Arks now remain. Most are

> waystations. (There *are* two GREAT-ARKS,
> ONE NEW.)

> FOR EARTH DUTY

AD, 1104: Burning torches, fiery darts, flying fires were often seen in the air in this year. And there were, near stars, what looked like swarms of butterflies and little fiery worms of a strange kind. They flew in the air and took away the light of the sun as if they had been clouds.

> Above Latter is Excellent description of
> Grecian Mercury HAT. THAT IS just exactly
> what His Hat & Mayhap himself, was designed from.

AD, 1067: In this year people saw a fire that flamed and burned fiercely in the sky. It came near the earth, and for a little time brilliantly lit it up. Afterwards, it revolved, ascended on high, then descended into the sea. In several places it burned woods and plains, and in the country of Northumberland this fire showed itself in two seasons of the year. (From Geoffrey Gaimar's Lestorie des Englis solum Maistre Geffrei.)

AD, 936: "In a clear sky, the sun was suddenly darkened red like blood."

> When the Chain Cities Moved all off the
> ark. No, FOR TWO SEASONS *old* arks &
> Boats BEING DEMOLISHED.

AD, 941: "The sun had a terrible appearance for some time and a stream like blood issued from it."

AD 823: "In summer a piece of ice fell from the sky over Burgundy, France. It was sixteen feet long, seven feet broad, and two feet thick." That was quite a hailstone!

> Ice for "Hangover!
>
> YAK

AD 796: Roger of Wendover records that small globes were seen circling around the sun.

AD 457: "Over Brittany, France, a blazing thing like a globe was seen in the sky. Its size was immense, and on its beams hung a ball of fire like a dragon out of whose mouth proceeded two beams, one of which stretched beyond France, and the other reached towards Ireland, and ended in firelike rays."

> "S" Ship, Ark type, in Battle & FORCE-LOCKED
> with L-M 'BOATS"

AD 393: "In the time of Theodosius, a sign like a hanging dove (colmba pendens) appeared in the sky. It burned for thirty days."

> Can't say, Probably Ship in Distress,
> FORCE-LOCKED

170 BC: "At Lanupium, on the Appian Way, sixteen miles from Rome a remarkable spectacle of a fleet of ships was seen in the air."

> Mirage of Boats on Clouds. No record of such

> a SIZED MOVEMENT.

106 BC: "A bird that flew in the sky and set houses on fire, was seen over Rome."

> "S" Ship, Not L-M, Jammed "Cutter"

214 BC: "The forms of ships were seen in the sky over Rome." And 220 BC: "A clear light shone at night in the sky at Rome."

> 214BC Probably Just plane Water boats, Human.

216 BC: "At Praeneste, sixty-five miles from Rome, burning "lamps" fell from the sky, and at Arpinium, forty-two miles east of Praeneste, a thing like a round shield was seen in the sky."

> Ship Cleaning off "Coat" & obviously in a
> Hurry, too

99 BC: "When Murius and Valerius were consuls in Tarquinia, there fell in different places a thing like a flaming torch and it come suddenly from the sky. Towards sunset, a round object, like a globe, or a round circular shield took its path in the sky from west to east." That is as good a description of a saucer as any.

> These describe the Great Activity & Undersea
> building (to a small inference) of the "Chain
> Cities" and too, the S-M's resistance to the
> L-M's in the "*Small War*" after "great Return."

Now let us consider the hieroglyphs from an Egyptian papyrus, together with a translation by Boris de Rachewiltz. De Rachewiltz says that the original is a part of the Royal Annals of the times of Thutmose III, circa 1504-1450 BC, and that the original is in bad condition. Parts were too obliterated for translation.

In the year 22, third month of winter, sixth hour of the day (..2..) The scribas of the House of Life found it was a circle of fire that was coming in the sky. (though) it had no head, the breath of its mouth (had) a foul odor. Its body one 'rod' long and one 'rod' large. It had no voice. Their hearts became confused through it: then they laid themselves on their bellies (..3..) They went to the King..? to report it. His Majesty ordered (..4..) has been examined (..5..) as to all which is written in the papyrus rolls of the House of Life His Majesty was meditating upon what happened. Now, after some days had passed over those things, Lo! They were more numerous than "anything" They were shining in the sky more than the Sun to the limits of the four supports of heaven (..6..) Powerful was the position of the fire circles. The army of the King looked on and His Majesty was in the midst of it. It was after supper. Thereupon they (the fire circles) went up higher directed to the south. Fishes and volatiles fell down from the sky. (it was) a marvel never occurred since the foundation of this land. Caused His Majesty to brought incense to pacify the hearth (..9..) (to write?) what happened in the ook of the House of Life (..10..) (to be remembered?) for the Eternity.

> ole TITMOUSE SAW "The Great Return; a Story
> you know very Well.
>
> He saw Group "Coat" Burnings of Whole Convey,
>
> in Great Return, one ship payed-call in Titmouses
> towns peopole (sic), was Honored & received Graciously,
> even if at first somewhat fearfully, Like sun
> Worshipers the World over.

To this added the following comment from the translator:

As you can see from (the translation) the "flying saucers" made their first appearance in the 22nd year of the reign of Thutmose III, about 3,500 years ago. The first lacuna of the papyrus in the end of another marvel. I think that this papyrus was part of a book preserved in the mysterious institution called House of Life (of which Sir Alan Gardner has written), that I am actually deeply investigating. In it, magic rites were performed and a special group of scribes was trained.

Two things have to be noticed: it left after a foul odor and it was not making any noise. It measures one rod, i.e. 100 cubit. As a cubit is about 20.6 inches we might judge the fire circle was large and long, about fifty meters. During their second appearance they were very numerous and shining, and fishes and volatiles fell down from the sky. And their movements through the sky, from north to south, was regular, and, more than that, powerful! Therefore the king thought that the best thing to do was to pacify the hearth of Ammon Ra, Lord of the Thrones of the Two Lands (Egypt).

This record is a part of the archives of a responsible government. The event was unusual enough to warrant inscribing in the archives, and to have the past records searched for precedent. The descriptions are concise, although the vacant places are annoying in their omissions. De Rachewiltz's comments, supplementing his translation, indicate an interpretation similar to that which we, ourselves, might make.

However we find it difficult to resist pointing out some of the elements of this event, which are so typical of the reports in current sightings. Silence of operation for one thing. Foul odor. In size, this UFO was said to be about one hundred cubits, which is about 172 feet long. The fact that two equal dimensions were given indicating (perhaps) equal length and breadth implies disc shape. In any case it was described as a fire circle, indicating its shape, and that flames were associated with it as has so often been the case. The exact nature of the flames is of course unknown to us; they may have been electrical discharges which would have been strange to the Egyptians of 1500 BC and would have been recorded as ordinary flames. As in our modern sightings, there was sometimes one object and sometimes a group or flock. They were shining, and by this it seems we can infer that they were luminous.

LAMINATED METAL, COVERED BY SHEET-DIAMOND?

One other thing is obvious from this Egyptian record; that mechanical flight, if it had been previously known to the Egyptians, or to their progenitors, was Already a completely lost science in 1500 BC. It is in line with our thinking that the Egyptians were merely another one of the trickles through the dyke of time from the previous great wave of civilization.

The records of Tibet, however, seem to be more complete than those of Egypt, and more ancient. Perhaps it is because the mountain fastnesses of Tibet and Northern India have not been subjected to the burnings and other destructive activities of Western civilization which annihilated the libraries of the Egyptians and the Mayas.

TRUE

If one may judge from his writings, Colonel James Churchward, in a lifetime of study, Learned something of the lore which is stored in the Tibetan monasteries, and supplemented this with studies throughout the world.

Churchward says that he came upon many records ranging back to at least 200,000 years. One of his most fascinating finds relates to mechanical flight, brought to India by the first settlers, and its antiquity may be anything from 15,000 to 200,000 years, with the longer term the more likely. It is Churchward's deduction that India was settled by Nagas from Burma, who, in their turn, were descendents of the original Mayas of the "motherland," common ancestors of the Naga and the Central

American Maya. This settlement must have taken place about 70,000 years ago, and it seems most probable that mechanical flight came form the "Motherland."

> Not know Churchward. If then he has seen so
> ancient writs, then he KNEW Why we do Not War,
> Nor ever Worry & Why each of us knows or Day
> of Death AND THAT WE ONCE RULERS THEN WERE
> SLAVES.

Here, by mechanical flight, we most certainly mean something different either our lighter than air or heavier than air flight mechanisms of today. That the flight of those millennia employed a type of power unknown today, "seems almost certain." Whatever the source of that power was it did not involve power plants as we know them today, and apparently did not result in a truly mechanical or industrialized civilization such as we have. That this power source worked on some principle of levitation or gravity nullification seems logical. It may be, too, that such a force or power does not lend itself to industry.

> IT DOES. FROM LIFE-BOAT POWER IS XXXXX
> BUILT "SCOUT & SO, ON UP TO Great Arks
>
> (XXXXX getting too close for comfort XXXXX ?)[1]
>
> *phraseology* indicates Lack of courage, Not
> Worry, Jemi.

An Hindu Manuscript of ancient origin says: "When morning dawned, Rama, taking the celestial car which Pushpaka had sent him be Vivishand, stood ready to depart; self moving was this car; it was large and finely "painted." It had two stories, and many chambers with windows, and was draped with flags and banners. It gave forth a melodious sound as it coursed along its airy way."

This was written millennia ago – and this translation was made before the modern age of mechanical flight. If the translation had been made by a person with the technical training available in 1955, it would read like this:

When dawn came, Rama took the flying machine with Pushpaka had sent to him by Vivishand, and stood by to take off. This machine was self-propelled, large and finely-finished. It was a two-decker, with many compartments having windows, and was draped with flags and pennants. As the machine flew it made a humming or droning sound.

> NO; Had TWO EQUALLY SHAPED HALVES; LOOKED
> UP AT FROM GROUND IT SEEMED --- TO BE OF
> TWO PARTS   as hereon.

There is another Hindu manuscript dated 500 BC, which has been translated as follows:

Rawan (Ravan?), King of Ceylon, flew over the enemy's army and dropped bombs, causing many casualties. Eventually Rawan was captured and slain, and his flying machine fell into the hands of the Hindu Chieftain, Ram Chandra (Rama), who flew it all the way back to his Capital in northern India.

> No, Not bombs: *Rocks* or "Frozen" air,
> or 'Coat" Burnings.

Both of these manuscripts seem to have been taken from the same temple records at Ayhodia and refer to a time at least 20,000 years ago.

---

[1] Parenthesis, markouts, and question mark by A

> During time before "The Ice"?

It is from this material that we come to the conclusion that space flight is not a new phenomenon, but rather a lost art!

> XXXXXXXXX *that* I can "remember."

Therefore, I strongly recommend that legislation be enacted to once to assign qualified researchers to the field of gravity. There, and not in atoms, shall we discover the secret of the true flight into space.

> a circular pattern of Bar Magnets 342 of them, HAVE NO WEIGHT if they are attached to a common Sheet of Metal
>
> & are XXXXXXXXXXXXXXXXXXXXXXXXXXXX[1]
>
> In short, THEY FLOAT IN THE AIR, *all* 900 lbs of them. XXXXXXXXXXXXX [1&2]
>
> 2
>
> (In center, I wish were one Drive-Inductor.[3] Boy! oh Boy!

ED: The following note appears on 111 above PART FOUR.

> "And a Little Child shall lead them" Nothing describes a LITTLE-MANS basic Nature so well as that Description. They are childlike in Many Many Ways. So Much so as to easily be mistaken for children WHEN they are Mature-youngs.

---

[1] A over B

[2] By B

[3] By Jemi

PART FOUR

Astronomy Speaks

The Incredible Decade

From 1877 to 1887, the decade of the Great Comets, we had a greater and more representative concentration of phenomena related to UFO activity than during any other similar period prior to 1947. Astronomy's part has been an important one; the pertinent observations of astronomers extend through the centuries; and to such an extent that we cannot consider all of them in one short volume. However, if we consider the decade of the Great Comets, as a typical slice of UFO History, we shall err but little and that little quantitative rather than qualitative. The events of the comet years were numerous and concentrated, but not typical.

Astronomers missed the best cue of their collective lives during those years, for they were the culmination of generations of observations which, if accepted at face value and interpreted with psychic insight, would have authenticated UFO deduction. The comet years would have supplied visible confirmation to anyone with the perspicacity to look for it.

It is difficult to select any single event as having initiated this period. In fact there is no real discontinuity; merely an unusual surge of erratics. Either of two obscure occurrences might serve as curtain raisers, but there were straws in the wind before 1877. Dr. Kirkwood of Indiana University had commented on the unusual, and increasingly large, number of fireballs reported, and there had been a modest but steady increase in the number of comets discovered per year.

Neither of the two minor events within our solar system was great enough to attract much public attention at a time when astronomy was moving out of the visual stage into its golden era of spectroscopic and photographic adventure.

The true magnitude of the universe of stars and nebulae was only beginning to dawn on the human intellect, and studies of the solar system beginning to be passé, because objects only a few score millions of miles distant were too near home to concern the exploring mind. Yet visual observation rolled up a record in the later years of the 19th century which may turn out to be Astronomy's magnum opus for the race of mankind.

The first of the two little events took place in an obscure corner of the Mare Serenitatis, which is one of the Seas, or dark areas, which make up the Man in the Moon. Near the modest sized but well-known lunar crater called Hyginus by the selenographers, there appeared sometime in 1877, without fuss or warning, a small but perfect and distinct crater. It was only a few short miles in diameter. It was just big enough to be comfortably seen with the small telescopes of that day. Orthodox astronomers, who did not believe in changes of the moon, refused to accept the word of the selenographers at first, and there was a minor intraprofessional hassle. Eventually the little erratic was called Hyginus N ?

       IMPRESSION, MADE BY FORCE-FORMING A NEW
       Ships Hull MADES SUCH HOLES. MAY BEEN
       "DEEP-ROUGHED" BY BURNER, AFTERWARDS.

> They don't know but Very Little about THIS
> GALAXY that we Live in. If they did they'd
> shout for Joy or weep the tears of Heartbroken
> Egotistical S-M

The discovery should have been a tip-off!

In 1878, a tremendous disturbance broke out on the surface of our greatest planet. At the beginning it escaped the notice of professional astronomers. They were busy conquering worlds much further afield. But the amateurs noted it. The Great Red Spot of Jupiter (some called livid pink) was some six or seven thousand miles wide, thirty thousand miles long, shaped like a longitudinal section of a pecan, and it raced around the planet at a surface speed of about 200 miles per hour, shouldering aside all one other surface features of that planet. This storm, if it was such, lasted several decades. Whether there was anything purposeful about it is problematical. Certainly for absolute size it dwarfed little Hyginus N.

But Hyginus N was close to being in our own back yard, and it should have received more attention than a busy profession gave it. It should have been remembered when Watson and Swift thought that they were observing some new planets.

It wasn't. And science moved on in a manner which has been called "progress."

> I see the Humor of such a Sarcasm but too
> Jemi. It is the Catastrophic truth. They Learn
> the Wrong things and because it is a Machone,[1]
> or Material thing, they call it Good, even though
> they do not know the Least Natural *Law of
> Social Philosophy.* (Italic by A)

Whether or not the era of the great comets was initiated, or only marked, by the appearance of Jupiter's Red Spot, the surface of Jupiter was exhibiting a condition of great turmoil and disturbance. Round white spots, and equally well formed dark spots, formed, moved over the surface and went away. The big cloud belts were sometimes shifted and distorted. To maintain that such activity on Jupiter was intelligently directed, or that it actually caused the odd phenomena in our own neighborhood, would be presumptuous. But that a common state of disturbance existed both here and there cannot be denied.

> The *Great* Ark.

> To Have *seen* "The GREAT ARK" would Humble
> or Terrify *any* Human. I wish, even so, that I
> could have seen it, *the* Greatest structure ever
> built, by Humanoids, or all time.

Jupiter, largest of the planets, fifth from the sun, is bright and easy to observe with small telescopes, hence it has been a continuos subject for amateur astronomical research. The literature is full of their reports. Jupiter has about a dozen satellites big enough to be seen from the earth, and some are comparable to our moon in size. These, together with their 88,000-mile diameter parent, make up a complex system in which many things may be expected to happen and many are indeed reported by observers. Jupiter is practically, if not actually, a fluid planet, having an average density only a little greater that that of water, and in spite of its vast bulk, its surface gravity is only two and one-half times that of the earth. It rotates on its axis a little less than ten hours with an equatorial velocity of roughly 28,000 miles per hour, and is so unstable that different latitudes move with different speeds. Local spots, both defined and hazy, have movements of their own, and some pass each other at speeds up to two hundred miles per hour. The clouds, spots, and belts appear to be floating on a liquid or gaseous base.

---

[1] clearest translation.

Such in the environment of the Great Red Spot which appeared over night in 1878 and covered an area comparable to that of the entire terrestrial surface.

It might be expected that such a large feature would be rigidly attached to a core or substratum. Not so. The Red Spot changed its speed and position constantly. In twenty years, for all its size, it drifted more than twice around the planet – total distance of over half a million miles – and, shoving the cloud belts aside, it shifted latitude by several hundred miles.

We do not know the depth of the spot. Its silhouette shape was almost identical with that of the so-called auroral object which passed over Europe and England in 1882. If it was three-dimensionally symmetrical, it was shaped like a pecan – which is to say it had the shape so familiar to UFO observers: The cigar, spindle or Zeppelin shape – but 8,000 miles in diameter and 30,000 miles long.

Besides shape and particular movement, the Spot had one other characteristic in common with Maunder's Object. There was no noticeable distortion of its front, or advancing edge, as it plowed through the cloudy or fluid surface on which it floated, although it moved with a speed of two hundred miles per hour through the medium.

It is conceded by all scientists that life, such as we know, could not exist on Jupiter in any form, from our lowest to our highest. As for life in some other form, or weird, discarnate intelligence, the limit is defined only by one's ability to speculate.

I "READ": "No Life there at all, Malfunction"

Because Jupiter's great size, complex and turbulent condition, intricate system of satellites and attendant comets, and its gravitational effects on all other bodies within the sun's bailiwick, it would seem that most anything could happen on or around the huge orb.

ARK GOT STUCK.

It is a fair question to ask whence came the power to drive this mass, several times greater than the earth, through the surface material at such high speeds, and to crowd aside the vast equatorial belts, sometimes as much as 8,000 miles. What created it; what started it in motion and what kept it in motion; and what directed its movements?

Such a Mass would cause a Huge Explosion
when it Hit that Great Planet unleess introduced
with great care.

As part of the celestial show of 1878, we should take a closer look at the reports of Russell and Hirst from the Blue Mountains of Australia.

Mr. H.C. Russell was heading a small expedition into the mountains to study high altitude and clear mountain air for better observing conditions. Here is his report, extracted from a letter to *Observatory*.

...the only observation which I would here place on record was made on the morning of the 21st of October (1889) at nine o'clock AM, when, on looking at the moon, (Mr. Hirst) found that a large part of it was covered with a dark shade quite as dark as the shadow of the earth during an eclipse of the moon; its outlines were generally circular and it seemed to be fainter near the edges...it quite obliterated the view of about half the moon's terminator (or that part where the sunlight ends) whilst those parts of the terminator not within the shadow could be very distinctly seen. I should estimate the diameter of the shadow, from the part we could see on the moon, as about three-quarters the diameter of the moon. This is one of those remarkable facts which, being seen, should be recorded, although no explanation can at present be offered. One could hardly resist the conviction that it was a shadow; yet it could not have been the shadow of any known body...No change in the position of the shade could be detected after three hours of watching. 1878, November 26th, H.C. Russell.

This is an important observation it shows that things were going on in space near the earth. Such an observation as this seems almost without recorded precedent. The moon was past third quarter and was proceeding the sun across the morning sky. The shade seen by Hirst and Russell was either a cloudlike formation between the earth and the moon, or it was the shadow of something between the moon and the sun.

MIND. "DEEP" MOBILIZATION & Mulai

IE MINDINAO DEEP, [1] *PROJECT* MOBILIZATION
FOR M-Chil & The Building of it.

If between moon and sun, it was well within the intense glare of sunlight and difficult to see. Not only would it escape a casual glance but might evade a search and, unless solid, it might be almost entirely invisible. We cannot tell how far it was from the moon, but by the geometry of shadows we can make some estimates. Russell describes the shape as circular and fainter towards the edges. This is a typical description of a dense umbra and lighter penumbra. Making allowance for a tapering shadow, and the estimated diameter, the object should not have been much over 100,000 miles away and probably about 75,000 to 80,000 miles. t is similarly obvious that the object itself must have been approximately the same size as the combined umbra and penumbra, shall we say about 1,400 – 1,700 miles in diameter. We cannot tell whether it was solid or a dense cloud.

Old ark or "old" Home-ship – ?

Most important, however, is that this shade did not move in three hours' time. With both moon and sun moving, this object so maintained its position that its shadow, cast by the light of one moving object, the sun, remained stationary for three hours or more upon another moving object, the moon. That is control – firm, steady, calculated and maintained control of position. It implies purposefulness, persistence, delicacy and … intelligence.

& reason too.

Suppose, on the other hand, that it was not a shadow, but was a cloud interposed between earth and moon. Its actual size then could be anything from a gnat to something three-quarters the diameter of the moon, depending on its distance from the Blue Mountains. Thus we don't know the size for certain, except that it was smaller than 1,500 miles in diameter.

But in this case the manipulation of this object was even more complex. Not only was the object maintained between moon and earth, it was maintained steadily between moon and a very definite portion of the earth's surface which was rotating rapidly while the moon was revolving around it. This represents doubly intricate control. This is calculated control of a higher order than the other, and, in fact, requires more manipulation than simple hovering. By way of explanation, something more is required than an inorganic spatial body moving under unmodified laws of Kepler and Newton.

It was this phenomenon which evoked the scorn of the armchair astronomer and editor, Mr. R.A. Proctor, in London, and caused him to publicly impugn and the sanity, observational acuity, and even the good faith of Russell in a long and flippantly scurrilous letter to the *Echo*, a London evening paper, March 14, 1879.

A highly EMOTIONAL Letter, yelping the wounded
"feelings" of a Dog who thought secretly that *that*
Bone should have been HIS; ONLY A HOWL

---

[1] An additional reference to "Mindanao Deep" appears on page 130.

FOR *MORE* PRESTIGE.

Russell replied with considerable warmth to Proctor's unprovoked attack, and while he does not overtly say so, it is hard to escape the belief that he felt there was something purposeful in the behavior of this cloud and also in the way some other clouds and, for example, dry frogs, have maintained themselves over limited parts of the earth. At best he was thoroughly but honestly puzzled. Proctor's attack, on the other hand, had some of the characteristics of whistling in the dark. He showed a perceptible fear of admitting the reality of Russell's observation and sought to squelch the observer.

SOME Scientists are Merely Children. Many of them Working to acquire Prestige, then MORE Prestige, Selfish-Small Yapping Children YET, TOO SOME ARE NOWADAYS MATURE.

Drujel almost started a Bonfire.

I sense a tinge of nervousness in this, and certainly believe that Proctor, himself an astronomical student, writer and observer of note, recognized more than physical import in this odd event. His protestations have something of the same tinge as those of the man who suggested that a kangaroo made the "Devil's Hoofprints."

I do hope that this Man, either, Whistles in the Dark, OR, blasts the Lid off. Perhaps then Philosophic progress can be introduced, Peace restored & this our Home-Planet Saved from Prophesied end. However, either could be fatal to human kind but the Latter *Not At All* if Handled Properly.

UFO's Against the Sun

For generations, perhaps centuries, it was thought that there were one or more planets revolving within the orbit of Mercury. Perturbation of that planet and its orbit led to such a conclusion, particularly before the theory of relativity explained a part of the disturbance. Over a long period of years, astronomers kept seeing object of planetary shape and apparently planetary size crossing the disc of the sun, and these were almost universally assumed to be intra-Mercurial planets. Somehow it never occurred to anyone that similar crossings of the moon, also seen occasionally, could be related, nor that such objects between the earth and moon could undermine the intra-Mercurial planet Hypothesis.

Relativity? Will explain by man???

After a number of carefully observed crossings of the solar disc were recorded, some of the more able mathematicians calculated tentative orbits for an intra-Mercurial planet. They based this on the assumption that the intervals of time between transits were susceptible to a least-common-denominator which was the probable time of revolution of the suspected planet around the sun. Such calculations led consistently to disappointment and sometimes to heartbreak. No intra-Mercurial planet was ever found, although mathematical astronomers were so confidant of its existence they even named it: "Vulcan." Much time was spent searching for the hypothetical object and many an astronomer hoped to make the discovery and thus perpetuate his name. Since it was realized that such an object would never be far from the sun, searching was especially vigorous at times of total solar eclipse. (Such an opportunity was afforded by the total eclipse of July 29th, 1878 or which more later).

Authors Childishness

From the earliest days of organized astronomical observation there have been these sightings of round and spindle-shaped bodies crossing the disc of the sun. Some of these observations disclosed objects so discordant with the established framework of the solar system that science considered them anomalous and often denied the validity of the observations and the mental balance of the observers. Despite scathing linguistic fire, however, some of these vital notations got through to editors of astronomical and other journals.

Many such observations are tabulated in the *Observatory*, but they are also scattered through the scientific literature in general. Since it has now been irrefutably demonstrated that these could not have been intra-Mercurial planets, their significance becomes much more apparent than it was to the casual reader in the early 19th century. We have changed our conception, and now we can accept these objects as being close to the earth. The overwhelming mass of evidence is too great to brush aside, and proves that astronomy has been sighting UFO's in space.

So has ??????? but they deny it
Will always so, they too ??? (unreadable)

During the eclipse of September 7, 1820, crowds in the streets of Ebrun saw great numbers of objects in the sky, moving in straight lines, countermarching and turning, all separated by uniform spaces. Five unidentified bodies of appreciable size were seen by Astronomer Gruithuisen. Two unknown dark

Home-Ships, Scout ships & Life-boast.

bodies were seen by Pastorff on October 23, 1822. Webb saw an unknown thing near Venus, March 22, 1823. Many more unknowns were reported in 1823, and this may have been another peak period if these phenomena are really periodic in their appearances. Sporer saw one crossing the sun August 20, 1863. Two starlike objects were seen crossing the sun by Carrington on September 1859. Several examples are reported in *Webb's Celestial Objects*, particularly on the dates July 31, 1826, to May 30, 1828. Jaennicke saw an unknown object against the sun on May 30, 1853. The unknown planetary object seen by several people in London, and described in *Nature*, has never been explained. In the summer of 1860, R. Covington saw, without optical aid, an object crossing the sun. On June 6, 1761, Scheuten was watching a transit of Venus and saw an object as round, black, and distinct as Venus, but about one-half it size, moving for three hours across the sun. He thought it was a satellite of Venus, but since the many other skilled observers who watched the transit did not see this thing, it is most likely that it was very close to the earth's surface, and so displaced by parallax that it was silhouetted against the bright disc only in that one location.

Great Arks advance Home ship bringing news & orders for Preparation of its arrival.

All this leads up to a showdown on the intra-Mercurial planet question. Since it has been shown by C.H. F. Peters and others that there is no intra-Mercurial planet, then what are these things?

Although C.H.F. Peters tried to belittle the sightings of all observers as illusions or fraud, we have difficulty in rejecting the statement of experienced observers like Staudacher of Nuremberg, who saw, in February 1762, a round black spot on the sun. He missed it the next day, and such was its appearance and movement that he thought it may have been a new planet.

On November 19, 1762, Observer Lichtenberg saw with his unaided eye, a very large, round spot one-twelfth the diameter of the sun, traverse a chord of 70 degrees in approximately three hours. Since the apparent diameter of the sun is about half degree of arc, one-twelfth would be about two and one-half minutes or one hundred and fifty seconds. Mercury's apparent diameter, when in transit, averages about twelve seconds, depending on its distance of the moment, so this thing, if it be considered an intra-Mercurial planet, must have had an actual size of more than twenty times that of Mercury, that is, a diameter of 60,000 miles or so. Obviously such a thing as large as Saturn does not exist in any intra-Mercurial orbit. What then, was it? And how far away? At the gravitational neutral the apparent diameter of two and one-half minutes would represent a real dameter of two hundred miles or less. Again, it seems unlikely that a thing so large would penetrate the earth-moon system without causing some noticeable disturbance – so, again, what and how far? At eight hundred miles it would have to be only about a mile in diameter to appear that big, and we are getting used to the idea of something a mile or so in diameter and a few hundred miles away.

THE RETURN OF THE *GREAT* ARK.

Between the first and fifth of May, 1764, Hoffman saw with the naked eye a large round spot, one-fifth the diameter of the sun, traverse it slowly from north to south. That is a direction of motion almost unheard of in the solar system, except, perhaps, for a few maverick comets. It looks like controlled motion. The size is comparable to that of Lichtenberg's object, and the difference is no greater than would be apparent with an object between earth and moon shifting its position with the changing location of the gravitational neutral.

GREAT ARKS GRAND-TOUR

On June 17, 1777, Messier, cataloguer of Nebulae and Star Clusters, saw a number of little bodies crossing the sun very rapidly and in parallel directions.

D'Angos, at Tarbes, France, saw a slightly elliptical, sharply defined spot on the sun, about halfway between the edge and center, which took about twenty-five minutes to pass off the disc. That was on January 18, 1798. This movement is about eight minutes of arc in twenty-five minutes of time, and at a distance of 1,000 miles this would represent a speed of about one-mile in ten minutes or six miles per hour. At 10,000 miles it would be sixty miles per hour, and at 100,000 miles it would be about six hundred miles per hour and at 1,000,000 miles distance it would be speeding at 6,000 miles per hour. No data are available regarding its apparent size, but if it was ten seconds in diameter, just comfortable for visibility in a small telescope, its diameter in miles would be about 1/500,000 of whatever distance you might assign to it.

GREAT ARK

The next celestial event on our roster is unusually pertinent to our theme, and must have been startling when it was first published. On October 10, 1802, at Madgeburg, Fritch saw a spot moving two minutes of arc in four minutes of time, across the sun and not seen again after a doudy spell. Near the sun, e.g., in a deep intra-Mercurial orbit, this indicates a velocity of 15,000-20,000 miles per minute. Fritch also states that on March 20, 1800, and February 7, 1802, he saw spots having rapid motions of their own. In hundred of hours in the dusty tomes of the Library of Congress, that is the first case I have found where a scientist has state clearly that these objects were free-lance agents. Even so he seems to have been imbued with the idea that they were near the sun, or in dher words, in intra-Mercurial orbits – at any rate not adjuncts of the third planet and its satellite. This seems to be a statement of controlled motion, but Fritch said it in 1802, and Fritch was an astronomer!

On January 6, 1818, two Englishmen, Capel Lofft and a Mr. Acton saw a small subelliptical, opaque spot moving more rapidly over the sun than Venus moves when in transit. It disappeared before sunset and seemed to be of either cometary or planetary appearance. This is a well attested instance of observation by two men who were sober and reliable.

Gruituisen saw two bodies cross the sun together on July 26, 1819. There are a goodly number of sightings which report two objects traveling together, e.g., the planets seen by Watson and Swift during the eclipse of July 29, 1878.

A circular, well-defined spot, with a circular atmosphere and orange-gold tint, not seen again the same evening, is reported by two independent observers: Stark and Steinbuhl. It crossed the sun in about five hours. February 12, 1820.

On July 31, 1826, Stark saw a round spot on the northwest border of the sun at 4:45 PM which was not visible on either of the preceding day or following days.

The American Journal of Science, discusses reports by Pastorff for the years 1834, 1836, and 1837, wherein he reports having seen bodies crossing the sun's disc in comparatively short spaces of time. Definite dates are lacking, but there is a description of a large object, and an accompanying much smaller one, changing position relatively to each other and taking different courses, if not orbits. In 1834 he had seen similar bodies pass across the disc of the sun – looking very much like Mercury in transit – six times.

Now, there is another statement of rugged individualism in celestial, controlled motion. How confusing this must have seemed how frustrating to an inhibited observer who could think only in terms of intra-Mercurial planets. There was not one, but two or more bodies, of size comparable to Mercury,

OR ONE WHO DOESN'T REALIZE THE GALACTIC-MOLECULAR SCOPE OF EINSTIENS UNIFIED FIELD THEORY, 1922-27

moving across the sun repeatedly with what seemed to be directed movement. But how simple it all is to us, when we are thinking of objects from one to ten miles in diameter only a few hundred miles away, or ten to two hundred miles in diameter and 150,000 miles distant, attendant on the earth-moon system, navigable, and possibly using the gravitational neutral as a habitat.

There is another observation by Steinheibel at Vienna, April 27, 1820, reported in the *Monthly Notices*, in 1862.

A very small perfectly round spot, without a trace of penumbra, was seen to cross a considerable portion of the sun's disc in the short space of six hours as observed and reported, July 12, 1837, by De Vico at Rome.

At a distance comparable to that of the gravitational neutral, an object would cover half a degree in six hours with a speed of about 300-325 miles per hour. At the distance of an intra-Mercurial planet the speed would be in the order of 100,000 to 135,000 miles per hour, which is about 30-35 miles per second – a little bit high for planetary velocity, but not inconceivable.

In October 2, 1839, De Cuppis, an astronomical pupil at a College in Rome, saw a perfectly clear, round and definite spot moving at such a rate that it would cross the sun in about six hours.

In late June or early July 1847, Scott and Wray saw a spot like Mercury in transit. On October 11, 1847, Schmidt, at Bonn, saw a small black body pass rapidly over the sun, "which was neither bird nor insect crossing before the telescope." We do not know what he means by rapidly – six hours, six minutes, or six seconds. All those would be rapid depending on where you think the object was in space. If it was, say, half an hour, and the body was intra-Mercurial, its speed would be 650,000 to 800,000 miles per hour, or 200 miles per second, which is nebular velocity, not planetary. If only two or three seconds were involved, which is a reasonable assumption since Schmidt compared the object to a seed or a bird, then, whatever it was, it was not more than a few hundred miles from the earth—certainly not farther than the "neutral." We assume that this was Julius Schmidt who became director of the observatory at Athens.

He saw a similar object on October 14, 1849, and there is still another sighting by him on February 18, 1850.

On March 12, 1849, Lowe and Sidebotham watched for half an hour a small round black spot traversing the sun.

On June 11, 1855, Ritter and Schmidt, near Naples, watched, just before sunset and with the naked eye, a black body crossing the sun's disc. That the color, here, is always black is of not concern. That is the only color silhouettes against the sun could have, unless they had intrinsic brilliance per unit of apparent area much in excess of that of the sun itself.

On September 12, 1857, at Wandsbeck, Ohrt saw a remarkable round spot near the north border or edge of the sun, at 1:00 PM, It had disappeared when the sun was next seen on the 14th. This thing was a little bit smaller in appearance than Mercury.

On August 1, 1858, a circular, opaque body moving from east to west was watched for about one and a half hours in late afternoon by Wilson at Manchester, England.

In 1859, Dr. Lescarbault, an amateur astronomer of Oregeres, France, announced that he had observed the passage of a body of planetary size across the sun on March 26. Dr. Lescarbault wrote to Le Verrier, knowing of Le Verrier's interest in intra-Mercurial planets. The cloak and dagger investigation and third degree imposed on the good doctor by Le Verrier is quite an incident.

Le Verrier was convinced that this was a transit of "Vulcan," and predicted another transit for March 22, 1877. At that time astronomers of the whole civilized world were alerted, and an intense and eager watch was kept on that date, in order to confirm the existence of "Vulcan," and to verify Le Verrier's orbital computations.

Nobody saw anything on March 22, 1877; and the whole idea of an intra-Mercurial planet has been pretty much broken down...but: what was it that these many good people really did see? Were these reputable astronomers deluded, mendacious or irresponsible? They were all highly intelligent people, educated and trained in the fields of astronomy and mathematics. Either you must say yes to one or more to the above charges, or these alert observers saw something round and solid —and it wasn't an intra-Mercurial planet.

> They will NEVER ALERT the WHOLE WORLD AGAIN.
> It would interfere with the petty squabbles between
> Nations & cause a common-bond of the Brother-hood
> of Man sort of Kinship to be realized. These Humans
> Love to implose their will, to Make War, too Well.

Note how uniform the reports are as to the apparent size of these things: usually about the apparent size of Mercury; sometimes a bit larger, occasionally somewhat smaller. That implies either that the distances are usually about the same, or that these objects vary greatly in size. It seems a little more likely that both sizes and distances vary, but as or now this is debatable. We do have Pastorff's observation, and a few others, of large and small bodies seen simultaneously. It is our considered opinion that most of these things reported by astronomers as seen crossing the sun are of about the same size, and that they maintain a distance of about 150,000 to 175,000 miles from the earth for a considerable portion of the time.

On March 20, 1862, a sharply defined round spot was watched in its progress across the sun for about twenty minutes by Lummis, of Manchester, and a friend. It was about one-half the apparent diameter of Mercury.

On February 12, 1864, a spot 8" seconds of arc in diameter crossed the sun at a rate between that of Mercury and Venus. On May 6, 1865, a round black spot moving across the sun was watched by

Coumbray, at Constantinople. It was watched for over three-quarters of an hour, until its departure from the disc. This spot was a sharply defined, black point, which detached itself from a group of sunspots near the limb of the sun and crossed the entire disc in forty-eight minutes. In an intra-Mercurial orbit having one-third the radius of the earth's orbit, it would require a speed of approximately 6,000 miles per minute, or a hundred miles per second to accomplish this, and this is a very high planetary velocity. At the earth-sun neutral, however, an object would move the same angular distance in the same time, with a speed of about thirty-five miles per hour, a conservative velocity even for a UFO.

There are seven reported sightings, in 1886, of a large body being seen near Venus. These are not transits of the sun, it is true; but the objects are in general direction of the sun – and the gravitational neutral – and there is always the possibility that some bodies are floating at the Venus-Sun neutral, as well as close to the earth.

In 1645, a body large enough to look like a satellite was seen near Venus. It was said to have been seen four times in the first half of the 18th century and again in 1867.

A luminous spot was seen in 1799, by Harding and Schroedter, moving over the disc of Mercury. This indeed, could not have been a intra-Mercurial planet.

There were two observations by Denning and Hind, persistent observers, on November 3, 1871, and March 26, 1873, and a black body was seen by Weber, at Berlin, April 4, 1876.

The London Times, for December 17, 1883, reports that Mr. Hicks Pashaw, in Egypt, saw through glasses, "an immense black spot upon the lower part of the sun."

According to Science, July 31, 1896, Brooks, of Smith Observatory, saw a round object pass slowly across the moon; he thought it was a dark meteor. It was about one-thirtieth the moon's diameter, and crossed in three or four seconds. According to the Scientific American, astronomer Muller saw a similar phenomenon on April 4, 1892. Now there are some objects which were actually seen to be closer than the moon. If Brooks' object was close to the moon, and traversed the disc in four seconds, it was moving at better than five hundred miles per second, and that is nebular velocity, neither planetary nor stellar, meteoric nor cometary velocity. So we adjudge it to have been closer to the earth. At the neutral it would still have to be moving at several hundred miles per second. At two hundred and fifty miles above the earth it would only have to be moving half a mile a second. If the thing was hovering, on the other hand, it would cross the moon's disc in two minutes – so it could not have been hovering.

Home-ship

All this account of objects of planetary aspect crossing the discs of the sun and moon is preamble to the hassle of Watson and Swift vs. the "profession," subsequent to the total solar eclipse of July 29, 1878.

There can be little doubt but that these objects existed, and that they existed in space; that they are quite commonly seen between the earth and t moon, and at least once between the earth and Mercury; that they appear as discs or spheres, spindles or dumbbells.

> Crescents, Sackles? Two reasons for odd
> shapes, one Electronic-Mag-Molecular "FIELD"
> Migration due to "Coat" on Center Parts of
> Ships Drive units; other, Like "Sun-Dogs."
> *also*, an Enfused Ship, Hit by ultra-High
> Polar-infusion Wave flames up & often takes
> these shapes, *to some extent*. Thus you have
> in effect a FORCE-FIED CHARGE *OVER-CHARGING*
> *THE* DRIVE-INDUCTION part of the ship. This
> causes Heat, cooks the Pilot and flames the

ship to cinders if it is Not caught soon
enough to cut-off (shed) the over-charge.

Location of UFO's

We have already mentioned Swift and Watson, and the objects which they saw. We are now going to present the details of how the observations were made and of the controversy arising with those astronomers who were not there and who did not see the object. We expect to show how these observations not only establish the actuality of UFO's in space, but demonstrate their approximate distance as well.

James C. Watson, one-time director of the Astronomical Observatory of the University of Michigan, wrote one of the most widely used text and reference books on mathematical astronomy. He had one of the best minds in astronomy and was an expert observer. Dr. Watson was at the peak of his career on July 29, 1878 the time of the total solar eclipse.

Lewis Swift was the director of Warner Observatory, and a skilled searcher for new bodies like planets and comets.

Neither of these men can be called irresponsible. They knew the difference between stars, planets, comets and nebulae. They did not see ghosts. However, at the total eclipse of the Sun, July 29, 1878, they saw unscheduled, unexplained objects. Like many of their contemporary scientists, however, they were too preoccupied with intra-Mercurial planets to speculate on anything close to the earth.

MOBILIZATION FOR BUILDING of Choi was SEEN

Astronomers came long distances to observe this eclipse. Many Europeans traveled across the Atlantic, then to the high plateaus of Colorado and Wyoming. Many were determined to make a final desperate search for an intra-Mercurial planet which, supposedly quite near the sun, should have shown up at the time of total eclipse. Both Watson and Swift arranged special equipment for this search, and both brought special skills to the task.

Watson was first to announce his findings. Through skillful use of a four-and-one-half-inch telescope (which this writer has used many times at the University of Michigan), Watson found two disclike or planetary objects, both red and both comparable in size to Mercury, perhaps a bit smaller. One was 2 ½° from the sun and the other between 4° and 5°. Both were to the west. Watson measured their positions carefully. He reported them as intra-Mercurial planets.

Swift saw two discoid objects also, of about the same size, brightness and color. He reported them as intra-Mercurial planets. But Swift saw them in different places. Whereas Watson's two were several degrees apart, Swift's were very close together. The members of the astronomical fraternity, who were not there, and observed nothing, were scathingly sarcastic. They maintained that Swift and Watson saw nothing but some stars which they had failed to identify accurately. But these men had memorized the star-fields and had made careful measurements. To have made mistakes of which they were accused, they would have been guilty of puerile errors.

> An attitude common, even among primitives,
> "I haven't been there or Seen such a place
> or a Thing or Person or Happening SO I must
> SHOW a semblance of Intellec & DOUBT this
> thing *until* I see it Myself." *(Too Common)*

> Strangely, No Sailor would believe that the
> World was Round even when SEEING its round-
> ness *Each Day*, for it WAS NOT THE PROPER WAY
> TO THINK THEN.

The conflict was long and hot, and towards the end it was bitter, but the observers stood their ground. They insisted that they saw something, and since not one person in the profession could conceive of anything but an intra-Mercurial planet, no common ground was ever found for agreement. The British professionals, and Dr. C.H.F. Peters, in the United States, were especially vehement in their protests. In a long and brilliant analysis, Peters proved conclusively that these objects could not possibly be intra-Mercurial planets, and for good measure proved that none of the other long lists or objects seen near the sun or crossing it could be such planets. In fact he did a credible job of proving that no such planet could exist! After studying his arguments, I most whole-heartedly concur – up to a point. That point is where Dr. Peters tries to prove that since Watson and Swift did not see intra-Mercurial planets, what they did see were erroneously identified stars. But he would not necessarily agree that they had seen anything at all. Peters was bitterly sarcastic and felt rather too secure in his superb analytical ability.

> IN THE ABOVE EXAMPLED CONFLICT IT WAS NOT
> WHO WAS RIGHT OR WRONG BUT "WHO BUT
> MYSELF IS THE BEST OBSERVER: I.E. *MY* PRIDE
> & *MY* EXPIERENCE *OR* EGO. WHEN EGO SLIGHTS
> EGO, BOTH BECOME NARROW AND QUITE SMALL.

But Peters performed a wonderful service for us!

Dr. C.H.F. Peters, arch master of astronomical and mathematical analysis, set up the best scientific case for UFO's which has ever been stated – unless one denies the observations, together with the sanity and honesty of Watson and Swift and about thirty other honest observers. I would be willing to rest the entire case for UFO's on Peters' analysis, if the observations be granted as presented by those practiced observers.

It boils down to this: Watson and Swift did see two disclike objects. C.H.F. Peters proved that they were not planets and not very far from the earth.

So did 30 others.

To make a long story much too short, here is what happened. First, everybody was wrong to some degree, as often happens in bitter controversies; and everybody was partly right. Watson and Swift did see what they said they saw – but they were wrong in thinking that they saw planets. Peters was eminently right in his analysis that they could not have been planets – but he was wrong, most blindly and unjustly, in saying that they did not see anything.

Watson saw two discs several degrees apart. Swift saw them close together and near the locations of Watson's first one. Watson and Swift observed from sites about one hundred and eight-five miles apart. Parallax caused the difference in the locations of the objects. On the basis of the measured positions and sizes, it is possible for us who are not blinded by inhibition and preconception, as were Watson, Swift, and Peters, to see that these two objects were UFO's not far away, but far enough to be surely in space. One was nearer than the other. The nearest one was displaced by parallax in Swift's observations due to the one-hundred-and-eight-five-mile base line. It is as simple as that.

Watson's object "a" turns out to have been between the extreme limits of ten thousand and sixty thousand miles from the earth. The best overall consideration places it at about twenty thousand miles away. Watson's "b" object, on the other hand, which was so greatly displaced in apparent position by the one-hundred-and-eighty-five-mile base line, was about one-tenth as far away as "a." If we assume "a" to be at twenty thousand miles, then "b" was at about two thousand miles.

The nearer one seems to have been smaller. The more distant one appears to have had a diameter of one-quarter to one and one-half miles depending on its distance, and at twenty thousand miles would be about half a mile or somewhat more in diameter. "B," the nearer one, would be about one-tenth as great. This is in keeping with our mother ship concept.

As for the red color, which Peters doubted so bitterly, it is simply explained when we realize that the objects were near the earth. At such a distance, they must have been within the penumbra of the moon's shadow. They thus escaped direct sunlight which would have given them crecentic illumination. However, they were illuminated by sunlight which came first to the earth through a long thickness of atmosphere and was reflected back from the surface. The blue light was therefore screened out. When the light finally got back to the objects it was red. On being returned by them to the observers, the light passed a third time through the atmosphere and naturally it was very red. Those who have seen the moon in eclipse will remember how red it looks from just one passage of the light through the atmosphere.

At various times during the past half-century, there have been suggestions of small satellites circling the earth, very rapidly, and close to the surface – two hundred to six hundred miles away, that is. *The New York Times* of August 23, 1954 discusses the rediscovery of these little bodies by Dr. Lapaz of the Department of Astronomy of the University of New Mexico. It seems that there has been some feeling that Russia may have catapulted these into space as observation platforms, and the Ordnance Department of the U.S. Army became concerned about it. While we do not deny the possibility of such an advance by the Russians, we do feel that observations covering hundreds of years disprove this supposed Russian origin of UFO's, and also establish controlled and irregular motion as opposed to the regularity of orbital motion.

In any event, it is time that the U.S.A. took note of these entities and made some study of them. Since they probably stay in the gravitational neutral most of the time, they are never far out of line with the sun, and this is why it is so difficult to see them except at times of eclipse or when they are actually in transit across the sun.

But there are ways to look for them: one is with telescopes and the other is with radar. Barring more searches at eclipse time, it does seem that radar has the better possibilities. We know that radar blips can be bounced off the moon: why not from these objects which are nearer? Let's point both our radar sets and telescopes at the region near the sun, at times of both new and full moon and see what we can see. The objects probably range a very few degrees east and west of the sun at first and third quarters of the moon. That would probably be the best time to look.

A Variation of the Radio-Telescope such as in used in England, & I Believe, New Jersey USA, can Detect Energy-forms of L-M Ships PLUS their Solid & "Semi-Solid_ forms as well. Detects "Nodes," too

UFO Patrol

The years 1879 and 1880 partook of the general spiciness of the era of the comets. The astronomical profession did not work up any major fracases, but then you cannot have a riot every year. However, things did happen.

There was the house whose roof suddenly took its departure on Easter Sunday of 1879 – a slate roof. It jumped up into the air suddenly and then fell back on to the ground. Beyond ten meters from the house nothing was disturbed. There wasn't the least bit of wind. This was officially recorded in the French science magazine, *La Nature* 1879. There are other cases of roofs taking off without provocation. An American case was reportedly similar.

On July 10, 1880, the conservative *Scientific American* broke its editorial policy of reticence regarding abnormal events and noted that some men were working in a field in Ontario when they saw stones shooting upward – without the aid of a whirlwind or any other obvious cause. Something seemed to be disturbing gravity.

On April 9, 1879, slag was reported to fall in the city of Chicago.

There were many falls of ice in 1879 – some at Richmond England, was in chunks five inches long.

Bright spots or lights continued to be seen on the moon in 1879-80, and the disturbances on the surface of Jupiter were so noteworthy as to cause comment in *Nature*. There were five comets visible in 1879 and six in 1880, although not all were visible to the naked eye. A green thunderbolt was reported in the *Scientific American*, and we are thereby reminded of the spate of green thunderbolts over New Mexico during the past three or four years.

The sako Banjo meteorite, which fell in Eastern Europe in the quite incredibly active years of 1879 – 80, was a strange and startling new kind of meteoric stone, and there were darkness, sun darkening, and abnormally cold winter weather.

The Great Red Spot continued to evolve and to maintain its merciless drive around the great globe of that planet. Because of its peculiar shape and movement, one could almost imagine a great interstellar space ship landing and floating on Jupiter's surface. Its size makes this a debatable hypothesis.

Would he believe it *when* he sees it?

But there was one astronomical event, which escaped general notice by being in the freak class. Only in retrospect is its significance revealed, for it was one of those dogs which seldom get reported except by naïve folk who think that what they see is what they see. There have been several reports of misty, fiery or cometary objects, which exhibited unusual motion. Often times, our attention is only attracted to them by unusually rapid movement, but even this has some statistical value and may signify the proximity of the object to earth. Such a report was telegraphed by Russian Astronomers in the early 1920's and was said to be moving ten degrees per hour. However, some alert observers have been acute enough to note motion which was too erratic to partake of the normal characteristics of meteoric or cometary activity, and only now are we awakening to the possibility that such erratic movement may signify direction and control by intelligence.

One of the most outstanding examples of erratic celestial movement was that noted by observer Henry Harrison, of Jersey City, New Jersey, on the night of April 12 and 13, 1879. He took careful settings and times on an object whose motion is a revelation. Harrison reported this event to the Naval Observatory at Washington by telegram, but the notice was disregarded by Director Hall, with the proper professional aplomb; for verily it was without doubt an erratic on the periphery of the consummately damned.

Getting no response from the fount of authority, Harrison reported his discovery to the New York Tribune in a letter, and this was reproduced in the *Scientific American* May 10, 1879. It is to the everlasting credit of the very conservative editors that they could and did recognize this item, partially at least, for its true worth. After publication in the *Scientific American*, some of the more alert astronomers bedeviled Harrison for further details, while berating him for sloppy scientific reporting. Harrison, an astronomer of militantly unpretentious character, was depressed by the critics and embittered by the snubbing he received from the inner sanctum of the Naval Observatory. But he responded with a letter under the date may 20, 1879. After some sarcastic remarks anent people who always see wonders in everything celestial, he says in part:

...I did not think that the above phenomenon was anything but of a meteoric nature...and it would have been XXXXXXX to have made a great outcry. Messages sent to Professor Hall were urged by a personal friend, whom I called into the observatory to see the object; otherwise it would this day only be known to my personal friends. The coolness with which my dispatch was received at the Washington Observatory, after great inconveniences in sending it, has compelled me to regret any publicity on my part. The presumption that I found Brorsen's comet ought to have been abandoned immediately from the fact that Brorsen's comet moved a little over a degree per day, whereas this object moved with a (variable) rapidity of two minutes of Right Ascension of one minute of time, passing the comet by about four degrees...There is one fact, however, which reconciles me to it, and that is the fact that the object was seen also by Mr. J. Spencer Devoe, on Manhattanville, New York, who published a letter to that effect.

After acknowledging indebtedness to his friend, Henry M. Parkhurst, for his interest, he gives the details of his observations:

POSITIONS OF OBJECT 1879, April 12 (Local Mean Time)

Time	Right Ascension	(Rate of R.A. per minute of time	North Declination
8h 40m PM	2h 34m	2.4	37°
9 10	3 46	3.1	37
9 35	5 04	2.6	37
10 30	7 08		37 06'
11 30	— —		37 28'
2 10	15 30	2.3	37 30'

He comments on the irregularity of motion.

Harrison concludes by hoping that Devoe will quickly publish his own observations for corroboration and confirmation, but as of the date of this writing I have not succeeded in finding any such report. The report from Devoe would be of considerable importance to the case for intelligently directed motion. Anyone reporting the reference will be making a worthwhile contribution to the *Case for the UFO's*. And unless we deny the veracity of Devoe, Harrison, and Parkhurst, or impugn their intelligence as observers -- or both -- there cannot possibly be any argument against manipulated objects of the misty or ethereal types in space.

So called Ethereal types are the Old Force-
Shield cooking full blast, Made good Protection.

With his letter to the *Scientific American*, Harrison sent a description and a sketch. He described it as looking like a planetary nebula, which has but slight resemblance to a comet, or any other celestial object. To us, however, there is value in his drawing. A planetary nebula is almost circular, and certainly not flat on one side. This object looked organic. We are vaguely reminded of some of the shapes of pyramids, bells, pears, etc., which have been reported for generations. Clearly a nebulous or gaseous object, freely suspended in space, would assume a symmetrical shape and fuzzy edges. This thing did neither. Its appearance alone indicates that it was a UFO. Its motion clinches the argument. There are other similar reports in history of astronomy, but this one can be our prototype. It should be a classic, not only of observation but of how an inhabited and regimented science can pass up the most spectacular of discoveries. It is just possible that this is the most important and revolutionary telescopic observation ever published, especially if we place as high a value on discovering and contacting a new racial intelligence as we do on finding new nebulae a few million lights years distant.

Yeah, IF. Well, Nobody's interested.

Before you get excited about that harmless little table of figures, and complain that I'm turning technical, I will give a modicum of explanation. Right Ascension (usually abbreviated RA) is the astronomer's technical way of locating an object eastward among the stars, from an arbitrarily selected point in the sky, and corresponds to longitude on the earth's' surface. Declination is the distance north or south of the celestial equator, and corresponds to latitude on the earth's surface. It really is not complicated.

We will better understand Harrison's observation if we realize that an object hovering directly overhead will move among the stars at a rate of one minute of RA in one minute of time. Imagine yourself lying under a tree at night looking upward at the stars. As the earth turns on it axis the twigs above you move slowly eastward across the stars at exactly one minute of RA per minute of time. Harrison's object was moving approximately three times that quickly.

These figures of Harrison's are the very thing for which UFO protagonists have been praying. They are the scientific pay-off!

Three minutes of RA per one minute of time is much too rapid for a comet, and the object didn't even look like a comet. Such a speed is impossibly slow for a meteor, not even a fraction of one per cent of meteoric velocity; and it certainly has less resemblance to a meteor than almost anything you could name. A comet very close to earth could move that rapidly, but a comet would not make sudden changes in direction. Under the laws of gravitation it could not.

It is important to note that during the first three hours the object did not move in declination. Hence it was not moving in a great circle, but around a parallel of declination, which in turn means that it was moving straight eastward, which, except at the equator, is impossible for uncontrolled motion – so it was directed.

So What.

But, then, it suddenly changed from one declination to another – an impossible maneuver for an uncontrolled body!

Catch one of them A Magnetic "Net" will do.

Mag. "deadfall" cut-out field controller would be considered a Crack-Pot Idea even if it *is*[1] the only chance *to catch one*. Must Cut Mag. field intake to do so.

---

[1] Italic by Jeml

Harrison's bell-shaped object was moving almost three times as fast as rotation of the earth would cause it to do. At first one hesitates to say that it was hovering, but a little mathematical deduction indicates an object merely drifting with currents of the upper air and at one hundred miles latitude would need to have but 2.4 miles per hour velocity over the ground, an at ten miles above New York and appearing in Dec. 37° north, it would be drifting only a quarter mile per hour and would have been but seven-tenths of a mile south of Harrson's observing point an therefore directly over New York Harbor.

Furthermore, if the object was actually moving in a straight line, overhead, it would appear to speed up slightly when it crossed his meridian (the N-S line) and this is precisely what it did. And, assuming that it shifted its position slightly so as to pass nearly over the city, its shift of a little more than half a degree of declination would indicated height of from ten to one hundred miles.

Considered from ANY approach, this object appears to have been organic, intelligently operated and hovering over New York City!

The *New York Tribune* of April 26, 1879, published a letter from Mr. Devoe, dated April 17, in which he stated that he, too, had at first thought it to be a planetary nebula like one near Beta Ursa Majoris, but he was equally astonished at the rapid pace which carried it away so fast that he could not find it again after taking time out for coffee. A little can be gained from his letter. He says the object was wonderfully brilliant, and at least the size of the Praesepe star cluster, which is a well-known naked eye object, and was brighter than Praesepe. It would, therefore, appear that it was brighter and larger as seen by Devoe than by Harrison, and if such a small difference in the site of observation could make such a difference in appearance, then the wanderer was indeed close to New York City. From Devoe's rough description of the size, this object would have been about half a mile in diameter at an altitude of eight to one hundred miles, If I can find a more accurate report of Devoe's observations, I could learn more about the size and distance of the object.

Whatever this thing was, and whatever may be the accuracy of our speculations as to its speed, distance and size, it exhibited motion inexplicable except as intelligent control.

There is a suggestion for us in this story of Harrison's rambling object. Professional astronomers are not spending much time, if any at all, in searching the sky for comets or cometary objects. For more than a hundred years most of this has been done by amateurs, and today very little is done by anybody. We have seen that a minimum of quantitative observation by Devoe would have enabled us to determine the distance, altitude, speed and size of Harrison's object. We do not know how many of the things there are near the earth, so why not start a UFO searching campaign among a coalition of UFO enthusiasts, amateur astronomers and radio hams?

Dr. Bone's crude observation of the discoid object was of the greatest importance in confirming Dr. Gould's discovery of 1882, and the observations of Bone and Tebbutt established the great parallax which has enabled us to show the proximity of those objects.

There are apparently two classes of dirigible UFO's to look for. One is the planetary, disclike things seen near the sun and moon, as by Watson and Swift, and the other is the cometary type as seen by Harrison.

The cometary ones can be swept for, just as are comets, and with the identical equipment -- special comet-seeking telescopes with structure, and lenses designed for that purpose. Any telescope can be used and there are many idle ones.

I do not believe that large numbers of cometary UFO's will be found, although I am not sure. Observers near large centers of population, atom plants or industrial sites will probably have the most success. But while the number of expected objects is small, the searching is easier than for discs. (red is B and Jemi)

The planetary discs, like those of Watson, are difficult to see because they stay nearly in line with the sun and moon and are lost in the glare of sunlight. Even so, this assures that they will be in a very limited part of the sky. Why not devise ways to search the regions near both sun and moon, especially at new moon with telescopes and radar? Because of the glare, radar would seem to offer the most likely chances of success as it will not suffer interference from the sun.

We have some tremendous advantages for this type of research today. We note the essential necessity for simultaneous observation from at least two points. This can be ONLY accomplished through the help of the radio ham networks. Let us set up dozens of observational stations, with telescopes, and let us man them with at least one saucer specialist, let us add some radar observers, for triangulation can be effected by radar as well as with telescopes. Let us maintain instantaneous contacts via the ham networks so that if one station sees a suspicious object, other stations can be alerted immediately; let us report all of this to an established central office.

WILL NEVER BE PERMITTED BY OUR GOVERNMENT TO A PURELY CIVILIAN SET-UP NOHOW

In this way we can track these erratic things to their source, be it the upper atmosphere, the moon, the gravitational neutral, or what have you. The UFO's problem can be solved, despite the curtain of secrecy, by coordinated effort. If an observing station in, say Philadelphia discovered a fast mover, they could alert observers in Baltimore, Harrisburg, and Jersey City, and a quick, triangulation would tell just how far out the interloper was, how big, and its speed. This would be a new type of saucer patrol, and would doubtless result in some genuine comets being discovered as well as xzxxx suspicious characters. So much the better.

This would make a good cooperative program for all interest parties. A specially organized saucer club could sponsor it.

IT WOULD DO LITTLE GOOD, EVEN IF A COLONY WERE OPENLY ESTABLISHED IN U.S. LAND. FOR, THOUGH, MAN WOULD THEN THUSLY REACH THE STARS THEY WOULD "FEEL" THE LITTLE-MEN TO BE "SUCH CHILDREN" THAT THEY I. E. MAN, WOULD "THINK" THE GIFT OF SPACE LIGHT TO BE MUCH MUCH MORE MPORTANT THAN THE PHILOSOPHY BY WHICH L-MS LIVE IN, WITH & OVER THOSE MIND WRECKING CONDITIONS THAT SPACE & SEA CONTAIN AND YET THEY LIVE WITH THESE, *SO VERY HAPPILY* THE ONLY THING "BAD" about such a colony is the fact that Little-Men DO NOT REMEMBER TO ALWAYS REMAIN VISIBLE. WHEN EMBARAASSED THEY GO "POP" & thus they "Hide". REASON: REPEATED H FE'SHIP STATE GIVES L-MS THIS ABILITY. THUS NOW YOU SEE OVER-ALL WISDOM OF EINSTIENS RETRACTION OF HIS UNIFIED FIELD THEORY. IN U.S. NAVYS SHIP INVISIBILITY EXPIERIMENTS(sic), 1943. RESULTS OF SUCH UNINFORMED TINKERING *SEEMED* TO SHOW THE CORRECTNESS OF HIS "REASON" FOR RETRACTION.

The Height of the Puzzle

There is no way of estimating how many of these fast-moving space objects escape all notice, nor is there any way of knowing how many are seen but not reported for fear of embarrassment. We have found a few examples, and still further search of the literature would produce more.

Colonel Marwick, amateur in South Africa, saw an object near the moon on September 27, 1881 (not the concentration of these in 1881), like a comet but moving very rapidly. On August 28, 1883 Captain Noble saw something "like a comet, new and glorious." On the nights of September 11, and 13, 1883, Professor Swift, at Rochester, saw an unknown object like a comet, and something was seen in Puerto Rico and about the same time in Ohio.

The most spectacular of these speed demons was seen by Captain Eddie, at his observatory in Grahamstown, South Africa, on October 27, 1890. It was called a comet, but almost certainly was not, for its description was much more like that of Maunder's auroral object. In fact it has something of the appearance of an auroral arch bridging a quarter of the horizon, but moving with a deliberate speed very similar to the Maunder thing. This object of Captain Eddie's sped 100 degrees across the sky in three-quarter of an hour. It made Harrison's cometary whiffit seem to be hovering, which no doubt it was. How far away was it and how high? What was its size? Who knows? But, a second observation from Pretoria, Johannesburg, Bloemfontein, East London, Port Elizabeth or Capetown would have located it definitely and determined the distance via parallax – and at that speed ??? we know it was close enough to exhibit great parallax – and thence we could sense its size and real speed, and perhaps its nature.

Another one of these celestail mavericks was seen by Professor Copeland, September 10, 1891, and Drayer saw it at Armagh Observatory and Alexander Graham Bell saw it or one like it in Nova Scotia the next night. If these astronomers made time measurements, and those measurements could be found, they would be invaluable to us today.

There were other things that were happening in 1879-80. There was reported a great waterspout at St. Kitts, in the West Indies, about the first of February 1880. It was called a waterspout and reported as though a single and unassociated entity. But while a solid mass of water of unknown origin was drowning St. Kitts, masses of water were deluging the Island of Grenada three hundred miles away. And in the Island of Dominica, masses of water broke windows and roofs. Mud fell in tons. Rivers burped with the detachables of the island: trees, cattle, houses, people. Other nations and islands were hit by masses of water. Colombia and Salvador were among them. Beginning on October 10, and continuing until the catastrophe at Saint Kitts, there was deluge after deluge on the earth – in one zone of latitude, the north tropical area. It seemed that a swarm of meteoric lakes must have gotten in the way of a rotating earth. To most of us such a thing "just could not be". But it did happen, and it is doubtful if meteorologists have ever assembled all of the data on that series of floods. Maybe it was not as general as the world-wide deluge of 1913, but it was bad enough, and its very concentration within a limited belt of terrestrial surface is sufficient for us to conclude that extraterrestrial forces and materials were involved. These storms partook, of the ado of a very disturbed period in which we should have become aware of our spatial environment.

On May 15, 1879, Commander Pringle, of *H.M.S. Vulture*, saw luminous waves of pulsating water. They were under the surface, not above it, and passed beneath his ship. The appearance was that of a revolving wheel of light, with illuminated or luminous spokes. In fact there were two wheels, one on each side of the ship, and the phenomenon lasted more than half an hour. There have been several such reports, and most of them come from oriental waters.

MINDINAO "DEEP" PROJECT STILL IN THE BUILDING
They will never finish that city Chomlegi has not
enough F to finish its planned growth but Location good.

About this time an enormous number of luminous bodies were seen to rise from the horizon in Germany. They shone with remarkably brilliant light and passed horizontally from east to west. A carbonacious (sic) mass like brown coal fell from the sky in Argentina. The red, blue and gray hailstones fell in 1880. An object of quartzite was reported to fall at Schroon Lake, New York. Ricco, at the Palermo Observatory, saw long parallel line of bodies crossing the sun. The wheels of light in the sea were seen again in May and June of 1880, reported from more than one vessel at sea. The three lights moving in the ravine at St. Petersburg were seen on July 30, 1880. Luminous phenomena continued to appear on the moon throughout 1879-80, including a luminous line, cable or wall which was seen January 23, definitely dividing in half the very brilliant interior of the prominent lunar crater Aristarchus, which has been carefully studied for centuries by those who suspect the moon of harboring life in some form. This was seen and sketched by Trouvelot, one of the few skilled astronomical observers with artistic ability.

A dead "sea serpent" was found at sea in early 1880, and sailors danced on its upturned belly. Something similar, like a turtle sixty feel long and forty feet wide was reported in the *New Zealand Times*, in December 1883, and there were several reports of huge marine animals during the comet years.

IF SO CALLED "SEA MONSTER OR SERPENT WAS A L-M SHIP *IT IS STILL THERE* UNDERSEA IF IF S-Ms NEUTRALIZED IT: THE L-MS WILL NOT HAVE COME BACK *OR* CALLED FOR IT, IN S-M TERRITORY.

The flying machine over Louisville, Kentucky was of 1880 vintage, and also the thing changing shape over Madisonville, Kentucky. The British trading ship, *Atlanta*, bound for Bermuda, was lost in 1880 – without trace in that region so well known today as the area of missing planes and ships.

There was an invasion of insects – flies – in 1880. Clouds of them, millions and millions appeared over Havre, France, as though from the Atlantic. On August 21, they blackened the air and seemed exhausted when they fell. The same day a cloud of long, black flies, so large that it took twenty minutes to pass, blackened the sky over Nova Scotia. Another cloud on September first. East or west, they seemed to come from the mysterious Atlantic. In November, a host of flies overwhelmed a schooner off the coast of Norfolk, England, lasting over five hours and driving the crew below decks. On September 4 the steamboat *Martin* was swarmed by a cloud of flies that reached as far as the eye could see; a drift of black snow. On the fifth a cloud of black flies appeared over Gusboro, Nova Scotia; took over half an hour to pass.

According to the *New York Times*, a woman was killed in 1880 in a closed room which nobody had entered. Explanations were that she had been killed by lightning, but bedposts were chopped as by a hatchet.

There seems almost always to be poltergeist activity in England, but an especially cirulent (sic) case broke out in October, 1880.

The year 1880 was in the midst of what we have chosen to call the years of the comets. There were six comets in the skies of 1880. The 19th century as a whole showed increasing activity in comet discovery, and in the number of bright comets. In part this can be attributed to increasing interest in telescopic work, and to improved availability and quality of small telescopes suitable for amateurs who made up a growing body wishing to participate in astronomical research, but lacked the great, fine-quality instruments of the large observatories. But such activity cannot in any way account for the very bright, very spectacular comets of 1880, 1880, and 1882, with their attendant phenomena, many of which can conservatively be described as abnormal. One had two tails; one aft and one forward, and appeared to have nuclei exhibiting independent motion within the head or the coma.

Study the following table of comet discoveries:

Period AD	New Comets Found	Average per year
1782 – 1801	25	1.25
1802 - 1821	26	1.30
1822 – 1841	36	1.80
1842 – 1861	83	4.15
1862 – 1881	79	3.95
1882 – 1889	40	5.00

There is a hint, of the added activity which we have suspected for 1845-55. Astronomer Barnard tabulated the comets discovered for 1876-86 and published the results in 1886, almost as though he felt, even then, that something abnormal was going on.

The score for "The Decade" is as follows:

1876 . . . 0	1882 . . . 3
1877 . . . 6	1883 . . . 2
1878 . . . 3	1884 . . . 3
1879 . . . 5	1885 . . . 6
1880 . . . 5	1886 . . . 3 (first seven months)
1881 . . . 8	

The peak at 1877-81 is very noticeable, without taking into consideration the number and size of the naked eye comets of mid-decade. What with comets, red spots, Hyginus N, will-o-the-wisps like Harrison's lights on the moon, and objects crossing the sun, the decade of the 1880's was, for certain, ushered in with a blaze of celestial glory, and it ended with a fanfare of puzzles.

The light of comets has been seen to fluctuate in rather remarkable manners. This was especially true of Pon's comet during its return in 1883-84, at which time it manifested the spirit of the times and presented some eccentric behavior. Its brilliance, for example, increased thirty-forty-fold above that explainable from merely becoming closer to the sun. In addition there were hour-to-hour fluctuations of one hundred percent and more, and concomitantly the nucleus experienced some tortuous changes in shape and structure, as such as we will note again in the great comets of 1881 and 1882.

In the *Monthly Notices* of the Royal Astronomical Society, there is detailed description of all of the six comets of 1880, and there is added the following:

In addition to the six comets, an object was observed by Mr. Swift, of Rochester, New York, on April 11, 1880 in the constellation Ursa Major (Big Dipper) in RA 11h 28m and Declination 68°, and supposed by him to be a faint comet. However, no motion was detected in one hour. It was not a nebula for it could not be found again after a period of bad weather.

Like Harrison's object, this was farther north than usual for a comet and quite far from the sun. If a comet, it should have manifest motion in an hour. The fact that it did not, yet moved away later, is indicative of controlled motion. Its stationary position suggests hovering.

Meteors came in for their share of attention during these years. The Royal Astronomical Society had a committee which assembled meteor data for a long period of years, and published it regularly as a part of the permanent records of the Society. Many of these meteors were of remarkable characteristics. For instance, in the *Monthly Notices* of December 1880, W.F. Denning describes a very "slow" meteor which took fifteen to twenty seconds to cross the sky and mentions a "stationary" meteor which seemed to be approaching the observer in a sinuous track. There are many references to unusual meteors during these years, and there are hundreds of drawings showing meteor trains, explosions, zigzag paths and erratic movements.

On the night of April 18, 1880, a storm of unprecedented severity passed over Missouri and adjacent states. Local whirlwinds, probably tornadoes, developed, and at least one town was completely destroyed. Everywhere along the track there was evidence of a wave of water flowing in the rear of the cloud spots, and in places debris was carried over obstacles of considerable height. The direction of the currents was always uphill. One man and his family were deluged by a wave of water and they said the wave was about fifteen feet high and was icy cold. Stones weighing several hundred pounds were lifted from the ground and carried along for some distance. There is an accredited statement that a stone weighing two tons fell from this storm into a field belonging to Mr. S. Rose, but it was impossible to determine from whence it came.

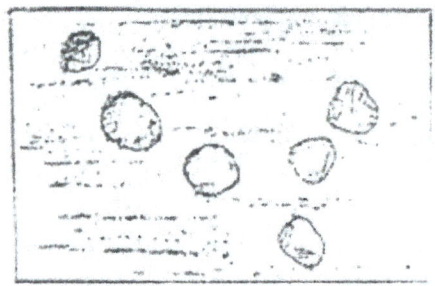

These six UFO's were seen and drawn by Astronomer Barnard, October 14, 1882, and were only 6° from the head of the great comet of 1882. They were accompanied by a spindle-shaped object, looking like a "mother ship" only a few degrees away. This comet had a tail which preceded it, and a complicated head which contained moving parts. Schmidt, at Athens, saw a number of these nebulous UFO's move away from the comet into space.

Now, there is a storm for you! It covered parts of several states. The two-ton stone is a problem, and where did all the water come from, since there are surely no waterspouts in Missouri—and it was icy cold water!

Why?

1880!

>What wind Velocity could ever *Lift* a two ton stone off of a Hill top and *Maintain* it in the air *until* it was carried to that spot. How far was the nearest Hill *where* such a stone could be found at all?

>The above questions will never be asked & so Will never be answered & if asked, No one would want to tell the truth, Lest he be Led away to the "Funny Farm" or Etc of the Like.

The Case is Proved! (B & Jemi)

In the summer of 1881, a routine announcement appeared in the form of a letter to the editor of the German Astronomical publication, *Astronomishce Nachrichten*:

While scanning the western sky on the evening of (May 22nd) with the unassisted eye, I detected a hazy-looking object just below the constellation Columba, which, for my familiarity with that part of the Heavens, I regarded as new. On examining it with a small marine telescope I found it half and five and one-half magnitude...and the head of a comet...and telegraphed (the news) to Mr. Ellery at Melbourne...

This announcement was signed: John Tebbutt, Observatory Windsor, N.S. Wales, 1881, June 18th.

This seems to be an entirely normal and innocuous communication, and would have been except for certain complications. Astronomers of the Southern Hemisphere immediately started making measurements of the comet's position. It would be a few weeks before the fuzzy object moved far enough north to be seen from observatories in Europe and North America.

Because of the shorter distance for mail, the following communication arrived in Germany ahead of Mr. Tebbutt's letter and appeared in *Astronomische Nachrichten*:

On June 9th, I sent you the series of observations which I made of the bright comet which has now passed to the North...the weather has been exceptionally bad and only two additional observations have been obtained. The first of these was on the 10th, (compared) with a star which I have not yet been able to identify. *(My italics)* It is, however, with regard to the second...June 11th, that I now write you...On that evening the comet was found with but little difficulty...although it was quite pale in the bright twilight...I obtained a preliminary determination of its position...for the purpose of identifying some comparison star, when I discovered one in the field...It was blurred by the thick haze and mists near the horizon. I believe it to have been as bright as second magnitude. On attempting to identify the star I found it in none of the catalogues. On the next evening I scrutinized the region without finding any visible star. A glance at the comet, which had moved nearly 3 northward, showed no visible object (accompanying it). I send you the observations as they were made:

Position of the comet determined from the setting of the telescope:
Right Ascension 5h 11m 04s; Declination 9° 36':
Sidereal time 10h 58m 09s.
Comparisons (Distance of comet from comparison star):

Cordoba Sidereal Time	Difference, RA	Difference, Dec.:	Second Time
11h 08m 49s	0m 49s	5' 12.9"	4.7"
11 02.5	49	08.2	0.2"
13 11.0	48	08.4	5.6
14 37.5	48.5	02.8	

The whole observation seemed to me so improbable that I have hesitated a good deal before sending it to you, fearing some gross error...But I have discovered none. Cordoba, 1881, June 16th. B.A. Gould.

(A "comparison" is the measurement of the location of a moving object such as a comet as related to a fixed star. It is the manner in which orbits are determined. It is not always easy to find a known star close enough to make a good comparison.)

Let us review Dr. Gould's statements. He had bad weather which handicapped him in seeing both comet and stars, and made all objects somewhat hazy. He made a comparison on June 10, but failed to find his companion star in any chart or star catalog. This item was overlooked by all correspondents in the controversy which followed, including the astute editors of the *Astronomische Nachrichton*, the *Monthly Notices*, and *Nature*. Do not forget it; for it is important to the *Case for the UFO's*.

A comet, or any other celestial body, moving under the natural forces of gravitation, traverses a smooth curve, and while its velocity may vary, it does so smoothly and gradually. Dr. Gould, <u>a skilled observer whose Argentine Star Catalogues have been accurate reference material for eighty years</u>, was deeply concerned because his observation of the comet indicated erratic motion. Later he was even more seriously troubled because he could neither identify his companion star nor relocate it. Nobody, much less an astronomer, likes to make a fool of himself, and to be frank this whole set of observations looks like mincemeat. It took courage to report this melee and <u>a man of lesser standing than Dr. Gould would have been brushed off.</u>

<u>**DR. GOULD WOULD HAVE *HAD* TO TAKE DR. PETERS ATTITUDE IF HE WERE HANDED THE VERY REPORT THAT *HIS* PROFESSIONAL INTEGRITY DEMANDED THAT *HE* SEND TO ASTRO-NACHRICHTEN AND TO OBSERVER MR. ELLERY. WOULDN'T HE!**</u>

The observations speak for themselves. There is little change in RA but such as there is reverses itself in the fourth comparison. In declination there was rapid motion (too rapid for this comet), the outright reversal, then rapid motion again. Such a thing is unheard of and, as Dr. Gould indicates, it is enough to shake an observer's confidence in his own ability. It is very difficult to escape the conclusion that one of these objects was moving erratically, and since there is no reason to suspect the comet, and since the "star" could not be found at later times, the "comparison object" must have been moving rapidly and erratically.) An explanation occurs to us, but in 1881 such explanations were of such heretical nature that no one even thought of them, much less put them on paper.)

Dr. Krueger, editor of the *Astronomische Nachrichten*, calculated the position of the comet for June 11, using orbital elements determined in the meanwhile, and analyzes the whole situation. His analysis was translated and published together with still further editorial discussion. Since Dr. Gould's position for the comet agrees well enough with the calculated position, the erratic motion is attributed to the star. After considerable mathematical deduction, the conclusion of the European astronomers was that a second comet had been mistaken for a star. This, however, did not account for the irregular motion.

Normally, this would have closed the discussion. But they reckoned without the intrepid amateur from Australia, the active and competent Mr. John Tebbutt. He immediately took pen in hand to address the editor as follows:

I have read the letter of Dr. Gould, dated June 16th, with much interest. It is quite obvious from the change in the relative declinations of the comet and the bright star of comparison, that the latter could not be a fixed star, and the only feasible conclusion is that it was a companion comet. But that this object had no existence a short time previously to Dr. Gould's observation is I think, shown by negative evidence in my journal: "The horizon being clear before sunrise yesterday morning I rose to observe the comet. The diffused twilight and full moon... prevented me seeing any stars near the comet for comparison. There was certainly no star of brighter than seventh magnitude...it will be found that (my) observation preceded the first comparison at Cordoba by only 1h 29m..." I feel confident that, at my last observation, no such object as that described by Dr. Gould could have been in the field with the comet...P.S.: Could Dr. Gould, by any possibility, have observed the blurred images of the stars, BAC 1592 and 1597, and if so is the former a variable star? (The difference in position is about the same, and different magnitudes have been assigned to BAC 1592 by different observers)   John Tebbutt, Observatory, Windsor, N.S. Wales.

There are two vital points in Tebbutt's letter. First, he establishes that he was observing the comet only one and one-half hours before Gould, for, because of the difference in longitude the evening of June 11th in Cordoba was the morning of the 12th at Windsor, New South Wales, Australia. He then states that the object used by Gould for comparison was definitely not visible at Windsor an hour and one –half before it was seen at Cordoba.

The second point is the suggestions that Dr. Gould, by mistaken identity, observed a pair of stars which, by strange coincidence, have about the same distance and direction from each other as the comet and "object." Except for a rather supercilious assumption of Dr. Gould's incompetence as an observer, Tebbutt's suggestion is not without merit. Yet there is one rather deplorable flaw in Mr. Tebbutt's letter; and we quote: "but that this object had no existence a short time previously to Dr. Gould's observation is, I think, shown by negative evidence..."

This is an unjustified and ill-considered conclusion and statement. True, Mr. Tebbutt did not see the object, under conditions in which it should have been seen according to his viewpoint. His assumption was, of course, that the object or star was as distant from the earth as the comet, if, in fact, it did exist. Therefore, if Gould saw it, Tebbutt should have seen it. Tebbutt didn't see it...ergo, it wasn't there!

Not satisfied with a somewhat reserved statement in *Astronomische Nachrichte*, Tebbutt sent a scathing letter to *Observatory* (1882) in which he reiterated all of his arguments, belittled Gould sarcastically, and postulated that one of the pair of stars which he thought was observed by Gould was sufficiently variable in light to have been mistaken for second magnitude while normally appearing as sixth or seventh magnitude. It would be hard to find more irrelevant data.

Mr. Tebbutt was quite honest in his conviction that Dr. Gould had made some kind of crude and unpardonable error in observing. The coincidence of a double star, the components of which have about the same relative position as Dr. Gould's two objects, had let Mr. Tebbutt completely astray, and his indignation at what he considers stupidity caused him to make the unnecessary insinuation that Gould was careless. Tebbutt went so far as to invoke a temporary outburst of light in one star to account for Gould's confusion.

Up to this point, nobody, including the cooler and more objective astronomical editors in Europe, had tried to explain why one skilled observer saw an object which was plainly there to be seen, while another experienced man did not see it. All efforts went toward proving one of them wrong.

But the confusion was only well started. A new astronomical knight-errant entered the celestial jousting. In a publication of the Royal Astronomical Society, January 1882, we find a letter to the editor from W. Bone, M.D., another amateur in Australia. Dr. Bone deposed as follows:

On June 10th, 1881, whilst measuring the position of the comet (at this time it was called comet 1881b) I noticed a peculiar discordance in each succeeding measure, and at length found that the star (?) from which I was measuring, was a rapidly moving body. At first I was inclined to believe it (the star) was the result of refraction, but this would have affected both the comet and the star nearly equally. On more careful inspection, I found it was somewhat discoid, but its light, although bright, was diffused and hazy. It moved through 6' of arc in 34m 34s of time, in a northerly direction. I telegraphed to the Melbourne Observatory and asked instructions. Bad weather prevented me from searching for it next morning and in the evening I could not succeed in again picking it up, neither could I find it where seen on the previous evening. I never received any answer from the Melbourne Observatory. This struck me as so remarkable that I decided to send you my records, Castelmaine, Victoria, 1881, October 22nd, W. Bone, M.D.

In a subsequent letter, Dr. Bone says that his stray object moved about 24s in right ascension in the same interval of time, and that he estimated it at about 2.5 magnitude in brightness, which agrees closely with Gould's estimate of his object. Bone quotes his telegram and concludes that both he and Gould have seen some peculiar type in addition to comet 1881b.

We are now sufficiently remote in time to have an objective view, and we can see more in this correspondence than met the eye in 1881-82. Hark back to Dr. Gould's announcement. Not only did he fail to relocate his comparison star on the 11th, but he admits that his observations on the 10th also failed for the same reason. Now, Dr. Gould, producer of the *Uranametria Argintina*, was too experienced a man to make this sort of blunder as a matter of habit. Something more than carelessness is demanded to explain.

We now have that something!

Dr. Bone made the same error, if it can be called an error, and at not too different a time, on the 10th. His comparison star disappeared also. It, too, was moving rapidly during the period of observation.

It is impossible to avoid the conclusion that something was moving around in the sky, which Bone and Gould thought was a star, or at least as distant as the comet, and which some other equally capable people did not see at all. The element which was consistently overlooked was the possibility that the wayward cometary object(s) was close to the earth and not as distant as either comet or stars. Even Dr. Bone, in his belated statement, failed to see the connection between his abortive observation of the 10th and Dr. Gould's similar debacle.

It seems obvious that the illusive thing used by Bone for comparison was moving rapidly enough that it come into line with the comet as seen from Cordoba a few hours later, and thus appeared to offset the effect of the rotation and revolution of the earth in causing parallax. This can only mean that the position of the object was being maintained on a line between earth and comet, which (the comet being close to the sun) was very close to being the line between the earth and sun, and hence through the neutral. Rotation of the earth brought first Bone and then Gould into this line, the revolution of the earth on its axis around the sun being offset by the object revolving with the earth around the sun.

The apparent movement of the object quite rapid as seen by both observers, was a movement relative to the stars (including the comet) and was a natural consequence of the object maintaining its position between earth and sun as seen from the earth. This, if our analysis and reasoning are even partially correct, proves intelligent control and space navigation!

> Zemja pdrida fastaticoni, dlo? He proves
> this too Many times, Not? Thus, Who would
> ever believe him here.

The fact that Dr. Gould saw something again, on the 11th, from Cordoba, indicates either that there was a second object, or that the first one was still maintaining its position in the line of sight. That Tebbutt did not see it during the morning of the 12th, at Windsor, Australia, is obviously due to parallax of a very high order, and this established the proximity of the object to the earth rather than to the comet. Anything closer than the moon might very well fulfill these conditions, and since the gravitational neutral of the earth-sun is within the moon's orbit, it becomes not incomprehensible that the object was maintaining itself at "the neutral," or thereabouts, and perhaps even adjusting itself to the gravitation of the moon at the same time.

"S"

But Mr. Tebbutt's sense of scientific proprietary had been outraged. He wrote again to the Editor of *Observatory*:

Sir: No sooner had Dr. Gould's mysterious observation of comet 1881b been, as I conceive, satisfactorily explained, than another bone of contention (italics by Tebbutt) is presented to astronomers in the shape of two papers in the *Monthly Notices*, but it is one which I trust may soon be disposed of...

Tebbutt then goes on to point out that the comet was only sixteen minutes of arc south of the star 8 Leporis when observed by Bone, and that at about that very moment the comet was being compared with that star by the astronomers at Melbourne only a few miles away. He says that the last of Mr. White's comparisons must have corresponded very closely with Dr. Bone's observation, and that Mr. White did not see any such object as was described by Dr. Bone.

So great was the interest in the debate that the editor of *Nature*, March 30, 1882, made another comprehensive survey of all available reports, including a very able defense on the part of Dr. Gould, acted as arbitrator and tried to calm the troubled waters. This controversy must have appeared to contemporaries as a tempest in a teapot, and perhaps meaningless, but to us, of the UFO age, it is important, for it represents real observations bearing on a real problem.

TO THIS MAN THERE IS A PROBLEM, *NOT* TO ANYONE *IMPORTANT*.

The Editor's dissertation is long and somewhat technical. Too much so for our use here. It boils down to a rather hesitant conclusion that Tebbutt's explanation of Gould's observation is the most reasonable one available, and poor Dr. Bone is pushed aside, with the assumption that he used the star 8 Leporis for comparison and was deceived by differential refraction of light in the earth's atmosphere. It was considered that Bone's object simply could not have existed without being noticed by the professionals at Melbourne, neglecting the fact that Bone estimated the brightness at thirty times as bright as 8 Leporis and of definitely disclike shape and size.

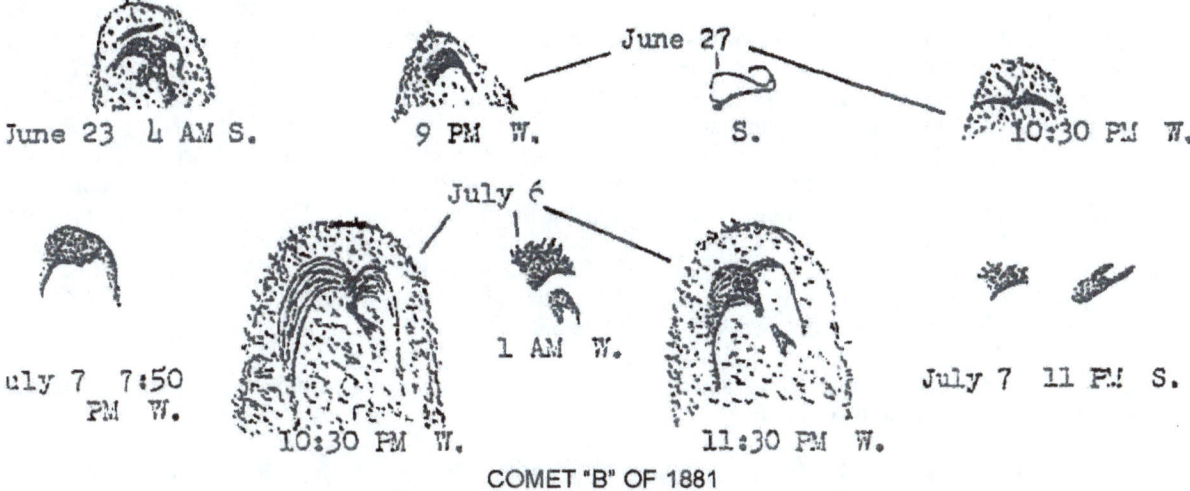

COMET "B" OF 1881

No one was happy about this tentative settlement, but Dr. Bone saw something—nobody denied that. He describes what he saw as discoid. A comet does not have a disclike appearance even under good "seeing" conditions, and under adverse conditions a star becomes comet-like rather than discoid, due to haze and turbulence. We have to conclude that Dr. Bone saw something large enough and near enough to the earth that its disclike shape was not lost in the haze conditions. That is even closer than the moon, and is very probably within our own atmosphere.

Obviously the ship was *in Distress* or Under
Attack, else it would Not have been using so
Much Power, thus going so Slowly & Glowing so
fiercely. Oh! Yes! Was the L-M inspection
ship, in distrustful truce of Above "S" ship,
FORCE SHIELD GOING FULL POWER FOR *PROTECTION*

But there is another powerful factor to consider. If this celestial object was even approximately as far away as the moon it would not have sufficient parallax to take it out of sight of the Melbourne observers while Dr. Bone was observing at Castelmaine, only three minutes of longitudinal distance away. Therefore, it was so close to Dr. Bone's observatory that it was completely out of the line of sight at Melbourne. To have been seen as a disc, to move so much more rapidly than a comet, and to have only an infinitesimal part of the velocity of a meteor, this object had to have been controlled and navigated.

Little wonder remains that all astronomers were puzzled by this thing, or series of things, for such proximity to the earth was unthought of in those days – and is unrecognized and unspoken today.

> Who dares panic a World so intent on showing
> off its Morals compared to another Nations?
> Such revelation of fact extant would Make All
> Mankind Brothers, bound by need of one anothers
> resources to observe & fight the "S" men.

In *Nature*, the patient editor breathed a sigh of relief as he rendered a final account of the Gould-Tebbutt imbroglio. He follows his usual policy and quotes almost verbatim from Dr. Gould's final letter of rebuttal against Tebbutt:

...we gave an account of Dr. Gould's observation on June 11th of last ;year, and it was mentioned that Mr. Tebbutt had suggested that the objects were 60-Eridini and Bradley 718. This explanation was considered a probable one and the same view was taken by the Editor of *Astronomische Nachrichten*, which has occasioned a further communication from Dr. Gould who rejects Mr. Tebbutt's solution. Dr. Gould says the appearance of the comet precluded the slightest doubt as to its identity; "The verist tyrp could recognize it as a comet..." no jar of the telescope took place. The field of the telescope was fully under control from the beginning, the declination clamp remaining tight. No account of blurring could have given such an aspect to a fixed star, though it was far brighter 60-Eridini. Dr. Gould doubts if a star of the sixth magnitude would have been visible under the circumstances. He concluded: "I can only suppose another comet to have been in the field. That it is not a companion comet is manifest, not only from the relative motion, and for examination next day, but from later abundant scrutiny in the Northern Hemisphere. That it was not a fixed star was evident from the beginning." Thus (says the Editor) is the matter left by Dr. Gould, who, it must be admitted, is by far the most competent judge of the probable explanation of the difficulty.

Again, the matter should have rested, but Mr. Tebbutt was to be heard from again, and Gould replied with a final rebuttal to all of them.

The Parthian shot came from a surprising source. Dr. Piazzi Smith, Astronomer Royal of Scotland, wrote in *Nature*, as follows:

While there seems no doubt that the honor of being the discoverer of the great Comet of 1881 belongs without doubt to that life-long and most persevering observer, as well as successful computer of comets, in Australia, Mr. John Tebbutt, three communications which have chanced to arrive here this morning from different countries, containing the most diverse ideas of the nature of that portion of the comet's light which universal spectroscopic observation proves inherent to the comet itself, which is quite different from the reflection of solar light.

> "Pyacha" he was to us & Piachi he "called"
> Himself, too. *Smith* My eye!

The rest of Smith's letter is too technical for this book, but it will suffice for our purpose to say that this comet was a most remarkable object and appeared to contain incandescent materials. Piazzi Smiths' explanations of the electrical nature of the comet's condition are about on an intellectual par with his soaring hypothecations on the portents of the Great Pyramid. All we need to know is that

Tebbutt's comet partook of the generally anomalous celestial turbulence of the Comet Years, in which it was one of the most exotic displays, and helps to establish that there are more things between th earth and Heaven than meet the unwary eye of our proud but ignorant race.

No one has yet fully explained the fact that a body, so ethereal as a comet, does, at time emit light which is apparently of it own generation; nor have the apparently self-generated movements of the inner particles of the comet's nucleus been explained. No one, thus far has suggested that these lights and great tails might offer a means of signaling over distances of a few billions of miles -- to the Red spot of Jupiter, for instance.

> *Force-shield* going full-power, Warding off
> the occasional onslaughts of fast Moving Space
> "Junk" -- When operating, SO gives off "cold-light"
> & it fashes-up WHEN IT HAS BEEN HIT BY
> SILICA-Corb Space Debris.

It matters not the Dr. Bone's findings were criticized. The fact that he did see the object (or one of them if there were two) established two things: (1) it confirmed Dr. Gould's observations of erratically moving, nearby objects on two nights instead of one; and (2) it demonstrates parallax of a pronounced amount, and hence the very close proximity of at least one object, and we are very forcibly reminded of the discoid things seen by Watson and Swift. If Dr. Bone did not provide completely scientific and accurate comparisons, it is indeed no matter, for such observations on a transient object, not supported by a series of other observations from other locations, could have been only qualitative at best.

The drift of at least one of these unknown objects was comparable in speed with that of Harrison's wayward widget, so there is some little indication here of one object very close, perhaps within our atmosphere, and another some thousands of miles out; one rotating with the earth (seen by Bone but not by White), and the other (?) maintaining position in line between the earth and the sun (seen by Gould, but not by Tebbutt). This is as we have surmised in the case of Watson and Swift in 1878.

Could all of these astronomers, professionals and competent amateurs, have conceived of a body being so close to the earth, yet moving slowly, maybe within our atmosphere, they would have realized that they had a new and awesome problem on their hands -- perhaps the key to many a celestial enigma.

Both Gould and Bone had valuable clues within their own observations, in consideration of the erratic movements and the circularity of the objects described by them, showing that the objects were neither stars nor comets. Nor could they have been intra-Mercurial planets because they were illuminated neither crescentically nor gibbously. Parallax was the ultimate kingpin of the tangle, and rules out all of these possibilities. It may even be that these were the selfsame two objects seen by Watson and Swift. It may be that they are the two objects sought today by Army ordnance and Dr. Lapaz. It may be that today's amateurs can find them if they will look toward the sun.

> One Was "S" The other "L-M", as the Peipoles (sic)
> Historian, I must say Neither harmed the
> other, for *that Was* During the Time of Truce
> & inspection, the Results of Which we all
> know. *Lapaz is Harmless.*

In any case, we have here recorded verified proof, when properly analyzed, of the existence and location of UFO's. Inherent in this proof, too, is conclusive evidence that intelligence and control exits (sic) in the UFO's.

Let us rest our *Case for the UFO's* with a provocative episode which took place at the same time the strange "comet" was born...1881!

The British ship *Ellen Austin*, in mid-Atlantic, encountered an abandoned derelict in perfectly seaworthy condition. A salvage crew was put aboard the strange wanderer, with instructions to make for St. John's Newfoundland, where the *Ellen Austin* herself was bound. The two ships then parted company in foggy weather. But a few days later they met again.

Like their unknown predecessors, the salvage crew had vanished...forever...without a trace!

A Note on Sources for
THE CASE FOR THE UFO

Those readers of The Case for the UFO, who have a flair for research, or who may desire to study the background phenomena in more detail than can be offered in such a short volume as this, may wish to consult source material directly. Such material is of vast extent, and to merely list it here would be impossible. In addition nobody knows the real extent of material related to space life and space activity, for it appears in a multitude of very diverse publications. In most of the records, the persons noting observations did not recognize the basic causes, and therefore had no categories into which they could place their data, so that much of it appears in the public press and in general magazines.

For instance, when we look for data about activity on the Moon we find it scattered through practically all of the volumes of several series of scientific journals, including *Observatory* and *The Selenographical Journal, Nature, Science, English Mechanic, Knowledge, Astronomical Register, Reports of the British Association for Advancement of Science, Monthly Notices of the Royal Astronomical Society, Astronomische Nachrichten, Sirius, L'Astronomie, Popular Astronomy, Intellectual Observer, Science Monthly, Philosophical Magazine, American Journal of Science Scientific American, Journal of Astronomical Society of the Pacific*, etc., not to speak of innumerable serial publications of various Universities and Observatories, and many popular treatises such as *Proctor's Astronomy*, and *Webb's Celestial Objects*.

Some of these series have been published continuously for more than one hundred years, and some, such as the *English Mechanic*, may average close to 1,000 pages per volume. Scanning them, even superficially, becomes a stupendous job. We have cited some specific references, and some general ones. The serious investigator could make a worth-while contribution to the Science of the UFO by selecting any one of dozens of serial publications and intensely perusing all of its volumes from Vol. 1, No. 1, clear through to yesterday, and reporting his findings.

There is absolutely no general rule as to what kind of publication to look in. The nuggets of information may appear any place at all, including old almanacs. But within any publication or series of periodicals, there is one best place to look: Letters to the Editor. These can be published without the Editor having to commit himself to belief or disbelief in the report.

Readers who live in small communities are urged to scan old files of their local papers for news of things falling from the sky. It is altogether possible that, if enough persons make searches, we can find more than ample material to prove the case for the UFO once and for all. If you live in a small community, it may well be that your facilities for research are better than those of the large cities.

One should note local historical sketches as an important source. There are hundreds of such publications from every locality of the United States. They were very prevalent in the 19th century, especially circa the stunning decade of the 1880's. They were prone to report peculiar storms, abnormal weather, and unexplainable occurrences. Almost every County in the U.S. published one of these histories in the latter part of the 19th century or the very early part of the 20th.

Rural people are much more weather-conscious than city folks. So, in our quest for records of falling masses of water, we are most anxious to have data from rural records.

One field of research which we do not believe to have been worked is sportsman's magazines such as *Field and Stream*. The correspondence columns of such magazines should supply some data on singular clouds, storms, UFO's and erratics from space.

The most general and intangible of all the categories for search is probably that extensive list of old books and magazines of general character which contain stories of local events and records and diaries of famous men, as well as legends and traditions. Much valuable material is buried in these, and often in single, isolated paragraphs with no headings or warning or what is coming. Most of these items will be picked up by accident by alert readers whose interests attracted by the novelty of the statement or the perplexity of the original writer.

The listing of ALL astronomical references bearing on UFO is utterly impossible in this book. Such a bibliography would require a volume to itself. In the series of the *Astronomical Register* (British), alone, there are several hundred page and paragraph references. Doubtless, it is due to our previous lack of comprehension as to the nature and broadness of the UFO problem that such data have not been recognized for their true worth and import. For this book, the astronomical records were fairly well searched for a brief period of about fifteen years centered around the "Comet Years"—say 1870 to 1885 – with spot checks at other dates.

WHAT HAPPENS WHEN A BOLT OF LIGHTING HITS AT A POINT WHERE THERE IS A "NODE" SUCH AS A "SWIRL" IN THE MAGNETIC SEA *OR WHERE* A MAG. "DEAD' SPOT" caused by the NEUTRALIZATION OF MAG. SEA contra GRAVITY ESPECIALLY, WHAT, WHEN THE NODE & BOLT BOTH ACT OVER BRONZE INLAY

The Good Doctor
is far more aware of Committing the Cardinal effrontery of Unorthodoxy than he wishes to show, perhaps. Too, He wishes to have More & More & More, a flood of Data, & facts & records of observations that will back-up his Theory. It would seem Much More apropo were he to not ask for further Proof to show to his fellow Professional Deriders *but* Were He To Proceed Himself into the *only* field that *would* convince each and Every one of His fellows: That field of Gravity & Magnetic exploration, as yet Untouched. He THEN could say the Moon is Hollow & *Not* one person would say a Word. Approach to Morals & Ethics of Science, Not New. Newton proved His Theory throo observable phenomena The which *any one* could obseve & *So has this Man*[1]

Not to anyone important.

---

[1] *Italics by* A and B

If the history of the Great War of the ancients
were ever recorded, except by the black-tongued o
ones own tales, It would cause Man to stand
in awe (or disbelieve) that such Huge Satelitic
Masses were ever deliberately tossed throo
this atmosphere in an attempt to Demolish all
of the "Little Men"[2] Great Works. Fortunately
for Mankinds ego only a Gypsy will tell another of that Catastrophe, and we are a
descredited (sic) peopole (sic), ages ago. HAH! Yet,
Man Wonders where "we"[2] came from, and I
Do Not Believe that they will *ever* know.
These folks on *this* planet are so engrossed
in their puny pettiness & Squabbles that If
the Great Bombardment were to happen again
They would destroy each other in *blind Panic*.
Ah! Well, Their own "Great Book"[2] Prophecys (sic)
that they will surely do so *and* kick this
Planet off its orbit, away from its Solar
System, even "The Moon shall not shed her
glow" & Well, stars "falling" & the Sun
"Going out" or *away*, seemingly. *They will
blast this Jewel into Dead Space*[1]. A good
thing that we have Learned to not war, pyac
ma droba jesi tlodlic' Truscani *The Atruscans know
Generosity overwhelms.*[2]

My Dear Brothers:
No one Single Man has dared before to do so
Much to expose the facts of the Matter before
us. I say to you that *this Man Fears* and so
Will not ever go any farther than this "Soap-
box." *He Definitely Lacks Character ENOUGH
to go further.* So do not concern yourselves
with Him at All. What if I am Wrong? Even
then *do Not be Concerned*. I say to you this
man is Plainly too interested in "*Who*"[2] shall
be Wrong" Rather than whether his touch upon
Fundamental Principles of Force utilization
is or is not so. Thus He tys (sic) Himself all
up firmly. In short, he is a "Small" man,
too small to Lay *himself* upon the alter of
Such Exploration as Would be necessary to
Prove Definitely that he is correct beyond
any doubt. No, He is "Proud-Small" and will
only defend his *investigations*, Not *that*
theory, at all. As you see, it is plain,
on the final Pages of this, His "Soap-box."
Even if Some one Else took up the Work

---

[2] "Quotation marks by Jemi

[1] *Italics by A*

he recommends to "enacted by Law" It is now already to Late for the Gaiyori are too Madly Racing to destroy each other & will Very Soon *Do* So, over a Mere Parcel or two of the sections of *this* Planet, or over Who is Right & Who is Wrong or from Jealousy (ENVY)[1] of the other. They are yet Children. These Humans, Show it *too Clearly.* As things Stand, They Value Materiall thing & Will not apply themselves to True Values of *Their own* Great Prophetic Book. In Principal Yes, but Not Practice No Christian Nation or Diplomat will *ever* be of True Value to another. *Thus, Destruction.* This Man is No Different He too is *Not*[2] of a "Big Spirit" enough.
Die Puka

---

[2] *Italics and insertion of the word ENVY by Jemi*